*The publisher gratefully acknowledges the
generous contribution to this book provided by
the Classical Literature Endowment Fund of
the University of California Press Foundation,
which is supported by a major gift
from Joan Palevsky.*

THE MATTER OF THE GODS

THE TRANSFORMATION OF THE CLASSICAL HERITAGE

Peter Brown, General Editor

THE MATTER OF THE GODS

Religion and the Roman Empire

Clifford Ando

UNIVERSITY OF CALIFORNIA PRESS

Berkeley   Los Angeles   London

The University of California Press, one of the most
distinguished university presses in the United States,
enriches lives around the world by advancing
scholarship in the humanities, social sciences, and
natural sciences. Its activities are supported by the UC
Press Foundation and by philanthropic contributions
from individuals and institutions. For more
information, visit www.ucpress.edu.

University of California Press
Berkeley and Los Angeles, California

University of California Press, Ltd.
London, England

Library of Congress Cataloging-in-Publication Data

Ando, Clifford, 1969-.
    The matter of the gods/by Clifford Ando.
        p.   cm. — (The transformation of the classical
    heritage)
    Includes bibliographical references and index.
    ISBN 978-0-520-25083-3 (cloth : alk. paper)
        1. Rome—Religion.   2. Title
BL803.A53   2008
292.07—dc22   2007044525

Manufactured in the United States of America
16   15   14   13   12   11   10   09   08
10   9   8   7   6   5   4   3   2   1

This book is printed on Natures Book, which
contains 50% post-consumer waste and meets the
minimum requirements of ANSI/NISO Z39.48-1992
(R 1997) (Permanence of Paper).

CONTENTS

PREFACE

What sort of knowledge did the Romans possess about their gods? What kind of information, of what status, motivated their religious actions? To those questions the first chapter of this book proposes simple answers: that in contrast to ancient Christians, who had faith, the Romans had knowledge; and that their knowledge was empirical in orientation.

The body of the book falls into two halves. The three chapters of Part 1 reconsider a set of problems in Roman religious history in light of chapter 1's conclusions. These are, first, the problem of materiality and representation in theology and cult; second, the relationship between naming and knowledge in Roman encounters with the divine in unfamiliar landscapes; and third, the influence on religious thought of doctrinal and theoretical developments in Roman law, and what these together might reveal about the metaphysical status assigned by Romans to their public institutions.

Part 2 contains a more strictly diachronic survey of the relationship between religious law and religious thought on the one hand, and different taxonomies and topographies of Roman, Italian, and provincial land on the other. It pursues this inquiry with an eye on two topics, the relationship between religion and imperialism, on the one hand, and the place of Rome in sacred topographies of the empire, on the other.

I was first provoked to ask what the epistemic basis of Roman religion had been by reading Augustine's *Contra Academicos.* That text was written, I came to feel, in response not to Cicero's *Academica,* but to his *De natura deorum,* and it was a rereading of the latter in light of Augustine's concerns that drew my attention to the very different epistemologies to which Velleius, Balbus, and Cotta subscribed and the precision with which Cicero respects that fact. But Augustine's response to Cicero has modern echoes, too, and the remainder of this preface seeks to elucidate some of those.[1]

. . .

For much of the twentieth century, the principal assumptions and often the principal questions motivating scholarship on Roman religion had to do with its demise: with some falling away from an originary state, during which process it came into contact with, and was corrupted by, first, Greek myths and Hellenistic philosophy and, later, Oriental mystery cults, one of which would ultimately supplant the cult of Jupiter Optimus Maximus in Rome and succeed the Roman empire in the West. Much of the work produced under this regime remains of great value, and I very much fear that, in dissenting from its terms of reference, we are in danger today of rejecting some great analytic work.

Then, in the 1970s, a group of scholars in England and France began to construct an alternative approach to Roman religion. Curiously, the same period witnessed a significant revolution in the study of Greek religion, which also took what we might describe as a ritual turn, but the theoretical affiliations of the new scholarship on Greek religion were profoundly different. For their part, those writing on Rome came to articulate their alternative in the first instance as a rejection of what they called the "Christianizing assumptions" of earlier scholarship. No target received more withering criticism than the twin pillars of Protestant historiography, namely the search for some Roman equivalent to Christian "faith" and the denigration of ritualism and its priestly devotees.

Where faith is concerned, we were instructed in those days, the search itself was misconceived. The Romans did not need faith; they had an orthopraxy. In John Scheid's terms, their religion was concerned with savoir-faire, not savoir-penser. On one level, this amounted to a reversal of the

---

1. Short essays on problems of method and the history of scholarship in the study of Roman religion, including much bibliographic material, may be found in Ando 2003b.

priorities of earlier scholarship: ritual itself became the privileged category, and faith was deemed irrelevant to Roman religiosity. And on another, this methodological turn harmonized with trends then emerging in functionalist anthropology, with its interest in the integrative function of rituals and their symbolic role as expressions of a particular cultural system.

.　　.　　.

The subsequent quarter-century of scholarship on Roman religion has produced much of great value. But the way in which "ritual" became naturalized as an object of study—its justification self-evident by virtue of its antithetical position in relation to a so-called Christian emphasis on faith—has occluded problems of two kinds, one set internal to the study of Roman religion, the other an order removed.

First, how are we to explain change within a religion devoted to orthopraxy?[2] Indeed, how are we to explain orthopraxy in the first place? How did Romans explain it to themselves? Mere statements on their part—or ours—advocating or describing an adherence to conservatism or formalism of a particular kind amount to little more than the echoing of an ancient ideologically motivated discourse, which was, so far as I can tell, mobilized in the face of continual processes of innovation, alteration, and renewal.

Second, the rejection of "faith" on the grounds that it was not a technical concept or constitutive category within Roman religion has itself produced an impasse and was probably misconceived. For the mere fact that "faith" was and is such a concept or category within Christianity should have led people to ask not whether the Romans had faith, but what they had instead.

Put another way, the radical assertion that (Protestant) Christians have faith, whereas the Romans had rituals, might have appeared self-consciously historicizing in the best sense, but in practice it has amounted to an assertion of incommensurate difference. We thus call many things religions, but in their study we ask of each of them different questions. Christian-

2.　Rüpke 1996b is one of the few essays known to me to study the causes and accommodation of change (other than the introduction of new gods) within Roman religion. Rüpke's questions are very different from mine, but neither his method nor his answer is discordant with my own.

ity's concerns are doctrinal and existential; Roman religion's concerns were political. To a skeptic, the subsequent dominance within the field of what we now call the "polis-religion" model looks little different from earlier generations' cynical descriptions of Roman magistrates manipulating rituals for political ends, except that we now speak not of hypocrisy but of ideology, and not of politics but of power.

.   .   .

The analytic isolation in which we continue to place Roman religion—the assertion of its difference, even its uniqueness—raises in my mind two questions. The first concerns the derivation and justification for the theoretical constructs through which we render ancient experience intelligible, and the second the audience whom we address. These are naturally related. For in privileging what I might call the "terms of art" or jargon of any given religion—in adopting, in other words, the terms and categories that participants in any given cultural system would have themselves used of their own culture—we restrict our theorizing to a set of first-order categories, and we condemn our inquiry to a kind of antiquarianism in which ancient data, however abundant or difficult of access, are ultimately situated only in relation to each other. To do that is to speak in the end only to our fellow classicists.

To some, this may not appear problematic. But to others, Classics appears overdue for an existential crisis. The relevance of classical antiquity both to contemporary cultural production more generally, and to humanistic scholarship in particular, is no longer obvious. One solution, of a very limited kind, lies in trying to speak to nonclassicists. By that effort I do not mean what Americans might call "outreach," or "popularizing," valuable though these are. Rather, I ask how we should address ourselves—or how we should present the ancient world—to scholars, and in particular to scholars of religion, to whom the ancient world seems little more than a curiosity.

To that question there are, of course, many right answers. I concentrate here on one, namely the assertion of incommensurate difference and the theoretical problems to which it gives rise. One solution to them might lie in the devising of second-order categories of the kind that make comparisons meaningful and cross-cultural study possible.

Rather than elaborate on this proposition in the abstract, let me now give three brief examples, each of which receives some attention later in this book. The examples concern myth, immanence, and faith.

The Romans had no myths.[3] Regardless whether they had once had Italic myths and lost them, or had never had any, the myths they retold in the historical period were either imported from Greece or products of a derivative mythpoiesis. This myth—the most pernicious legacy of Dionysius of Halicarnassus—has had a curious afterlife among scholars of Roman religion. For part and parcel of Greek religion's turn to ritual in the 1970s was the development of elaborate theories of "myth and ritual," among which various forms of Continental structuralism long held sway. This view of ancient myth produced in the study of Roman religion a fatal syllogism: religion lies somewhere at the nexus of myth and ritual; Rome had no native myths; therefore Rome had no religion. In no small measure, classical scholarship in this vein has sustained a fallacy that originated elsewhere in an ideologically motivated misconstrual: namely the insistence that "rites" are merely enactments or performances of "rituals," a term that in early modern usage designated a written script "directing the order and manner to be observed in performing divine service."[4]

The effects of this exogenous pressure on the study of Roman religion can be elaborated in several directions. I concentrate on one, namely that wrought by the reliance of contemporary ancient historians on literary texts for their knowledge of religious rituals. Put simply, those dependent on literary descriptions of rites tend to develop theories that privilege discursive interpretations of ritual over and against cognition-in-performance. And, once invested in problems of priority, largely under the influence of Hellenists and their fascination with aetiology, scholars of Roman religion could set aside literary accounts of rituals only by denouncing them as secondary reflections on rites whose original meanings had been lost.

3. Over the last few years, the possibility of genuine historical and philological inquiry into Roman myth has been placed on an entirely new foundation, a development to be credited to Peter Wiseman (2004, following on much earlier work) and Alan Cameron (2004a).

4. This is the definition of ritual offered by the first edition of the *Encyclopedia Britannica;* I quote it from Asad 1993, 56.

The last twenty years have witnessed the elaboration of two significant new theories in the study of myth and ritual at Rome. One situates myth in a realm cognitively autonomous from ritual and views the former as a type of exegesis upon the latter; the other understands Roman myths as what, with Beard, North, and Price, we might call "myths of place."[5] To my mind, these theories still operate on three questionable assumptions, none of which might be tenable in a Roman context. These are, first, that rituals are one thing, but their meanings, by virtue of requiring discursive elaboration, are another; second, that Roman rituals were fundamentally unintelligible, because they were old and had not changed; and, third, that proper myths are old stories about an ancient world in which the agency and the personalities of gods are described and subsumed within narrative.

But what sort of myth would an orthopraxy have? To answer that question we need to understand that Roman orthopraxy was invested not in rituals that did not change, but in correct performance per se. What is more, the correctness of any given performance was subject to empirical verification, and the results of that testing could and occasionally did provoke not merely an exact repetition of a performance but changes in the ritual itself. That is to say, misfortune in the aftermath of ritual performance could be interpreted as revealing error in the conduct of the ritual, in which case one could conduct an *instauratio,* a thoroughgoing repetition, or a fault in the construction of the ritual itself, which would lead to an *emendatio,* an alteration to its script. A Roman story about a ritual thus did not have to explain how the ritual originated, but only how it had come to be performed in the way it was at the moment of the story's telling. A theory of myth and ritual at Rome that searches for aetiological myths of the Hellenistic variety will, of course, find them, but it will miss the native relationship between historiography and religious practice at Rome.

.   .   .

Second, immanence. The issue of place in Roman religion has moved center stage of late, not least thanks to the attention paid by Beard, North,

5. Beard, North, and Price 1998, 1:167–210.

and Price to "myths of place." But what is a myth of place, and in what sense does having one or more of them distinguish Roman religion from other religions? What would a myth that is not a myth of place look like?

Myths qua narrative generally describe actions consecutively, and those actions are normally situated in place and time. I can think of one important exception to this rule, the story of the sacrifice of Isaac in Genesis 22. That episode was, of course, the subject of a famous chapter in Erich Auerbach's *Mimesis,* in which Auerbach contrasted Homeric and biblical narrative in their strategies for "representing reality."[6] The episodes that he read in that chapter were Eurycleia's recognition of Odysseus's scar and the sacrifice of Isaac. Auerbach identified the impulse of Homeric style as a desire "to represent phenomena in a fully externalized form, visible and palpable in all their parts, and completely fixed in their spatial and temporal relations." Of course, the interaction between two metaphysically equivalent subjects lends itself to such a reading. We might therefore ask why Auerbach contrasted the one encounter between two humans with another between a mortal and a god. Had Auerbach instead discussed the occasional arrival of Zeus or Poseidon from feasts of the Aethiopians—episodes to which he alludes in a single line—he might have had to confront the possibility that the representational impulses of any given myth or mythological tradition could have theological implications or, better yet, could be regarded as reifying particular theological presuppositions, as the representation of God in Genesis surely does.

I might clarify what is at stake here by turning to a very different example, namely the divergent attitudes to pilgrimage held by dyophysite and monophysite Christians in the fifth and sixth centuries. These were populations who shared to a very large extent the same myths, but who approached them in very different ways. For monophysites, who regarded Christ as having a single, divine, nature and therefore in some controversial way a divine body, did not recognize the possibility that such a body could leave traces in the world. Within such a Christology, Christ and the land—in some respects Christ and human history—were ontologically distinct. And for that reason, it seems, monophysite Christians did not recognize the value in visiting and viewing the locations where

6. Auerbach 1953, 3–23. On this text see also below, pp. 26–27.

Christ had appeared. If they had prevailed, the history of the Crusades—indeed, the history of tourism—would look far different.

Chapters of this book approach this problem in Roman religion from different angles, asking, for example, whether a singular metaphysical apparatus can account for Roman emphases on the residence of the gods in particular locations as well as their representation in cult objects (chapter 2). Another invokes Jonathan Z. Smith's distinction between utopian and locative cults (chapter 5). But doing so poses a challenge: how to make Smith's categories genuinely heuristic, rather than merely descriptive. Perhaps paradoxically, in light of the misgivings I expressed earlier regarding antiquarianism, one solution might lie in asking how his distinction might have been expressed in ancient terms. As an illustration, I offer the description given by Servius of the Penates in Lavinium: "They are called the Great Gods," he wrote, "because they are felt to be most present," *quod praesentissimi sentiantur.* Indeed, their presence in Lavinium was held to reflect their desire there to abide, and so generals about to go to provinces sacrificed before them at the place where they themselves had chosen to reside. In contrast, recall the first words of Isis to Lucius—*En adsum,* "Behold, I am present"—or those of Christ to his disciples: "Wherever two or three of you are gathered in my name, there I am in their midst."

The questions before us, then, when studying the "placing" of Roman religion, concern not so much its myths, but its gods, and those questions should be framed not narratologically, but philosophically: How was the relationship of Roman gods to the material world and to their representations conceived, such that it was largely impossible to conceive of the simultaneous performance of their cult in multiple locations?

.   .   .

To approach the third problem, that of faith, in light of what is written above, we should have asked long ago how the hapless, mythless Romans learned what they knew about the gods and, for that matter, whether it was knowledge at all. The answer is at some level obvious: they sought information through observation of the actions of the gods in the world—indeed, an enormous amount of the apparatus of state cult was directed toward this end. And insofar as that information was acquired through sense perception, it was knowledge of a very particular kind. The

Romans, I will argue, subscribed in matters of religion to an empiricist epistemology.

Its foundation thus described, Roman religion's devotion to orthopraxy becomes more intelligible, as does the conceptual possibility for change. For in light of the terrifying difference in power between gods and mortals, mortals had no choice but to consult the gods; and yet, the habit of Roman gods in particular of communicating with enormous indirection placed an exceedingly high standard on the correct performance of all such processes of consultation. What one knew to work on the basis of experience had therefore very precisely to be recreated, until such time as one learned through experience that something about the ritual had to be changed.

The problem of demise, too, might be rendered more intelligible as a result of viewing classical Roman religion in these terms. For the problem with scholarship that took demise as its explanandum turns out not to have been the search for faith, but the failure, upon having designated "faith" a peculiarly Christian concern, to frame a second-order category in which "faith" might sit alongside other forms of knowledge, privileged in other religions.

Measured in this light against Christianity, Roman religion paradoxically appears both more flexible and more vulnerable. A religion based on knowledge can always change, for knowledge presupposes error. Faith admits no such challenge. In a peculiar, limited, but important sense, the history of Christianity *is* the history of doctrine. For that reason, Christians could disdain to acknowledge massive historical events like the sack of Rome in 410 C.E. Adherents of Roman religion in late antiquity could not, and in the face of disaster on that scale, their faith—their faith in their knowledge—did not so much bend, but break.

ACKNOWLEDGMENTS

This volume represents the fruition of a course of research first outlined in a proposal to the American Council of Learned Societies many years ago. To the ACLS, and to the Huntington Library in San Marino, California, for its hospitality during a later fellowship, I extend my thanks for their support and patience.

In the event, several of the chapters in this volume were first drafted in response to invitations; at times, offers of publication followed. Credit to the venues of original publication may be found in the notes.

I should like here to thank the communities of scholarship that extended me their hospitality and wisdom during the writing of this volume, including institutes and departments at the Claremont Graduate University, the University of Chicago, Erfurt University, the University of Exeter, the University of Michigan, the University of Mississippi, the University of Münster, the University of Southern California, the University of Texas at Austin, the University of Virginia, and York University.

When I embarked on this project, Roman religion was a new discipline to me, and I have learned more than I can say from the kindness, example, and erudition of experts who have become friends, especially Mary Beard, Jörg Rüpke, and John Scheid. At the risk of diminishing debts of kindness and consultation over many years, I here simply name friends who helped along the way: Nicole Belayche, Sarah Blake, Andy Dyck,

Jonathan Edmondson, Catherine Feeley, Tom Harrison, Ted Kaizer, Kristina Meinking, Fergus Millar, Claudia Moatti, David Potter, Guy Stroumsa, Jody Valentine, and Jim White.

Laura Cerruti and Cindy Fulton have once again made working with the University of California Press a pleasure, while Paul Psoinos has likewise again much improved a manuscript by his care and attention.

I have profited more than I can say from the learning and friendship of Sabine MacCormack. She speaks my questions before I find the language to suit them and shapes my answers before I know what they are.

Nearly every day that I worked on this book, I had the companionship of my son, Theodore, with whom I share chocolate. To him last and first of all, my thanks.

ABBREVIATIONS

The abbreviations of titles of primary sources generally follow those in the *Oxford Classical Dictionary*, 3rd edition. They are also expanded in the Index Locorum.

AÉ	*L'Année Épigraphique*
AJPh	*American Journal of Philology*
ANRW	*Aufstieg und Niedergang der römischen Welt* (Berlin, 1972–)
Anth. Pal.	*Anthologia Palatina*
ARG	*Archiv für Religionsgeschichte*
ARS	A. C. Johnson, P. R. Coleman-North, and F. C. Bourne, eds., *Ancient Roman Statutes* (Austin, 1961)
ARW	*Archiv für Religionswissenschaft*
BÉFAR	Bibliothèque des Écoles Françaises d'Athènes et de Rome
CAH²	The Cambridge Ancient History, 2nd edition
CÉFR	Collection de l'École Française de Rome
CFA	J. Scheid, ed., *Commentarii Fratrum Arvalium Qui Supersunt: Les copies épigraphiques des protocoles annuels de la Confrérie Arvale (21 av.–304 ap. J.-C.)* (Rome, 1998)

CIG	*Corpus Inscriptionum Graecarum* (Berlin, 1828–77)
CIL	*Corpus Inscriptionum Latinarum* (Berlin, 1963–)
CJ	*Corpus Iuris Civilis,* vol. 2, ed. P. Krueger, *Codex Iustinianus* (Berlin, 1929)
ClassAnt	*Classical Antiquity*
CPh	*Classical Philology*
CQ	*Classical Quarterly*
CSSH	*Comparative Studies in Society and History*
CTh	T. Mommsen, ed., *Codex Theodosianus,* vol. 1, pars posterior, *Theodosiani Libri XVI cum Constitutionibus Sirmondianis* (Berlin, 1905)
DOP	*Dumbarton Oaks Papers*
EntrHardt	*Entretiens,* Fondation Hardt pour l'Étude de l'Antiquité Classique
FGRH	F. Jacoby, ed., *Die Fragmente der griechischen Historiker* (Leiden, 1923–)
HSCPh	*Harvard Studies in Classical Philology*
HThR	*Harvard Theological Review*
IG	*Inscriptiones Graecae* (Berlin, 1873–)
IGRR	R. Cagnat et al., eds., *Inscriptiones Graecae ad Res Romanas Pertinentes* (Paris, 1901–27)
ILS	H. Dessau, ed., *Inscriptiones Latinae Selectae* (Berlin, 1892–1916)
JECS	*Journal of Early Christian Studies*
JRA	*Journal of Roman Archaeology*
JRS	*Journal of Roman Studies*
JThS	*Journal of Theological Studies*
Lampe	G. W. H. Lampe, *A Patristic Greek Lexicon* (Oxford, 1968)

LSJ	H. G. Liddell, R. Scott, and H. S. Jones, eds., *A Greek-English Lexicon,* 9th ed. (Oxford, 1968)
MÉFRA	*Mélanges de l'École Française de Rome, Série Antiquité*
MÉFRM	*Mélanges de l'École Française de Rome, Série Moyen Âge*
NHLL	*Nouvelle histoire de la littérature latine,* ed. Reinhart Herzog and Peter Lebrecht Schmidt (Turnhout, 1993–)
NTh	*Novellae Theodosii,* in T. Mommsen and P. Krueger, eds., *Codex Theodosianus,* vol. 2, *Leges Novellae ad Theodosianum Pertinentes* (Berlin, 1905)
PBA	*Proceedings of the British Academy*
PBSR	*Papers of the British School at Rome*
PCPhS	*Proceedings of the Cambridge Philological Society*
PL	J.-P. Migne et al., eds., *Patrologia Cursus Completus, Series Latina* (Paris, 1844–1900)
PLRE	A. H. M. Jones, J. R. Martindale, and J. Morris, eds., *The Prosopography of the Later Roman Empire,* vol. 1, A.D. 260–395 (Cambridge, 1971)
RAC	*Reallexicon für Antike und Christentum* (Stuttgart, 1950–)
RDGE	R. K. Sherk, *Roman Documents from the Greek East* (Baltimore, 1969)
RE	A. F. von Pauly, G. Wissowa, et al., eds., *Real-Encyclopädie der classischen Altertumswissenschaft* (Stuttgart, 1894–1972)
RÉAnciennes	*Revue des Études Anciennes*
RÉAug	*Revue des Études Augustiniennes*
RechAug	*Recherches Augustiniennes*
RÉLatines	*Revue des Études Latines*
RHD	*Revue Historique de Droit Français et Étranger*
RHM	*Rheinisches Museum*

RHR	*Revue de l'Histoire des Religions*
RS	M. H. Crawford, ed., *Roman Statutes* (London, 1996)
SCI	*Scripta Classica Israelica*
SIG	W. Dittenberger, ed., *Sylloge Inscriptionum Graecarum*, 3rd ed. (Leipzig, 1915–21)
TAPhA	*Transactions of the American Philological Association*
VigChr	*Vigiliae Christianae*
ZKG	*Zeitschrift für Kirchengeschichte*
ZPE	*Zeitschrift für Papyrologie und Epigraphik*

I

RELIGION, LAW, AND KNOWLEDGE
IN CLASSICAL ROME

The historian Valerius Maximus, who compiled his nine books of *Memorable Deeds and Sayings* under the emperor Tiberius (14–37 C.E.), introduced the first section of his first book, "On Religion" (*De religione*), in the following terms:[1]

Our ancestors desired that fixed and formal annual ceremonies be regulated by the knowledge of the *pontifices;* that sanction for the good governance of affairs be marshaled by the observations of augurs; that Apollo's prophecies be revealed by the books of the seers; and that the expiation of portents be accomplished in accordance with the Etruscan discipline.

Also, by hallowed practice, observances are paid to divine affairs: by prayer, when something must be entrusted; by vow, when something is

---

1. Valerius Maximus 1.1.1a–b: "Maiores statas sollemnesque caerimonias pontificum scientia, bene gerendarum rerum auctoritates augurum obseruatione, Apollinis praedictiones uatum libris, portentorum depulsiones Etrusca disciplina explicari uoluerunt. prisco etiam instituto rebus diuinis opera datur, cum aliquid conmendandum est, precatione, cum exposcendum, uoto, cum soluendum, gratulatione, cum inquirendum uel extis uel sortibus, inpetrito, cum sollemni ritu peragendum, sacrificio, quo etiam ostentorum ac fulgurum denuntiationes procurantur. Tantum autem studium antiquis non solum seruandae sed etiam amplificandae religionis fuit, ut florentissima tum et opulentissima ciuitate decem principum filii senatus consulto singulis Etruriae populis percipiendae sacrorum disciplinae gratia traderentur."

demanded; by thanksgiving, when a vow is discharged; by entreaty [for a favorable sign], when an inquiry is made by entrails or lot; and by sacrifice, when something is accomplished through formal ritual, whereby, too, the warnings of prodigies and lightning are expiated.

So great was the desire among the ancients not only for the preservation but also for the expansion of religion [*religio*] that, at a time when the city was flourishing and wealthy, by decree of the Senate, ten sons of leading men were handed over to the peoples of Etruria in order to acquire technical mastery of their sacred rites.

Valerius Maximus possessed neither sharpness of intellect nor clarity of style, and it would be easy to impeach this passage for obscurity of many kinds.[2] But as an ostensive circumscription of Roman religion in a Roman formulation, it can serve as a point of departure, not only in our consideration of what Roman religion was, but also in our reflection upon its study. In this chapter, I concentrate on one specific aspect of that field of inquiry, namely the epistemological basis of Roman religion; as I shall argue, this basis by its very nature conditions the manner in which Roman religion can be studied. The chapters that follow will consider further problems of theory and practice, some consequent to this argument, and their contents will be flagged here.

We might begin by reflecting on the translation of *religio*.[3] "Religion" is but one possible rendering for *religio,* and Valerius's lists suggest that it might here be rendered more accurately by "the sum total of current cult practice."[4] It is not that "religion" does not capture the force of *religio* in one of its uses, but rather that this usage is not primary, and its field proves harder to map onto "religion" than one might expect. Consider the description of the *religio* of the Roman people offered by Gaius Aurelius

---

2. Compare his immediate inspiration for the first paragraph, Cicero *Har. resp.* 18: "First of all, I regard our ancestors as authorities and guides in the cultivation of religion [*religionum colendarum*] . . . they thought that fixed and formal annual ceremonies should be governed by the pontificate, sanction for the good governance of affairs by augury, the ancient prophecies of Apollo by the books of the seers, and the interpretation of portents by the Etruscan discipline."

3. On *religio* see Pease 1963, 580–83 on Cicero *Div.* 2.148; Michels 1976; Muth 1978; Schilling 1979, 30–93; Sachot 1991; and Bremmer 1998, 10–14.

4. Compare Cicero *Dom.* 121, translated below, p. 6; and see Bremmer 1998, 10.

Cotta, the Academic pontifex, in the opening pages of book 3 of Cicero's *On the Nature of the Gods* (*Nat. deor.* 3.5):[5]

> The entirety of the *religio* of the Roman people is divided into rites and auspices, to which is added a third thing, namely whatever warnings the interpreters of the Sibylline books or *haruspices* issue for the sake of foreknowledge on the basis of portents and omens. I hold that none of these *religiones* [*harum . . . religionum nullam*] should ever be neglected, and I have persuaded myself that Romulus and Numa laid the foundations of our state by establishing the auspices and rites, respectively, and that our state could never have become so great without the greatest appeasement of the immortal gods.

The tendency among translators has been to render *harum . . . religionum nullam* with a phrase like "none of these parts of our religion":[6] in other words, to efface entirely Cicero's discomfiting switch from the singular *religio* to the plural *religiones*. In time, *religio Romanorum* will come to mean something like "Roman religion" or, more accurately, "the religion of the Roman people," for the genitives "of the Roman people" or "of the Romans" signal an essential aspect to the classical Roman conception of religion, namely that it was of and for a political community or body of citizens, one that included both humans and gods.[7]

During the long opposition of "Roman religion" to the religion of the Christians, the meaning "religion" in a totalizing sense eventually occluded all other meanings of *religio,* and the fractious dialogue that required that binarism yields a portrait of Roman religion that the classical term *religio* cannot sustain.[8] So it is, even at the height of pagan-Christian conflict, that Quintus Aurelius Symmachus, prefect of the city of Rome in 383 C.E.,

5.   On this passage see Pease 1955 *ad loc.* See also p. 105 below.

6.   See, for example, the recent Oxford World's Classics translation by P. G. Walsh (1997, 109: "I have never regarded any of these constituents of our religion with contempt"); the Penguin Classics translation by H. McGregor (1972, 195: "I have never held any of these aspects of our religion in contempt"); and the Loeb translation of H. Rackham (1933, 291: "I have always thought that none of these departments of religion was to be despised").

7.   See Cicero *Nat. deor.* 1.115–16, quoted below, and cf. Scheid 1985a; 1985b, 69–76; and 1987/89. This emphasis on the group (and the here-and-now: see p. 13) stands in distinct contrast to Christianity's notional interest in the individual and the hereafter.

8.   See Ando 2000, 392–95; and Bendlin 2001, 200.

did not think to use *religio* to denominate the cultural systems to which he as a pagan, and the emperor as a Christian, separately adhered: "Of course," he wrote, "it is possible to list emperors *utriusque sectae utriusque sententiae,* of either sect and either conviction."[9] His turn to *secta,* "sect," which in classical Latin might refer to a philosophical school or code of conduct, betrays the huge gap that lies between classical *religio* and late antique "religion."[10]

We may likewise learn something from Augustine's dissatisfaction with *religio.* Writing in the decades before and after the sack of Rome in 410 C.E., Augustine delivered to the West its enduring portrait of Roman religion. Indeed, Augustine's critique of paganism became foundational for almost all Christian theorizing about polytheistic religions, and so has come to influence even those who have not read his work.[11] In the twentieth book of his refutation of Faustus the Manichee (*Contra Faustum Manichaeum*), written in the last years of the fourth century, Augustine sought to distinguish Christians' reverence for martyrs and saints from their worship of God. "We do celebrate the memory of the martyrs with religious solemnity," Augustine allowed, "but we neither build altars nor sacrifice to them" (Augustine *Faust.* 20.21):

> But that *cultus* which is called *latreia* in Greek but that cannot be rendered in Latin by any one word, as it is a sort of servitude owed exclusively to divinity [*cum sit quaedam proprie diuinitati debita seruitus*]— with that *cultus* we neither worship anything, nor teach that anything should be worshipped, other than the one God. Moreover, the offering of sacrifice relates to this *cultus,* whence we name "idolatry" the practice of those who pay sacrifice to idols.[12] Therefore, we never in any way offer anything of this kind to any martyr, or any holy spirit, or any angel, nor do we teach that such offerings should be made.

9. Symmachus *Rel.* 3.3. Compare Libanius *Or.* 30.53, viewing Hellenic paganism as a totality in opposition to Christianity.

10. On "philosophical allegiance," a topic deserving much further study, see Sedley 1989, and cf. Bremmer 1991.

11. For three quite distinct studies of Augustine's attack on Roman religion see Mandouze 1958; MacCormack 1998, 132–74; and O'Daly 1999, esp. 74–134.

12. The compound, first attested in the letters of Paul, derives from Greek εἴδωλον + λατρεία; in Greek (and often in Latin) it long remained uncontracted: εἰδωλολατρία = *idololatria.* See Waszink and van Winden 1987, 73–79.

If Augustine tacitly rejects *religio* as a signifier for the totality of Christian worship, he at least acknowledges his qualms about *cultus*. His rejection of *cultus* in its traditional meaning in classical Latin we may trace back to Cicero's *On the Nature of the Gods*, a text Augustine knew well. Twice in that work Cicero's characters gloss *religio* as comprising the *cultus deorum*, worship of the gods—a formulation that Augustine would himself embrace later in life.[13] But Augustine presumably came to do so because the field of *cultus* was capacious, and he could in a Christian context avoid the classical implications that had disturbed him a decade earlier.

Those classical implications we can excavate by turning to the speech delivered by Cotta at the end of the first book of *On the Nature of the Gods*. Cotta there refutes the criticism of traditional worship just offered by the Epicurean Velleius, and he concentrates on the network of obligations that bound humans and their gods (Cicero *Nat. deor.* 1.115–16):

> For why do you suppose men should have regard for the gods, if the gods not only do not have regard for men, but neither show concern nor do anything whatsoever for them? . . . What *pietas,* what devotion is due to one from whom you receive nothing, or what can be owed to one who does nothing deserving? For devotion is justice toward the gods, but what system of justice can there be for us with them, if there is no community of human with god? *Sanctitas,* piety, is the knowledge of giving the gods their due, but I do not know why they should be so treated, if we have neither received nor expect any good from them.

The word I translate in the first sentence as "have regard for" is *colere,* a word otherwise well rendered by "worship," for what is at stake in its use normally is what is due the gods, and that is cult. But Cicero through Cotta here emphasizes the asymmetrical reciprocity between humans and gods—they are, after all, members of the same community, albeit ones with very different status and power. Hence Cicero defines "piety" (*sanc-*

---

13.   Cicero *Nat. deor.* 2.8: *religione, id est cultu deorum* ("religion, which is to say, the *cultus* of the gods"), and 1.117: *religionem, quae deorum cultu pio continetur* ("*religio,* which is subsumed in the dutiful *cultus* of the gods"). Note Augustine *Civ.* 10.1: *dicere valeamus religionem non esse nisi cultum Dei,* "we can say that *religio* is nothing other than the *cultus* of God."

titas) as *scientia colendorum deorum,* as the knowledge of having appropriate regard for the gods, which I render above "the knowledge of giving the gods their due." The theme of reciprocity in Roman religion is integrally related to its conceiving of the gods as resident in and, indeed, citizens of particular communities, and the chapters of Part 2 will take up the nature of their membership and related problems. At present I want to consider only what it means—more at a foundational level than at the level of practice—for relations between gods and men to be characterized by "justice," and hence to be governed by *ius,* a system of justice or body of law.

We must first recognize that although Romans occasionally referred to "the law" as something that transcended any particular state—speaking in such circumstances of natural law or the law of nations (the *ius gentium* or *ius naturale*)[14]—they also understood that justice is both realized and actualized in particular contingencies and in any given society through statutes and institutions that are locally and historically constructed (an argument elaborated in chapter 4). The contingent specificity of the *ius* that governed relations between human and divine emerges with particular clarity in an aside in Cicero's speech *On His House.* Having described in a superficial way the process by which pontiffs consecrated buildings, Cicero allowed that he said *nihil de pontificio iure, nihil de ipsius verbis dedicationis, nihil de religione, caerimoniis,* "nothing regarding pontifical law, nothing regarding the words of the actual dedication, nothing regarding *religio* or rites" (*Dom.* 121).

Laws change (and other priestly colleges have their separate bodies of law); formulas vary; rites develop; religion . . . expands? We are returned to the puzzling diction of Valerius Maximus, and to the intellectual challenge presented by a religion that expands.

Roman religion was polytheistic. If the nature of polytheism has been an enduring source of ideological misconstrual, the historical development of Roman polytheism—namely changes in the identities of the gods worshipped at Rome, and the gradual increase in their number—has been an equally enduring object of historical inquiry.[15] To an outsider, perhaps the most obvious way in which a polytheistic religion can expand is

14. Gaius *Inst.* 1.1, with De Zulueta 1946, 2:12–13; Berger 1953, s.vv. *ius gentium* and *ius naturale;* and Grosso 1973. See also below, chapter 4, n. 28.

15. See Scheid 1987.

through the incorporation of new deities into the civic community and state cult, a problem taken up in chapter 6.[16] For now, I want to examine two further kinds of "expansion," namely the mere acknowledgment of the existence of deities outside Rome who were previously unknown, and the development of new forms of worship for gods already included in the state pantheon.

As an example of the former, we might turn to Oropus, a city north of Athens at the mouth of the Asopus river, famed in antiquity for its Amphiareion, the temple and precinct of Amphiaraus situated within its territory.[17] The Roman general and dictator Sulla had successfully attacked Athens in 87/86 B.C.E., when on his way to war in Asia, and stayed there again in the winter of 84/83. The chronology of these events is obscure, but it seems likely that in response to Sulla's victory in 86, the wardens of the Amphiareion expanded the scope of its games to honor both Amphiaraus and Rome.[18] They will have sent a delegation to inform Sulla of their decision, almost undoubtedly before his departure for Asia—the god, known for his prophetic powers, may have forecast a Roman victory. Delighted, Sulla took a vow to honor the god and, upon his return to Athens, fulfilled his vow by granting to the god ownership of a considerable body of land and a claim on the revenues of the city.[19] That land and those monies, insofar as they belonged to a god, were tax-exempt.

Sulla died in 79, and sometime thereafter the publicans attempted to collect taxes from Oropus for the valuation of the Amphiareion's land. Oropus sent a delegation to the Roman Senate in 74, in response to which the Senate convened a board of senators to investigate the rival claims and advise how to resolve the matter. (The board of senators included the young Cicero, who refers to this case twice in his theological works.) The consuls for 73, advised by the board, called witnesses and considered documents, whose testimony and contents are paraphrased in the Senate's final decree on this matter. The consuls rendered a decision on 14 October,

16. See Beard, North, and Price 1998, vol. 2, section 2.6.
17. On Amphiaraus see Pease 1955, 562 and 1080; and 1963, 251–52.
18. *SIG* 1064, with Dittenberger's note 4 on that text and note 43 to *SIG* 747.
19. On the historical and financial issues at stake in this episode see Kallet-Marx 1995, 272–83.

and it formed the bases of a decree of the Senate, which the city of Oropus then inscribed on a stele of white marble. I quote selectively from the sixty-nine lines of that document:[20]

> [Lines 1–5] Marcus Terentius, son of Marcus, Varro Lucullus and Gaius Cassius, son of Lucius, Longinus, consuls, to the magistrates, Council, and People of Oropus, greetings. . . . We want you to know that we . . . have reached a decision regarding the dispute between the god Amphiaraus and the publicans. . . .
>
> [Ll. 16–19] Whereas Hermodorus son of Olympichus, priest of Amphiaraus, . . . and Alexidemus son of Theodorus, and Demainetus son of Theoteles, envoys of Oropus, said:
>
> [Ll. 19–23] "Since in the law of contract [i.e., the censorial law governing the actions of publicans in the province of Achaea], those lands are exempt that Lucius Sulla set aside for the protection of the immortal gods and their sacred precincts; and since Lucius Sulla gave to the god Amphiaraus the revenues at issue in this dispute; in consequence they should pay to the publican no tax on these lands."
>
> [L. 24]) And whereas Lucius Domitius Ahenobarbus on behalf of the publicans said:
>
> [Ll. 25–29] "Since in the law of contract those lands are exempt that Lucius Sulla set aside for the protection of the immortal gods and their sacred precincts, but since Amphiaraus, to whom these lands are said to have been granted, is not a god; in consequence it should lie within the power of the publicans to collect taxes on these lands";
>
> [Ll. 29–31] In accordance with the decision of our advisory board, we have reached a decision, which we will bring before the Senate. We have also entered it into the record book of our proceedings.

The inscription continues, but the text thus far quoted already reveals how the case was resolved. For in describing the dispute as lying be-

---

20. *SIG* 747; *RDGE* no. 23. English translations include *ARS* no. 70 and Sherk 1984, no. 70. In support of their decision, the consuls then quote (1) the law of contract, (2) the decision of Sulla, insofar as it was later ratified by a decree of the Senate (3), which is also quoted. The consuls include a reference to an archive of senatorial proceedings: "Present on the advisory board were those same people who are named in the first book of Senatorial Proceedings, wax tablet 14."

tween "the god Amphiaraus and the publicans," the consuls gave away their decision. What the decree of the Senate, alas, does not clarify are the process and reasoning used to resolve what was, at heart, a theological problem. Hence, in Cicero's recollection, there had been no dispute about the law and, indeed, the speakers before the board did not disagree on the content of the *lex censoria*. Rather, according to Cicero, "the publicans discovered that the *lex censoria* exempted from taxation lands in Boeotia belonging to immortal gods, and so they denied that any were immortal who had once been human" (*Nat. deor.* 3.49). How many times must the Senate have adjudicated such claims to divinity, put forward by the gods who owned the myriad shrines dotting the landscape of its empire!

What obligation did the Senate incur on behalf of the people of Rome in recognizing Amphiaraus as a god? The answer is: none. Chapter 3 takes up one aspect of Rome's encounter with foreign gods, namely the need to determine whether those gods were already known at Rome in another guise and by another name, or were in fact previously unknown. Here I wish only to consider the striking authority arrogated by the Senate to adjudicate such claims to divinity. I say "arrogated" because it hardly seems appropriate for a body of mortals to render judgment on the gods. As a matter of law, the Senate had been granted authority in such matters by the Roman people, in whom final authority over such affairs resided.[21] The central question before us might seem to be one of power: Who was the Senate, who were the people, to decide who was a god, and

21. Livy 9.46.6–7: "Licinius Macer dedicated a temple to Concord in the precinct of Vulcan, to the great annoyance of the nobles. Cornelius Barbatus, the *pontifex maximus,* was compelled by the unanimous will of the people to recite the formula of dedication first [for Macer to repeat], although he argued that, by custom of our ancestors, no one other than a consul or general could dedicate a temple. Therefore, on the motion of the Senate, a law was passed by the people that no one should dedicate a temple or an altar without the consent of either the Senate or a majority of the tribunes." See also Cicero *Dom.* 136: "You [pontiffs] will find in your records the case of Gaius Cassius the censor: he reported to the pontifical college his desire to dedicate a statue to Concord; Marcus Aemilius, the *pontifex maximus,* responded for the college, saying that unless the Roman people specifically granted him authority, so that he were acting at their command, he did not think that the dedication could properly be performed." On respective roles of the pontifex and the dedicating magistrate see below, p. 192. On the authority of the people, see Cicero *Leg.* 2.19 with Dyck 2004 *ad loc.,* as well as below, p. 117.

who was not? Thus stated, the question seems to lead inexorably to an old-fashioned view of Roman religion as legalistic, as granting power to mortals to dictate to their gods.[22] Should we perhaps subscribe to such a view after all?

Let me attempt to shift our frame of reference and, in so doing, to formulate the question anew. I begin with an ancient question, one asked by the Roman Senate in 216 B.C.E. Not only had Rome recently suffered a sequence of brutal defeats at the hands of Hannibal, but two Vestals were convicted in that year of inchastity (Livy 22.57.4–6):

> Taking place among so many disasters, that impiety was interpreted as a prodigy. The Xviri were ordered to consult the [Sibylline] books, and Quintus Fabius Pictor was sent to the oracle at Delphi to learn by what prayers and supplications they might placate the gods and what end there would be to these disasters. Meanwhile, on the authority of the sacred books, several extraordinary sacrifices were performed: among them, a male and female Gaul and a male and female Greek were buried alive in the Forum Boarium, in a place walled by stone, already then stained by human sacrifice—a most un-Roman rite.

To ask of an oracle how to placate the gods situates the inquirer in a very different position vis-à-vis the gods than did the act of assessing their divinity. One could argue that the Romans humbled themselves in 216 under exceptional circumstances, their confidence shaken; and the period of the war and the quarter-century that followed it were without a doubt characterized by unprecedented political, social, cultural, and religious turmoil.[23] But other evidence suggests the Romans acted in similar ways from positions of strength.

In 186 B.C.E. the Senate erupted into action and savagely suppressed the private cult of the god Bacchus. For our knowledge of this event we depend principally on two sources, one literary and one documentary, and much toil has been spent in the struggle to reconcile the two, in par-

---

22. Warde Fowler 1911, 270–91, offers perhaps the most cogent and historically grounded argument for this view, but it has had many proponents.

23. A. Toynbee 1965, a monument of classical scholarship, studies the entire period. On its religious history see 2:374–415.

ticular to explain on their basis why the Senate acted then against a cult that had been present in Italy for some years.[24] What requires emphasis here is the seeming dissonance between Livy's description of the cult, on the one hand, and the actual stipulations of the Senate's decree against the cult, on the other. Livy opens his narrative of the year by announcing that the two consuls were ordered to conduct an investigation *de clandestinis coniurationibus,* "concerning secret conspiracies." For as the Bacchic rites spread and developed—and Livy offers an explanation for that process, too—they became more corrupt and more dangerous (Livy 39.8.3–7):

> To *religio* were added the pleasures of wine and banquets, by which
> the minds of many were corrupted. When wine inflamed their minds,
> and night and men mingled with women, and the innocent young with
> the old, then all power of moral discrimination was extinguished, and
> crimes of every kind began to be practiced: . . . not merely the shameful
> violation of freeborn men and women, but perjurious witnesses, false
> evidence, and forged wills.

Speaking before the People, the consul Postumius emphasized not only the criminality of the cult's initiates, but their identity as a political community of suspect allegiance—they constituted "another populace"—as well as the foreignness of the rites.[25] The narrative is remarkable for its sweep and power.

Livy closes the first stage of his account by summarizing the Senate's decree authorizing the consuls to suppress the cult.[26] It is our extraordinary good fortune to possess a copy of the Senate's decree, the one dispatched to the *ager Teuranus,* a territory in Calabria. Its central clauses run as follows:

> [Lines 3–6] Let none of them want to host a Bacchanal. If there are
> any who say that it is necessary for them to host a Bacchanal, let them
> come before the urban praetor at Rome; and concerning that matter,

24. For recent bibliography see Cancik-Lindemaier 1996, de Cazanove 2000a and 2000b.
25. Livy 39.15–16.
26. Livy 39.18.7–9.

when their words have been heard, our Senate shall render a decision, provided that not less than one hundred senators are present when the matter is deliberated.

[Ll. 7–9] Let no man, whether a Roman citizen or a person of Latin name or one of our allies, want to be present at a Bacchic rite, unless he approaches the urban praetor and the urban praetor permits it, in accordance with the will of the Senate, provided that not less than one hundred senators are present when the matter is deliberated. Decreed.

[Ll. 10–14] Let no man be a priest. Let no man or woman be a master. Let none of them want to have money in common. Let no one want to make either a man or a woman a master, or make a man or a woman serve in the place of a master; let no one after this want to swear oaths in common or make vows in common or pledge things in common or promise in common, nor let anyone swear loyalty to another among them.

[Ll. 15–18] Let no one want to perform [Bacchic] rites in secret; let no one want to perform [Bacchic] rites in public or private or outside the City, unless he approaches the urban praetor and the urban praetor permits it, in accordance with the will of the Senate, provided that not less than one hundred senators are present when the matter is deliberated. Decreed.

[Ll. 19–22] Let no one want to perform rites with more than five men and women together, and let not more than two men, nor more than three women, want to be present, except in accordance with the will of the urban praetor and the Senate, as is written above.

The most remarkable feature of the Senate's decision is not that it permits the worship of Bacchus to continue. Rather, it is that the Senate eschews any effort to regulate the forms that Bacchic worship might take, concentrating instead on the institutionalization of the cult and the financial and legal relationships among its members. The major exception, the injunction against male priests, can perhaps be explained by Livy's insistence that that had been a recent innovation, one not authorized by the god.[27] It is loyalty to other members of the cult, and not loyalty to Bacchus, that is the Senate's province. To describe the suppression of the Bacchanalia in terms derived from our study of Amphiaraus and the embassy

27. Livy 39.13.8–10.

of Fabius Pictor: once the Senate had conceded the divinity of Bacchus, it was no longer the Senate's place to decide "by what prayers and supplications" he wished to be worshipped.[28]

The Senate's question to Delphi returns us, somewhat unexpectedly, to the problem of *religio*. To say that it can often be translated as "the sum total of current cult practice" is not to denigrate Roman religion for being legalistic or ritualistic, for lacking a creed, a statement of faith to which individuals could adhere.[29] Nor should we be content merely to assert the inappropriateness of these terms: the negative assertion of incommensurate difference marks the start, and not the end, of inquiry. For what we need urgently to understand is what the Romans had, if not faith.[30]

The simple answer is: knowledge. For having learned from Delphi how to placate the gods, the Senate will have acted; those instructions, their performance, and their results will have been recorded; and the rites will have been repeated in analogous situations, so long as they were adjudged efficacious.[31] Roman religion was thus founded upon an empiricist epistemology: cult addressed problems in the real world, and the effectiveness of rituals—their tangible results—determined whether they were repeated, modified, or abandoned. Roman religion was in this strict sense an orthopraxy, requiring of its participants savoir-faire rather than savoir-penser;[32] and knowing what to do—*scientia colendorum deorum,* the knowledge of giving the gods their due—was grounded upon observation.

---

28. For this concession to the god that it should determine the form of worship appropriate to it see Ando 2003b, 141–46.

29. On the history of "ritual" as a concept in the study of Greek and Roman religion, see Bremmer 1998. For an indicator of the difference between Roman and Christian valuations of "faith," observe that *religio* (and *peccatum,* "sin") are things that cleave to individuals, not things to which one adheres: Cicero *Nat. deor.* 2.11 and *Div.* 1.30.

30. For a fuller exposition of a very similar argument, see M. Linder and Scheid 1993, an exceptionally clear statement of an important theme. See p. 54: "These convictions [actualized in ritual], these beliefs, were never collected in the form of a doctrine for instruction, and above all they did not correspond to an 'act of faith' in the Christian sense. The convictions exposed by the rites did not express a belief in the proper sense—because, for the ancients, belief was an inferior form of knowledge—but a knowing. . . . The verb 'to believe' and the substantive 'faith—just like the term 'pious'—were not technical terms in the religious domain."

31. See Livy 23.11.1–6: "The Senate decreed that the divine matters and supplications should be performed at the first opportunity, with care."

32. M. Linder and Scheid 1993, 49–50; on orthopraxy and seemingly related concepts like "formalism" and "invariance" see Bell 1997, 138–69 and cf. 191–97.

The Romans' famed rectitude and rigor in the performance of cult should be understood in this context: in light of the terrifying superiority of the gods, and knowing what had worked before, one had an overwhelming obligation scrupulously to recreate precisely that earlier performance.[33] For the gods' part, their willingness to abide by this *ius,* by this body of law, was the highest expression of both their *fides,* their norm-based loyalty to the other members of their community, and their goodwill.[34]

Illustrations and reflections of this principle lie near to hand. For example, the consul Marcus Claudius Marcellus was once forbidden by the *pontifices* from consecrating a temple to Honos and Virtus (Honor and Virtue), despite his having taken a vow to do so; the pontiffs argued that if some prodigy were then to happen in the temple, they would not be able to determine to which god the expiatory sacrifice should be made.[35] That is to say, an action in this world, once deemed portentous, required a response; and the need to respond precisely drove pontiffs to require, and architects and urban planners alike to produce, cities in which divine messages in the terrestrial landscape would be as clear as possible. Similarly, the correlative to pagan denunciations of Christian credulity (their religion was based on belief!) was pagan confidence that their practice was based on historical evidence.[36]

The study of Roman religion—as a system of embedded symbols and social actions and their institutionalization—must therefore take its epistemological foundation into account. The distribution and diffusion of

33. See M. Linder and Scheid 1993, 53, and below, p. 45.

34. On *fides* see Boyancé 1972, 135–52; and Scheid 1985b, 128–37. On the honoring of prayers as a sign of divine goodwill, Pliny *Nat.* 28.17, discussed below on p. 000. It is perhaps worth emphasizing here that relations between Romans and their gods were *not* governed by any principle such as *do ut des.* The Romans did not give in order that the gods should give. The Romans induced the gods to give by promising themselves to give, so long as the gods did. If the gods did not deliver, Romans simply omitted to fulfill their vows. On this topic see Scheid 1989/90.

35. Valerius Maximus 1.1.8.

36. For a pejorative view of Christian belief see Julian the Apostate quoted by Gregory of Nazianzus *Or.* 4.102. On the evidence supplied by historical events see Symmachus *Rel.* 3.8 (and cf. 3.9 and 3.15–16): "For insofar as all reason lies in darkness [where the gods are concerned], whence more properly can knowledge of the gods [*cognitio numinum*] come than from recollection and the evidence supplied by things that turned out well?" See also below, chapter 6, p. 126, on Roman claims that non-Romans, too, should be able to recognize the signs of divine favor toward Rome.

power and authority in the religious sphere among individuals, offices, colleges, and institutions reflect at every level the basic needs of Roman religion, to acquire, adjudge, and preserve *cognitio deorum,* "knowledge of the gods."[37] The expression of this epistemic basis at the level of practice and discourse might occasionally seem paradoxical. For instance, Roman religion was incapable of revivalism: assigning no priority to aetiological myths merely because of their antiquity (where they were ancient, of course), Romans could esteem the piety of their ancestors even as they recognized a necessity to act on the basis of more recent evidence. In other words, in matters of religion, their esteem for *mos maiorum* was dispositional and did not extend to practice. What is more, insofar as Romans expected to learn more about the gods over time, Roman aetiological myth *was* historical narrative: when a conflict arose, knowledge acquired during the Hannibalic war, for example, necessarily trumped information of hoary antiquity.[38] It is within this overall epistemological framework that we should situate the importance of record keeping among the duties of the priestly colleges and analyze the institutional and political impact of changes in the technologies of knowledge production.[39]

Finally, the Romans' understanding of the history of religion—as a set of practices developed in response to the gods' immanence and action in the world—lends to their writing on religion an historical awareness deeply at odds with virtually all widely prevalent Christian philosophies of history. The structure and reception of Marcus Terentius Varro's *Human and Divine Antiquities* illustrate this perfectly. Varro's work—written in the final years of the Republic[40]—now exists only in fragments, and the *Divine Antiquities* in particular survives almost exclusively in extracts quoted by Roman paganism's most relentless and influential critic, Au-

---

37.   On this theme see also Potter 1999.

38.   Note the wording used by the praetor Publius Licinius in 209 B.C.E., when he sought to deny the new *flamen Dialis* ex-officio membership in the Senate: "The praetor wanted privileges to rest not upon historical examples of tiresome antiquity, but in each case upon recent practice" (Livy 27.8.9). See also below, chapter 6, p. 140, on record keeping regarding *emendationes sacrificiorum,* changes to rites.

39.   Beard 1985, 1991, and 1998; Gordon 1990a, 184–91; Scheid 1990a, 1994, 1998a, 1999c, 2006; North 1998. See also pp. 000–00 below.

40.   On this work and its date see Jocelyn 1982.

gustine, who outlined and analyzed the structure of the *Antiquities* in the sixth book of *The City of God*.[41]

> [Varro] wrote forty-one books of *Antiquities;* which he divided into human and divine affairs; to human affairs he apportioned twenty-five books, and to divine sixteen.
>
> AUGUSTINE *Civ. 6.3* = Varro *Ant. div.* fr. 4 Cardauns

> Varro himself admits that he wrote about human affairs first, and then about divine affairs, because civic societies arose first, and subsequently the things established by them. But the true *religio* was not established by any terrestrial society; on the contrary, it was the true religion that established heavenly society. This in truth is revealed and taught by the true God, the giver of eternal life, to his true worshippers.
>
> AUGUSTINE *Civ. 6.4*, quoting from Varro *Ant. div.* fr. 5 Cardauns

Augustine's critique rests on a presupposition that is, for Christians, axiomatic: God's ontological priority sanctions the authority of his Scripture, and the myths contained therein provide aetiologies for Christian rites. Assuming for the sake of argument that Varro wrote under similar beliefs, Augustine construes the organization of Varro's work as surrendering ontological priority to humans. We can rather easily, and perhaps facilely, assert that Augustine was wrong to operate on that assumption, and that we would be wrong to follow him. It is rather more difficult to pin down the nature of his error.

We might start by identifying two rather paradoxical ruptures between the status of the gods and the truth content of the information that they provide. They are paradoxical from the perspective of classical metaphysics, and the ruptures exist between Roman and Christian religion, on the one hand, and between Roman religion and classical philosophy, on the other. So, despite Augustine's mockery, Varro's gods did exist prior to the foundation of Rome, but that (chronological) priority did not translate into a privileged role in the foundation of the city or in the establishment of its

---

41.   Note Linderski 2000, 458: "No student of religion can ultimately avoid or evade choosing between Varro (and Cicero) and Augustine."

religious rites. Again, though the passage of information and instruction from gods to mortals remained enormously indirect—so much so that Roman priests devoted much of their energies to the interpretation of divine communications[42]—the Romans nevertheless construed such information as they did receive as factual in basis, the object of knowledge rather than belief. They presumably did so because communication with the gods took place through physical things in the tangible world. Within an (ancient) empiricist epistemology, that would matter.

Viewed from a Roman perspective, the Christians' insistence that their god had once communicated with them directly and yet they did not so much know as merely believe the basic tenets of their faith betrayed not simply a point of philosophical difference, but one of fundamental error. But then to act—whether in the development of liturgy or in the rejection of traditional rites—on the basis of something less than knowledge! To persist in such behavior required the obstinacy of a depraved mind.[43]

Varro himself offered a justification for treating human before divine affairs, which Augustine, alas, only paraphrases (Augustine *Civ.* 6.4):

> Varro confesses that he wrote about human institutions first, and later about divine ones, because divine institutions are established by humans. This is his reasoning: "As painters are prior to paintings, and builders prior to buildings, so civic communities are prior to the things established by them."

But Augustine has no sympathy for this argument. Any part of the true nature of the gods would have to be preferred to mortal affairs, and hence treated first. On the basis of the extracts quoted by Augustine—and here we are truly dependent on him—it appears that Varro left himself open to Augustine's attack by slipping between speaking of *res divinae* and *natura deorum,* between speaking of human institutions established for the worship of the gods and the nature of the gods itself. Augustine seizes on this slippage (Augustine *Civ.* 6.4):

42. For this view of Roman priests see esp. Potter 1999, and cf. 1994.
43. See Pliny *Ep.* 10.96.3.

For, as Varro himself says, if he were writing about the entirety of the nature of the gods, then that nature ought to be preferred in the order of writing. Moreover, as the truth itself declares while Varro falls silent, the nature of the gods certainly ought to be preferred to *res Romanae*, even if it were not all, but merely part of the nature of the gods about which he were writing. And therefore, insofar as the nature of the gods in his treatment is rightly placed after his treatment of human affairs, it is rather none of the nature of the gods that he treats.

Augustine continues by positing, more or less tacitly, that different kinds of things are the objects of different kinds of knowing. In so doing, Augustine reveals himself a typical (Platonic) metaphysician. But the cleavage between divine and human presupposed by Augustine then allows no scope either for cultural-historical approaches to the history of religion, or for empiricist approaches to the study of the divine. As gods precede men, so religion precedes human knowing. What follows is a decisive rejection of the cardinal basis of Roman religious practice, a rejection so fundamental that it precludes sympathetic understanding (Augustine *Civ.* 6.4):

> It is not, therefore, that he wished to privilege human affairs over divine ones, but that he did not want to privilege false things over true. For in what he wrote about human affairs, Varro followed the history of actual deeds; but concerning those matters that he calls divine, what did he follow except mere speculation about nonexistent trifles?

Augustine's mockery cunningly allows for the possibility that Varro agreed with him. That is, pagan readers of Varro in late antiquity could henceforth salvage his respectability only by conceding that he treated "not the truth that belongs to nature, but the falseness that belongs to error." That Varro wrote not about "nature," but about practice; that what he wrote was intended to be true only for the moment at which he wrote it; that a theology of practice fundamentally identifies "religion" with "the history of religion" and still seeks "the truth": these possibilities lay beyond Augustine's reckoning. Augustine's legacy to us is a rupture between our conception of religion and the Roman search for *cognitio deorum*, knowledge of the gods, knowledge that was for them as historically specific as the institutions that developed in response to it.

PART I

THE LIMITS OF ORTHOPRAXY

2

IDOLS AND THEIR CRITICS

Data in an empiricist episteme must be susceptible to sense perception. Where Roman religion is concerned, one or the other of two things must be true: either the actions of the gods in this world in their effects, or the gods themselves, must be material. Of course, the former in no way requires the latter. But much of Roman ritual, and many strands of Roman religious literature, do, in fact, situate the gods in this world, whether as recipients of cult or as inhabitants of particular spaces. What is more, many but by no means all of those actions and representations focalize such relations upon a particular visible manifestation of the divine, namely their cult objects. And yet, already in the ancient world, such patterns in religious behavior were construed by critics of contemporary religion as misconceived or even as fundamentally confused—as directing worship toward the representations themselves rather than toward the gods: hence idolatry, a contraction for "idololatry," from εἴδωλον + λατρεία, the worship of idols. The critique of idolatry has since had a long and distinguished history in the philosophical and religious literatures of Greece and Rome and, indeed, of Christian Europe,[1]

An earlier version of this chapter appeared in James Boyd White, ed., *How Should We Talk about Religion?* (Notre Dame: University of Notre Dame Press, 2006), 33–54.

1.   Besançon 2000 provides a wide-ranging overview. Bevan 1940 and Barasch 1992 survey attitudes to religious art in the ancient Mediterranean. On Greek and Roman critics of idolatry see Clerc 1915, Borries 1918, and Geffcken 1916/19. On iconoclasm in Byzantium

and the sophistication of that tradition, and of its modern students, has in many ways overdetermined the study of idolatry itself, as though ancient philosophers or medieval or early modern Christians could be expected to describe accurately and faithfully the workings and presuppositions of Graeco-Roman religiosity.[2]

This chapter explores the problem of theorizing the materiality of the gods and their susceptibility to representation through consideration of two strands in ancient philosophy: first, that tenet of ancient theories of representation that required idols either to be or to represent the gods; and second, the problem of matter—which is to say, what sort of thing a material god might be. The latter is offered by way of suggestion only; for as a matter of method, it would be perverse to denounce the corrupting influence of ancient philosophy in its theories of representation while co-opting its understanding of matter. What that understanding offers, I suggest, is but one resource among many, for the imaginative work now required to understand and ultimately to describe gods who are and are not idols.

THE STONE THAT WAS THE GODDESS

Our ability to recognize the particularity of Roman religion and to comprehend its rituals depends in large measure on our understanding of its idols.[3] Reconstruction of Greek and Roman rituals reveals that virtually all included the gods as participants.[4] Indeed, the few rituals held without the gods inevitably observed their absence: the *sellisternium,* for example,

---

see Hennephof 1969 and Pelikan 1990; on iconoclasm in Judaism, another important ingredient in the afterlife to ancient religious art, see Bland 2000.

2. Pietz 1985, 1987, and 1988 explore from this perspective the development of the modern anthropological category of the fetish. For other recent histories of religious historiography see Ando 2003b, 373–75; and below, chapter 5, pp. 96–99.

3. I would not follow Vernant 1985, 325–51, in arguing that the converse was true, that idols functioned as idols rather than objets d'art only insofar as they were used in rituals (see esp. 337 and 343–45). If that were true, one would expect many more cult statues to perform miracles, and one might expect famously beautiful statues by renowned artists to account for a disproportionate number of such miracles. But famous Greek sculptures were rarely more than sculptures. Roman anxieties about the efficacy of ritual in desacralizing objects also suggests that Vernant's association of image and ritual needs modification.

4. Gladigow 1985/86 and 1994 survey the use of cult statues in Greek and Roman ritual; cf. Estienne 1997.

consisted in part of a parade of empty chairs, in direct contrast to the *lectisternium,* a feast at which wicker representations of the heads of gods rested on couches and shared a meal.[5] Richard Gordon called attention to this problem in a famous article on religious art in which he observed that Pausanias was as likely to refer to "Athena" as to "a statue of Athena" when he described any given temple.[6] At one level, Gordon did no more than revisit a long-standing puzzle, namely the tendency of participants in Greek and Roman cult to confuse "image and prototype, represented and representation."[7] As Johannes Geffcken observed long ago, this charge had been the mainstay of rationalizing critics of idolatry throughout antiquity; Geffcken could do little more than document that fact, however, because he affirmed it. According to him, this confusion of categories was symptomatic of the "simplistic habits and superstitions *des Volkes.*"[8]

Few recent scholars have taken up the challenge presented by Gordon's observation, namely that of explaining the seeming confusion of ontological categories implied by Pausanias's diction, in large measure because they, like Geffcken, unwittingly subscribe to a theory of representation incompatible with pagan religiosity. For example, although several scholars have catalogued rituals in which idols were treated as gods and fed, washed, and clothed, none of them has sought to explain the philosophical or theological underpinnings of this behavior.[9] Scholarship on ritu-

---

5. On the *lectisternium* see esp. Festus s.v. *struppi* (472L) and *capita deorum* (56L: *capita deorum appellabantur fasciculi facti ex verbenis*), and cf. s.v. *stroppus* (410L), together with Livy 40.59.7 (*terra movit; in fanis publicis, ubi lectisternium erat, deorum capita, qui in lectis erant, averterunt se, lanxque cum integumentis, quae Iovi adposita fuit, decidit de mensa*) and pseudo-Acro on Horace *Carm.* 1.37.3 (PULVINAR DEORUM pulvinaria dicebantur aut lecti deorum aut tabulata, in quibus stabant numina, ut eminentiora viderentur). On the *sellisternium* see Taylor 1935, correcting a long tradition of overreliance on Valerius Maximus 2.1.2.

6. Gordon 1979, 7–8; cf. Schnapp 1994 and Burkert 1970, 360.

7. Geffcken 1916/19, 286: "Für das ursprüngliche Gefühl, den naiven Glauben, fallen Bild und Original, Darstellendes und Dargestelltes, jederzeit zu einer gewissen Einheit zusammen."

8. Geffcken 1916/19, 287; cf. Link 1910, 34: "Antiquissima enim aetate simulacra sunt di ipsi, cuius opinionis recentiore quoque aetate reliquiae manserunt, quoniam auxilii numinis participes esse, si eius simulacrum possiderent, opinabantur. Cuius vetustioris sententiae reliquias cognoscimus ex eo, quod vivendi signa simulacra dedisse feruntur: rident, loquuntur, se avertunt, sudant, se movent, quin etiam ulciscuntur iniurias sibi illatas."

9. Kuhnert 1883; Gladigow 1985/86 and 1994. Vernant 1985, 333, constitutes an important exception, observing of the *kolossos* in the archaic Greek world that one swore "by the stone": it was, as Vernant shows, a double in this world for something invisible, associated alike with the soul and with εἴδωλα (325–38; cf. MacCormack 1975 on the *genius*). But

als in which humans took the place of gods has with few exceptions been similarly abortive: extensive research has revealed that such rituals continued to be performed well into the Christian era, but they are labeled the relics of earlier religiosity and their survival evidence of institutional formalism.[10] Jas Elsner's discussion of "image as ritual," in his essay arguing for a "religious way of viewing images," and Greg Woolf's kindred study of the Jupiter columns constitute two important exceptions to these generalizations, both explicitly indebted to Gordon's work.[11]

Research in other areas of Greek and Roman religion has made significant advances in unpacking ancient descriptions of religious art. For example, Greek and Latin terminology for statuary always reflected the ontological status of the individual depicted and could record whether or not a given statue had been ritually consecrated.[12] Similarly, Greeks brought to the appreciation of religious art a complex aesthetic that differentiated it from other forms of artistic production and assimilated it to a specifically literary theological discourse.[13] For their part, the Romans positioned artwork in their temples in patterns that reflected ontological hierarchies, from god to human, whose appreciation might well aid modern investigations of Roman theological literature and imperial cult.[14] But this ancient sophistication in

---

Vernant merely records rather than explains the disappearance of the conceptual framework that underpinned the use of such doubles, and so he does not ask what one had to believe of both visible and invisible things in order to assert their identity.

10. Back 1883 concludes a fascinating chapter with the judgment that "Hae actiones, quas proprie sacerdotales dixerim, non ab ipsius religionis initiis repetendae sunt, sed manifesto pertinent ad id tempus quo cultus deorum patriarchico illo statu relicto jam suae potestatis factus erat atque ad maximam partem in sacerdotum manus pervenerat. Attamen demonstrant, quamtum antiquitus apud homines Graecos ipsa, ad quorum similitudinem illae celebrabantur, spectacula floruerint. Recte igitur Augustinus civ. 7.18: ex cuiusque dei ingenio moribus actibus casibus sacra ete sollemnia instituta sunt" (28–29). Kiechle 1970 ends a similar survey with the judgment that humans replacing gods in rituals was a feature of "der magischen Vorstellungswelt früher Religiosität." Scheid 1986 constitutes a very important exception to the scholarship in this area, as in many ways does Link 1910, esp. 46–48 and 55–56.

11. Elsner 1996, Woolf 2001.

12. Schubart 1866, Estienne 1997.

13. Madyda 1939, Gladigow 1990.

14. Among earlier work I single out Link 1910. Link investigated the term *sanctus* and had to confront its application to widely disparate things: gods, places, and people. His argument about the development of Roman belief does not persuade—his chronology is in any event indistinct—but his work is conspicuously free of the anachronisms that cloud much work

marking and observing metaphysical boundaries, through language, ritual, and law, has not elicited a correspondingly sophisticated and sympathetic explanation for the theology of idols and sacrality of material objects.[15]

Let me start with an episode from the history of Rome, whose narratives, ancient and modern, neatly illustrate the particular nature of my concerns. In the last years of the Hannibalic war, the Romans were told to bring Cybele, the mother of the gods, from Pessinus to Rome.[16] Rejoicing in the many omens and prophecies that presaged its ultimate victory, the Senate gathered to deliberate *quae ratio transportandae Romam deae esset,* "by what means the goddess should be transported to Rome."[17] It is not mere captiousness that leads me now to quote the Penguin translation of Aubrey de Sélincourt, who wrote for this clause, "the best means of transferring the *image* of the Goddess to Rome."[18] For the anxiety felt by the twentieth-century translator when confronted by a goddess who was a rock, which led him to replace the goddess with her image, was shared by Livy himself, and it is the history of that anxiety, as much as anything, that requires—indeed, demands—elucidation.

I say that Livy shared this anxiety because he vacillated in his estimation of the metaphysical or existential status of Cybele's *baitulos.* In Livy's narrative, the Senate sent legates to Attalus of Pergamum and sought his aid in obtaining the goddess. I quote: "Attalus received the Romans amicably, led them to Pessinus in Phrygia, gave them the sacred stone *that the natives said was the mother of the gods,* and ordered them to take it to Rome."[19] The qualms reflected in the diction of that sentence had disappeared by the time the *lapis niger* arrived in Rome: there Publius Cornelius Scipio was ordered to meet the *goddess* at Ostia; there he received *her* from the ship; and in the temple of Victory on the Palatine he installed the *goddess* on the day before the Ides of April 204.[20]

---

of that era, and his insistence that pagan gods dwelled in particular locations is welcome. See also Scheid 1996 and 1999b; Ando 2003b, 141–46 and 247–50.

15. On the sacrality of objects see Whitehouse 1996, esp. 13 and 19; and Glinister 2000.

16. Beard, North, and Price 1998, 1:96–98, discuss this episode and cite earlier literature.

17. Livy 29.10.8.

18. Sélincourt 1965, 579.

19. Livy 29.11.7.

20. Livy 29.14.10–14.

Ovid's narrative of Cybele's arrival shares this feature with Livy's history: he referred to the stone as the goddess at every opportunity but one, when he described Claudia Quinta fixing her gaze *in imagine divae,* "on the image of the goddess."[21] But not everyone felt this need to be distanced from those who identified idol and goddess. Writing four centuries later in defense of the altar and statue of Victory in the Senate house, Quintus Aurelius Symmachus asked the emperor, "Where shall we swear to obey your laws and decrees? By what scruple will the deceitful mind be terrified, lest it perjure itself under oath? To be sure, all things are full of god, nor is any place safe for perjurers. Nevertheless, the *praesentia numinis,* the presence of the goddess, is a powerful inducement to a fear of wrongdoing."[22] It is, I think, insufficient to say that Symmachus has done no more than elide a distinction between image and prototype, even in the service of a psychological or emotional understanding of religious art, for what was at stake for him in his quarrel with Ambrose of Milan was a great deal more than a philosophy of representation.

Let me provide two more examples, one historiographic, the other historical, the better to articulate my concerns by way of triangulation. In the first chapter of *Mimesis,* Erich Auerbach famously contrasts Homeric and biblical narrative in their strategies for "representing reality." The episodes that he reads in that chapter are Eurycleia's recognition of Odysseus's scar and the sacrifice of Isaac in Genesis 22. Auerbach identifies the impulse of Homeric style as a desire "to represent phenomena in a fully externalized form, visible and palpable in all their parts, and completely fixed in their spatial and temporal relations."[23] Of course, the interaction between two metaphysically equivalent subjects lends itself to this reading; the question is why Auerbach contrasts the one encounter between two humans with another between God and a man. Although he alludes in a single line to the occasional arrival of Zeus or Poseidon from feasts of the Aethiopians, he refrains from suggesting that Homeric poetry and its representational impulses could have theological implications, as the representation of God in Genesis surely does; indeed, by refusing to select true comparanda, he denies the texts equiv-

21. Ovid *Fasti* 4.317.
22. Symmachus *Rel.* 3.5.
23. Auerbach 1953, 6.

alent sacrality. Classical literature is, on his reading, not religious litera-ture at all.

Second, in a homily delivered late in the 390s, Augustine berated his audience for celebrating the birthday of Carthage in a public feast for the *genius* of the city. Had they not known that they were practicing idola-try? "'It is no god,' someone says, 'because it is the *genius* of Carthage.' As though, were it Mars or Mercury, it would be a god. But learn how it is regarded by them: not for what it is. For you and I know that it is a stone. . . . But they regard [the *genius*] as a *numen,* and they accept that statue in the place of the *numen;* the altar testifies to this. What is the al-tar doing there, if the *genius* is not regarded as a *numen?* Let no one tell me, 'It is not a *numen;* it is not a god.' I have already said, 'Would that they knew this, as we all do.' But that altar testifies to their belief con-cerning the *genius* and the statue and to their practice. It convicts the minds of those who worship it; let it not convict those who recline before it."[24]

To the evident concern of an Ovid or a Livy with the representational capacity of religious art, Augustine added an indictment against the ma-teriality of the idols themselves—he and his fellow Christians knew that the statue was merely a stone—as well as a denial that pagan divinities had a metaphysical status equivalent to that of the true God.[25] These re-lated concerns, the seemingly irreducible materiality of idols, on the one hand, and the seeming impossibility of representing anything invisible and incorporeal in or through matter, on the other, formed the basis of all critiques of idolatry in Graeco-Roman literature. I want now selec-tively to review that literature, in terms that draw out its origins within a specific philosophical tradition, in the hope that doings might clarify some difficulties in writing about religion in the ancient and modern worlds, and in reading what has been written.

IDOLS AS (MIS)REPRESENTATIONS: PLATO AND THE TRADITION OF CRITIQUE

Even the limited fragments that we now possess reveal Presocratic philoso-phers to have been absorbed with the issues that were to exercise Augus-

24. Augustine *Serm.* 62.6.10.
25. Ando 2001, 26–30.

tine, albeit in different formulations and on the basis of different postulates and preoccupations. Xenophanes' famous attack on anthropomorphism, for example, censured it as more than a strategy of representation. Of course, he argued, cattle that could draw would draw gods that looked like cattle, as humans drew gods with human forms; but anthropomorphism also concretized theological and metaphysical presuppositions of far greater moment, of which the joke about cattle and horses and lions was merely a reductio ad absurdum.[26] And although Heraclitus attacked the forms of contemporary religious ritual with particular vehemence, like Xenophanes he did so because he believed that ritual expressed beliefs that he found insupportable. Insisting that idols as material objects had the same metaphysical status as other such objects—he likened praying to a statue to conversing with one's house—he lamented that devotees of idols did not understand the true nature of the gods.[27]

It was Plato, not surprisingly, who exercised the greatest influence on the critique of idolatry. He might have expected to do so through his attack on the immorality of traditional mythopoiesis, but those sections of the *Republic* were largely ignored until their arguments and their data were appropriated by Christian apologists of the second century and beyond.[28] Rather, it was his complex subordination of representation and epistemology to metaphysics that sounded the death knell for sympathetic appreciations of idolatrous religiosity among later intellectuals, both pagan and Christian.[29]

Of course, Plato had severe misgivings about the status of images of even material objects. Early in the *Cratylus,* for example, he drew an analogy between producing images of Cratylus and reproducing the number

---

26. Xenophanes frr. 166–69 KRS, esp. 167 (Clement *Strom.* 5.109.2): mortals think the gods are born and have clothes, voices, and bodies like their own.

27. Heraclitus fr. 241 KRS.

28. Weinstock 1926.

29. Vernant 1979, 105–37, provides an exceptionally useful overview of Plato's theory of representation but does not consider its connection to materiality or its specific connection to religious art. Osborne 1987 offers a trenchant reading of Plato's criticism of mimesis in *Republic* 10, but her discussion of its "repercussions" is deeply ahistorical, leaping from Plato to Byzantine iconoclasm, and she is in any event not concerned with cult practice. Her choice of "incarnation" as a term when discussing mimesis in religious art was unfortunate: it seems implicitly to justify (or it simply reflects) a decision not to come to grips with the materiality of gods and idols outside Christian thought.

10. Take anything away from 10 and it is no longer 10. So, a perfect image of Cratylus would be another Cratylus. What, then, is the principle of correctness with which we can judge images?[30] Where representation as such was concerned, Plato answered this question most fully early in the *Sophist*. Writing there of the art of image making, which he called ἡ εἰδωλοποιική or εἰκαστικὴ τέχνη, Plato argued that artists must necessarily leave behind the truth in order to give their creations not the actual proportions of their exemplars, but such proportions as *seem* to be beautiful. For this reason, plastic images, which are called "likenesses" because they are "like" their prototypes, do not even deserve that name, but should be called φαντάσματα, "appearances."[31]

In the *Cratylus,* the quest for a provisional principle of correctness by which to judge images soon yields to a very different question, one framed as a choice between starkly opposed alternatives. Is it better to learn about the truth of things from images of them, and from those images to conjecture about the accuracy of the image itself? Or is it better to learn the truth from the truth, and on that basis to judge its representations?[32] By equating paradigm or prototype with truth, Plato transformed a problem of representation into one of epistemology. This argumentative sleight-of-hand has its analog in the *Sophist,* too. In that work, Theaetetus and the Stranger had reached a seeming paradox, that insofar as being belongs to what is true, and images are inherently false because inaccurate, neither images or idols nor appearances can exist at all, in any way, at any time.[33] But they soon satisfied each other that both false speech and false opinion were possible, and this allowed them to concede a form of existence to imitations of things that really are.[34]

Plato has shifted ground once again. For what are these things that really are? Not Cratylus, of course, nor any corporeal object: for all such things are subject to generation and corruption, and insofar as they are always in flux, no knowledge of them is possible. What had seemed an argument

---

30. *Cratylus* 432b–d.

31. *Sophist* 235d–236c.

32. *Cratylus* 439a–b.

33. *Sophist* 264c–d: ὡς οὔτε εἰκὼν οὔτε εἴδωλον οὔτε φάντασμα εἴη τό παράπαν οὐδὲν διὰ τὸ μηδαμῶς μηδέποτε μηδαμοῦ ψεῦδος εἶναι.

34. *Sophist* 264d: ἐγχωρεῖ δὴ μιμήματα τῶν ὄντων εἶναι.

about epistemology has its foundation in a simple—indeed, simplistic—ontology. It informed much of Plato's work, including analogies he drew with image making. So, for example, he likened the particular examples used by geometricians to so many images in water, εἰκόνες ἐν ὕδασιν, used for seeking realities that are visible only through intellection.[35]

These varied strands of argument find their nexus in the *Timaeus*. Early in that work, Plato distinguished between two kinds of things: those that are and have no origin, and those that are always in a process of becoming but never are. The former are apprehended by intelligence along with reason; the latter by opinion with the aid of sense perception.[36] Understood in these terms, Plato observed, the world itself is an object of sense perception and must have been created through participation in some object of intellection: the world, in other words, is a copy of something.[37] But applying words like "image" and "paradigm" to cosmogonic processes made Plato uneasy. He had earlier deliberated whether to designate the universe by οὐρανός or κόσμος or some other name, and lamented that it would be impossible to speak even the little that one might know of the father and maker of the world.[38] He no longer hesitated. In speaking in this way, he continued, we must assume that words are akin to what they describe: when they relate to the lasting and permanent and intelligible, they ought to be irrefutable and unalterable, but when they express only likeness, words need be only similar or analogous to what they describe. The problem of representation was thus resolved by the paradoxical assertion that the words of discursive language can represent the truly existent more accurately than objects of metaphysical status like unto themselves, namely those subject to generation and decay. "As being is to becoming," Plato could then conclude, "so truth is to belief."[39]

Plato had begun by positing a direct connection between a particular ontology and a set of epistemological distinctions, and only a few pages later used the same two assertions, before either had been proved, to complete a syllogism about representation. Later in the *Timaeus* he returned

---

35. *Republic* 510d–e.
36. *Timaeus* 27d–28a.
37. *Timaeus* 29a.
38. *Timaeus* 28b–c.
39. *Timaeus* 29b–c.

to problems of representation, asking whether one can designate corpo-real objects using ταὐτόν, "the selfsame thing," "the very one," since do-ing so would make a complex assertion about the identity and ontolog-ical integrity of the object in question. Plato concluded that only what receives all bodies and all forms can be so designated, because it never de-parts from its own nature and never participates in any way in any form. It is the mother and receptacle of all created and visible and sensible things, and yet it cannot be called "earth" or "air" or "fire" or "water," but is an invisible and shapeless form; all-receiving, it participates in some way in the intelligible and is itself utterly incomprehensible.[40]

So far, so good. But Plato closed this section by turning once again to epistemology. "There: I have put forth my argument. If mind and cor-rect opinion are two different categories, then there must be self-existent ideas, which are not susceptible to sense perception but are apprehended only by the mind."[41] The formulation of the final argument as a condi-tional is a typical Platonic sleight-of-hand. For its articulation invites one unreflectively to assent to precisely what had been and largely remained at issue, namely that the distinction between knowledge and belief cor-responds with or, rather, rests upon a metaphysics conceived in ontolog-ical terms.

ART AS REPRESENTATION

What has all this to do with idols? A great deal. In what follows, I shall follow modern trends in the study of ancient philosophy and treat the twin foundations of idolatry critique separately, concentrating first on rep-resentation and only later on materiality.[42] But these problems cannot be entirely divorced. On the contrary, I shall argue in closing that it is pre-suppositions about materiality and metaphysics that lead us, as they led Augustine, to insist that idols must be—indeed, can only be—idols of something. Pagan understandings of the representational capacity of idols

---

40. *Timaeus* 50b–51a.

41. *Timaeus* 51d.

42. Cf. chapter 7 below, which attempts to break down the distinctions drawn by modern scholars between Christian and pagan theories of the sacralization of space. Pagan rituals of sacralization, and Christian reliance on sacred narratives and the contingent location of holy relics, presuppose very similar theories of divine immanence.

and the ontological premises of pagan ritual turn out to be far more fluid, complex, and potentially conflicting than any interpretation consistent with a Platonic metaphysics would allow.

Philosophizing defenses of idolatry existed in a variety of forms, but they all accepted the premise that the function of idols was *to represent,* and not in any way *to be,* the god. I label these texts "philosophizing" in part because their authors are demonstrably familiar with Plato, but especially because defending idolatry by recourse to theories of representation itself takes place only within a particular intellectual and discursive tradition.

The problem for idolatry's champions was twofold: first to defend the use of images and only secondarily to defend anthropomorphism. As so often, we know the most influential defense of images in the Western tradition only from its opponents. For it was the first-century Roman polymath Varro who introduced the Latin-speaking world to the allegorical interpretation of religious statuary, and we know his works on religion almost exclusively through the extracts of them quoted by Augustine. We are, therefore, in no position to say whether Varro developed this theory of religious art himself, on analogy with Stoic allegorizing interpretations of Hesiod, although it seems clear that both he and Cicero knew Zeno's reading of Hesiod's *Theogony.* In any event, according to Augustine, Varro argued that the material objects used in religious rituals served to draw the eyes' attention to them in order to direct the sight of the mind to invisible things.[43] Augustine placed a terse formulation of Varro's argument in the mouth of a fictive pagan in a sermon delivered during the closing years of the fourth century: "Suppose some debater stands forth, one who seems learned, and says: 'I do not worship the stone. I merely venerate what I see, but I worship him whom I do not see.' Who is this? 'An invisible *numen,*' he says, 'that presides over that idol.' People who defend the use of images in this way seem learned only to themselves: they may not worship idols, but they still worship demons."[44]

Other advocates for idolatry similarly accepted the premise that idols had to be defended as *representing* something. Although both Dio Chrysostom and Porphyry ultimately defended anthropomorphism, each began

43. Varro *Ant. div.* fr. 225 Cardauns = Augustine *Civ.* 7.5.

44. Augustine *En. Ps.* 96.11. On Augustine's critique of idolatry and its philosophical bases see Ando 2001.

his defense of religious art by reflecting on its function and power. Dio admitted that it was difficult for humans to gain access to and secure knowledge about the divine. He identified four sources of accurate information: poets, lawgivers, artists, and philosophers. Although he knew the story that Pheidias had been inspired by Homer, he also insisted that artists could become the rivals and peers of the poets, as "through their eyes they interpreted the divine for their numerous and less experienced spectators."[45] By allowing that artists ἐξηγούμενοι τὰ θεῖα, "interpret the divine," Dio implicitly elevated them to rivalry with the philosophers, as he had explicitly compared them with the poets, for it is the philosopher, according to Dio, "who interprets the divine in speech and most truthfully and perfectly proclaims its immortal nature."[46] In *On Images*, Porphyry followed Varro and Dio in construing the interpretation of statues as material objects on analogy with the reading of words as material signs. In the preface to that work Porphyry promised "to those who have learned to read from statues as from books what is written about the gods" that he would reveal "the thoughts of wise theology, in which men have revealed God and God's powers through images susceptible to sense perception, by rendering the invisible in visible forms."[47]

All these authors shared with Plato the basic metaphysical assumption that incorporeal deities and, indeed, incorporeal ideas exist not simply on a different but on a higher plane than embodied humans; it was this assumption that triggered the need for the divine to be interpreted rather than merely depicted and that required artists to render the divine not from a corporeal model but from some outstanding form of the beautiful that existed in their minds.[48] The philosophical basis of these debates is nowhere more apparent than in Origen's refutation of Celsus or the first book of John of Damascus's *On Images*.[49] Celsus had argued that

45. Dio *Or.* 12.46.

46. Dio *Or.* 12.47; Madyda 1939, 9 and 38–39.

47. Porphyry *Περὶ ἀγαλμάτων* fr. 351 Smith (fr. 1 Bidez). See also fr. 353: Ἀλλ' ἐπεὶ πάντα τὸν περὶ τούτων ἀπόρρητον δὴ καὶ μυστικώτερον λόγον εἰς ἀσωμάτους δυνάμεις μεταφορικῶς ἀνῆγον, ὥστε δοκεῖν μηκέτ' ἐπὶ τὰ ὁρώμενα μέρη τοῦ κόσμου τὴν θεοποιίαν αὐτῶν συντείνειν, ἀλλ' ἐπί τινα ἀοράτους καὶ ἀσωμάτους δυνάμεις, σκεψώμεθα εἰ μὴ καὶ οὕτως μίαν χρὴ τὴν θείαν δύναμιν ἀποθαυμάζειν, ἀλλ' οὐ πολλὰς ἡγεῖσθαι.

48. Cicero *Orator* 2.8–9; Madyda 1939, 16 and 27–29.

49. See esp. John 1.7.

Christians were both idolaters and poor metaphysicians because they believed humans had been created in every way similar to God. Did they not depict God saying, "Let us create man in our image and resemblance [κατ᾽ εἰκόνα καὶ ὁμοίωσιν ἡμετέραν]?"[50] This was impossible, Celsus continued, because God did not make humans in his image, nor does God resemble any other visible being.[51] Origen defended Christians first with a specious semantic argument, insisting that God made man only in his image but not in his resemblance, a claim for which he offers no proof but a formulation that achieved lasting influence. Origen also undertook a more rigorous defense of Christian metaphysics. Celsus has clearly misrepresented the Christians, Origen wrote, when he suggests that we think what is made "after the image of God" is the body, whereas the soul, which is better, is deprived of what is "after his image." For none of us, Origen asserted, thinks that your idols are actually images of gods, as you do, as though such things could depict the shape of an invisible and incorporeal deity; still less do we imagine that anything created after God's image could be ἐν τῷ φθαρτῷ σώματι, "in a corruptible body."[52]

THE MATTER AND MATERIALITY OF RELIGIOUS ART

What is a corruptible body? Are there incorruptible bodies? These questions return us to theories of matter and to the reception of Plato's *Timaeus*. For among ancient readers, that text remained to the end of antiquity a touchstone in debates about creation and hence about matter. Not surprisingly, the features that make it most characteristically Platonic—its peculiar and misleading claim to debate first principles, and its use of myth to describe things it elsewhere labels unrepresentable in discursive language—serve as lightning rods in subsequent debate. In reviewing that literature, I turn first to Aristotle, Plato's most influential reader and most powerful critic.[53]

50. Origen *Cels.* 4.30, and cf. 7.62.

51. Origen *Cels.* 6.63.

52. Origen *Cels.* 6.63 and 7.66.

53. Two recent overviews of the Platonist tradition obliquely relevant to this chapter are Gerson 2005 and Karamanolis 2006. They have quite distinct perspectives, though each is concerned to explicate Aristotle's place in that tradition. Neither is invested in the questions foregrounded here.

In his engagement with Plato's physics, Aristotle reacted above all to two related problems, the first having to do with theory, and the second with the particular articulations by which theory was elaborated. So, according to Aristotle, Plato offered no theory of matter or, rather, none that satisfied Aristotle's demand for logical coherence. The theory of Forms, for example, demanded the existence of unformed matter, whether of chronological or merely logical priority. This demand Plato signally failed to meet. Hence Aristotle asked whether Plato's universal receptacle or his so-called "space" might be interpreted as prime matter but declared the text insufficiently precise to allow any certainty.[54] It was not that Plato failed to appreciate the existence of this problem, as Aristotle pointedly observes. For his part, Plato wants the Forms to preexist, to be prior to corporeal matter. But as Aristotle notes, Plato's own illustration of formation—that of a goldsmith imposing a design on previously unformed gold—did not require that the design exist before the gold, nor, in fact, could it explain the existence of the gold at all.[55]

I do not want to belabor the details of Aristotle's reading of Plato. It is, however, crucial to understand two things, both connected to the paradoxical reception of Aristotle's critique among later Platonists. The first has to do with the elaborate connection Aristotle drew between forms and particulars, on the one hand, and the ontological status of the different kinds of matter from which each is made, on the other; the second principally with the tools for discussing materiality that Aristotle bequeathed to Graeco-Roman posterity.

As regards the first legacy of Aristotle's critique of Plato, although Aristotle insisted that prime matter existed prior to its formation only in potentiality and not in actuality—only, that is, logically and not temporally—he did concede to Plato that the metaphor of the goldsmith may have been useful as a narrative representation of processes that were themselves atemporal.[56] Writing in the *Metaphysics* of the making of a bronze sphere

54. Plato *Timaeus* 51e–52b; Aristotle *De generatione et corruptione* 329a5–24, with Joachim 1922, 194–95; cf. *Metaphysics* 1035b31–1036a13 and 1028b33–1029b13; and Ross 1960, 565.

55. Plato *Timaeus* 49a–50b; Aristotle *De generatione et corruptione* 329a5–24, and cf. *Metaphysics* 1033a24–1034a8 and 1050b6–28.

56. On the logical priority of prime matter see Aristotle *De generatione et corruptione* 329a24–b2, with Joachim 1922, 198–99, as well as Ross 1960, 47 and 50, on *Physics* 206b12–16.

from unformed bronze, he observed that we call the particular and the form by the same name, and yet what we call the form cannot have any existence—is not, in his terms, a self-subsistent substance—merely because we have a name for it.[57]

If Aristotle resembles Plato in having connected problems of epistemology, representation, and metaphysics, he did so in radically different ways. So, for example, Aristotle conceded that most people defined processes of generation and corruption, γένεσις καὶ φθορά, by drawing an incorrect ontological distinction between perceptible and imperceptible matter.[58] On the other hand he insisted, first, that some matter was potentially susceptible not to sense perception, but only to intellection; and second, that both kinds of matter were properly speaking unknowable prior to their formation. That is why we assign the same name to both forms and particulars.[59]

The second crucial legacy of Aristotle's critique of Plato is more subtle. It consists of the conceptual and terminological apparatus that Aristotle developed to correct Plato, which was appropriated by later Platonists merely to supplement him. Of particular importance were the assimilation of Aristotle's logically and potentially extant matter, what he calls the πρώτη ὕλη, to Plato's universal receptacle, on the one hand, and the complex belief that "intelligible" particulars had some form of imperceptible matter, different in kind from ὕλη γεννητὴ καὶ φθαρτή, sense-perceptible matter subject to generation and corruption, increase and change. This endowed Plato's ontological framework with a form of underlying and unchanging ὕλη νοητή, intelligible matter, that could be the object of reason and νόησις, to correspond to the corruptible matter that was the object of opinion and sense perception.[60]

The complex afterlife of these debates within middle Platonic physics lies to one side of my project, concerned as it is with pagan and Christian theorizing about idolatry. I therefore concentrate here on two prob-

---

57. Aristotle *Metaphysics* 1033a24–1034a8.

58. Aristotle *De generatione et corruptione* 318b18–27; cf. *Metaphysics* 1036b32–1037a5

59. Aristotle *Metaphysics* 1035b31–1036a13 and 1036b32–1037a10.

60. As both Joachim 1922, xxxiv and 143–44, and Bostock 1994, 156–57 and 165–66, make clear, Aristotle regarded intellectual matter as nothing more than an imaginary logical postulate, useful for discussing the application of concepts like "place" and "touch" to τὰ γεωμετρικά.

lems: first, the gradual evolution of a specifically Latin vocabulary for matters of materiality prior to Augustine (and so prior to his historically decisive articulation of a Latin idolatry critique), and, second, the recursive application of an Aristotelian vocabulary to problems of theology raised (or discovered by later readers) in the *Timaeus*. The testimony of Cicero's *Posterior Academics* is crucial to both problems, both for its account of the eclecticism of Antiochus of Ascalon and for its explicit discussion of problems of translation. These issues became intertwined when Cicero turned to ὕλη, "matter," because in brief compass he equated Aristotelian prime matter with Platonic space, called them both *materia,* and identified *corpus,* or body, as the product of this matter and Stoic ποιότης, which he rendered with *qualitas.*[61] Cicero implicitly acknowledged the eclecticism of this brief essay on *initia,* "first principles," when he assigned authority for its various components to Antiochus, Aristotle, or the Stoics, but he often labeled the whole as the thought of the Greeks.[62]

But the full extent of Aristotle's influence on Platonic physics emerges with particular clarity in the philosophical handbooks of Alcinous and Apuleius. Alcinous took from Plato his correlations between knowledge and intellection, on the one hand, and sense perception and opinion, on the other.[63] Indeed, like Plato, Alcinous accepted this distinction as axiomatic: it is because intellection and opinion are categorically different that their objects possess differential ontological status; there must be primary objects of intellection, πρῶτα νοητά, as there are primary objects of sense perception, πρῶτα αἰσθητά.[64]

Post-Aristotelian metaphysicians, lacking the courage of Aristotle's rigorous empiricism, and adhering to a Platonizing physics that would have dismayed Plato and Aristotle alike, concluded quite naturally that objects

---

61. Cicero *Acad. post.* 24–27.

62. I set aside here consideration of philosophy at Rome between Cicero and the late first century C.E. There is, however, much of interest in this material. Seneca's extended meditation on first principles, for example, would repay careful study, both for its Platonic smith who imposes form on Aristotelian bronze, and for its vocabulary, which is largely independent of Cicero (see, e.g., *Ep.* 58.16–31; cf. *Ep.* 65.8–9 and 90.28–29). Indeed, Seneca's language reveals just how fluid the Latin philosophical tradition remained in the middle of the first century.

63. Alcinous 4.3–4.

64. Alcinous 9.4; cf. *Timaeus* 51d–52a.

of intellection and sense perception each require their own kind of matter. What Alcinous provided, therefore, is a thoroughly Aristotelianized account of the *Timaeus*. Not only did he accept without hesitation that the universal receptacle, the mother and nurse of all things, and space are one and the same, but he equated them with an Aristotelian substratum inaccessible to sense perception and consisting of matter.[65] This substratum is neither corporeal nor incorporeal, but is body in potentiality.[66] That there was neither a continuity in language nor in any meaningful sense a continuity of meaning in the concepts of "substratum," "matter," and "potentiality" between Plato's time and his own would not have concerned Alcinous; the doxographic tradition, as we would term it, was not concerned with history in that sense. So it was that Alcinous could conjoin those equations by adapting an argument from Aristotle's *Metaphysics* and so identify matter as a first principle, from which the world was created, and then ask by whom and with reference to what it was fashioned.[67] The answers to those questions were, of course, God and the Forms, the former imposing the latter on a chaotic, imperceptible preexistent substratum of matter.[68] If on the one hand we have here traveled far from the *Timaeus,* we are far from the *Cratylus,* too, and reside now among gods with a far more complex, if somewhat nebulous, relationship to matter.

Apuleius provides our best glimpse into the Latin reception of Plato between Cicero and Lactantius. In book 1 of *On Plato* he described Plato's first principles: God, matter, and the Forms. According to Apuleius, prime matter is *improcreabilem incorruptamque,* by which he meant it is not subject to γένεσις καὶ φθορά, generation and corruption.[69] This matter is potentially recipient of form and is the substratum of creation. It is, finally, indeterminate and imperceptible: it is infinite insofar as its magnitude is indeterminate; it is neither corporeal or incorporeal. It cannot be body, since it lacks form; but without body it cannot be said to exist.[70]

---

65. Alcinous 8.2: Καὶ πρῶτόν γε περὶ ὕλης λέγωμεν. Ταύτην τό νυν ἐκμαγεῖόν τε καὶ παν-δεχὲς καὶ τιθήνην καὶ μητέρα καὶ χώραν ὀνομάζει καὶ ὑποκείμενον ἁπτόν τε μετὰ ἀναισθη-σίας καὶ νόθῳ λιγισμῷ ληπτόν.

66. Alcinous 8.3.

67. Alcinous 9.3, following Aristotle *Metaphysics* 1032a12–20.

68. Alcinous 12.2.

69. Apuleius *De Plat.* 1.5.

70. Apuleius *De Plat.* 1.5.

Alcinous drew his correspondences between epistemology and metaphysics in a section of his handbook separate from that on first principles. Apuleius for his part understood that knowledge of first principles was inseparable from our capacity to articulate or represent it. So, for example, he tentatively concluded that prime matter was unsusceptible to sense perception but accessible to intellection.[71] He grew more certain when he turned to the distinction between objects of intellection and their essence, and objects of sense perception and their essence. The former are visible to the eyes of the mind and exist always in the same way, equal to themselves; the latter must be judged by opinion, whether rational or irrational, because they are created and pass away. What is more, the essence of objects of intellection, insofar as it is the subject of discourse, offers grounds for rational and abiding true statements; the essence of objects of sense perception, which are like the shadows and images of true things, offers ground for disputation and words that are inherently inconstant.[72]

It would be interesting to trace the development of this conceptual framework in greater detail, for its influence on theology and the exegesis of creation narratives from the Jewish diaspora to late antiquity, from Philo to Hermogenes and Tertullian, to Calcidius, Proclus, and John Philoponus. In this area as in so many others, Plotinus broke with his predecessors: his model of divine immanence, that of a mirror reflecting images, created conceptual space for growth in new directions.[73] Julian the Apostate's writings on embodiment similarly allowed for new understandings of ritual practice, which have been largely ignored by those convinced that paganism was on the wane by the mid-fourth century.[74] At present, however, I want only to return to the problem of gods and idols, and I do so by way of Augustine.

AUGUSTINE, IDOLS, AND
THE AFFECTIONS OF THE MISERABLE

In his great commentary on Genesis, written early in the fifth century, Augustine was concerned to reconcile his own form of a Christian Pla-

71. Apuleius *De Plat.* 1.5.

72. Apuleius *De Plat.* 1.6.

73. Plotinus 4.3.

74. See, e.g., Julian *Ep.* 89.293a–d, together with R. Smith 1995.

tonizing metaphysics with a narrative of creation that rather unfortunately concretized very different theological presuppositions.[75] Yet analysis of and writing about such issues raised irresolvable problems of representation, ones that Augustine sought to explain by appeal to the very metaphysical postulates that had motivated his project in the first place.[76]

When, therefore, Augustine asked how it was that God had said, "Let there be light," he wavered between two possibilities: God had spoken either in time or in the eternity of his Word. The first option he dismissed: *si temporaliter, utique mutabiliter,* if God had spoken in time, then his words would have been subject to change, for material words inevitably sound and pass away; their matter is subject to generation and corruption.[77] "But this is an absurd and fleshly way of thinking and speculating."[78] Augustine's diction, *carnalis,* "fleshly," invoked two closely related problems. Being embodied souls, not only did humans interact with the world through sense perception, but their language and their physics had developed to explain the physical and not the intelligible world. Genesis had, therefore, to accommodate its narrative to the limitations of discursive speech and the patterns and habits of thought that human speech could articulate. Genesis 1.2, for example, represented the "waters" as preexistent not because matter participated in God's eternity in any way, but because God had *to be said* to be stirring above something: in actuality, Augustine insisted, the verse referred not to spatial relations, but to God's powers, which were transcendent over all things.[79]

As this example indicates, Augustine took pains throughout the commentary to be as precise as possible in matters of priority, both logical and temporal, and never more so than in matters of matter. Unformed matter, he insisted, was created at the same time as the things made from it: just as a speaker does not utter sound and then fashion words from it, so God did not first make unformed matter and then impose form upon it. Unformed matter is thus prior not in time, but in origin; and Scripture has, in narrating with the material words of discursive language, sep-

75. The following paragraphs treat material studied in depth in Ando 2001.
76. Ando 1994; cf. Ando 2001.
77. Augustine *Gen. litt.* 1.2.4.
78. Augustine *Gen. litt.* 1.2.5.
79. Augustine *Gen. litt.* 1.7.13.

arated into a temporal sequence actions that God did not separate in time in the act of creation.[80] Augustine extended his concern for precision about materiality to the theology of demons and angels: demons may be animals, but they are ethereal ones. Their ethereal bodies remain ever strong and do not suffer corruption in death.[81] Formed not from corporeal matter but from what Augustine called spiritual substance or what Apuleius might have called intelligible matter, the bodies of demons were not susceptible to sense perception. The anthropomorphism of their idols was thus doubly corrupting: the familiarity of their appearance was as reassuring as it was deceptive, and it granted to them such power as they had over the affections of the miserable.[82]

The particular metaphysics and theory of matter that underpinned Augustine's understanding of Genesis and the bodies of demons also framed his view of idolatry. In a sermon delivered in Carthage in 404, he once again posited a fictive interlocutor as a learned defender of pagan practice. "'When I worship Mercury,' he says, 'I worship talent. Talent cannot be seen; it is something invisible.' We readily concede that talent is something invisible [*aliquid inuisibile*], and insofar as it is invisible, it is better than sky, or earth, or sea, or anything visible. Indeed, invisible substances [*substantia inuisibilis*], such as life, are better than every visible substance, since everything visible is a physical thing [*quia omne uisibile corpus est*], and talent is indeed a great thing. Nevertheless, if you were to consider the talent that they say they worship, what does it do? For do not many with great talent err? Perhaps they err greatly who think that talent is to be worshipped using an image of Mercury."[83]

. . .

What, then, of Cybele? Was the black stone really the goddess? Did the Romans get the one and only black stone that may have been the goddess? Might they, in fact, have received a duplicate of the stone housed

80. Augustine *Gen. litt.* 1.15.29.

81. Augustine *Gen. litt.* 3.10.14.

82. Augustine *En. Ps.* 113.2.6. Augustine regarded Plato's inability to conceive of "spiritual substance" as the principal failing of Platonic theology; on this problem see Ando 2001, 38–43.

83. Augustine *S. Dolbeau* 26.24; cf. *En. Ps.* 113.2.4.

at Pessinus, or even one copy among many? Let me suggest one way to answer these questions without looking at the history of Pessinus.

Plato's metaphysics of representation has influenced the reading of this episode and others like it in two ways. On the one hand, because we assume that copies are not only different from but inferior to their exemplars, we insist that religious artifacts cannot be duplicated. Hence the Romans must have received the one and only black stone. Paradoxically, because we assume that the divine exists on a higher plane than the corporeal, we also believe that the black rock must have *represented,* rather than *been,* the goddess. But surely a sign or a symbol or an image can be reproduced?

I suggest that ancient understandings of materiality, and the philosophy of representation underlying religious ritual, provide a means to obviate this most Platonic of false binarisms. Recognizing further hypostases beyond or between the divine and the corporeal, people in the ancient world might well have understood that Cybele somehow was, and yet was not coextensive with, their black stone; and in that way, she might also have been, but not been identical with, other black stones.

I do not know what the Romans brought from Pessinus to the Palatine in 204 B.C.E. But I suspect that the metaphysical and epistemological doctrines bequeathed to us from Plato are not going to help us to find an answer. What I do know is that Cybele's shrine in Pessinus remained an active site of cult and focus for pilgrimage for at least 560 years after her *baitulos* went to Rome. For that reason alone, I suspect that Lucius Cornelius Scipio received both more and less than the black rock that was the goddess in the port of Ostia twenty-two hundred years ago.

3

INTERPRETATIO ROMANA

Among scholars of classical religion, the terms *interpretatio Graeca* and *interpretatio Romana* commonly refer to the "broad identification among Greeks and Romans of a foreign godhead with a member of their own pantheons." These identifications are generally studied at the level of naming—not least because most easily collected evidence for them is linguistic, namely the epigraphically attested use of "theonyms as appellatives." What is more, many argue that the central interest of *interpretationes* lies more or less exclusively in the act of naming, and not in the act of identification, and that *interpretatio* itself is "therefore a phenomenon in the linguistic-conceptual realm."[1] This seems to me shortsighted. It is the object of this chapter to suggest that an inquiry into *interpretatio Romana* might well reveal as much about Roman gods as it does about Roman language. For *interpretatio* is not, at its heart, an act of translation, but one of naming, and its unpacking conjoins two complex problems. There is first that of knowledge, of discerning what god one is dealing with and the name by which he or she would like to be known; and second one of theology, of gods who exist in particular locations, some of whom might or might not

An earlier version of this chapter appeared in *CPh* 100 (2005), 41–51, © University of Chicago.

1. Graf 1998b.

be identical with (and yet different from) gods known by other names and in different guises elsewhere. In chapter 6 we shall find these issues raised again by the ritual of *evocatio,* "summoning forth," by which gods, properly addressed, were invited to abandon one location (among Rome's enemies) for another (at Rome itself). The problem of identification thus lies not with language per se, but in recognizing and theorizing the identity of gods across landscapes and linguistic and iconographic traditions.

We might start with *interpretatio Romana* itself. The phrase occurs in extant Latin literature only once, in a famous passage of Tacitus's *Germania* (43.4; trans. after M. Hutton and E. H. Warmington):

> Apud Naharvalos antiquae religionis lucus ostenditur. Praesidet sacerdos muliebri ornatu, sed deos interpretatione Romana Castorem Pollucemque memorant. Ea vis numini, nomen Alcis. Nulla simulacra, nullum peregrinae superstitionis vestigium; ut fratres tamen, ut iuvenes venerantur.

> Among the Naharvali is shown a grove, the seat of a prehistoric ritual. A priest presides in female dress, but the gods commemorated there are, according to *interpretatio Romana,* Castor and Pollux. That, at least, is the power manifested by the godhead, whose name is Alci. There are no images, no trace of any foreign superstition, but nevertheless, they worship these gods as brothers and young men.

What did Tacitus mean by *interpretatio Romana?* Did he, for example, assume that the gods in question were *both* ontologically prior to human language *and* everywhere the same, and that their names in different languages arose arbitrarily? In which case, does he intend no more by *interpretatio Romana* than the identification of a referent by its Roman sign? Or did he assume that names arise organically, in which case Castor and Pollux were in some yet-to-be-determined sense different at Rome and among the Naharvali, and nonetheless still the same? In which case, does *interpretatio Romana* refer not simply to the translation of natural signs, but to the intellection necessary to recognize the identity of their referents?

This development of Tacitus's diction takes us in a rather different direction than does traditional scholarship on the passage and its context. *Interpretatio Romana* has generally been studied not for what it reveals about a specifically Roman form of polytheism, or in particular about its epistemic and linguistic premises, but rather as a phenomenon of religion in the provinces of the empire. To scholars so minded, Tacitus has provided a name for—and is often supposed to have intended no more by that name than—a simplistic form of translation, kindred to contact syncretism, by which Romans and Germans, in this case, recognized some identity between the *vires* of the *numina* of gods whom they knew by different names.[2] (I note in passing my own astonishment that this mode of understanding the divine has not provoked more reflection than it has; it seems to me an extraordinarily perilous way of being in the world.)[3] And scholars subscribing to such a reading of Tacitus have compiled vast catalogs of correspondences between Roman and provincial gods, drawing on both epigraphic and literary evidence.[4]

My concern with this body of scholarship lies not with its aims or achievements, but with the unreflective way in which Tacitus is made to serve its proponents. For what few scholars other than Georg Wissowa

2. This is the usage foregrounded by Graf 1998b. See also Henig 1986, 159–69 at 160–61, or R. Bloch 1973, 55–61 at 55: both scholars assume that *interpretatio* was a (simple) matter of naming and therefore, as it seems, unimportant in cult and largely irrelevant to individual religiosity.

3. Perilous, that is, because the processes of recognizing a god on the basis of some exercise of its power and then naming it properly were so fraught with difficulty and simultaneously so essential. See Ando 2003b, 141–46; and chapter 1 above.

4. For two recent studies of *interpretatio Romana* along these lines, see Webster 1995 and Spickermann 2001, each of whom uses the term more or less with the meanings it has acquired in twentieth-century usage. The principal development of recent years in scholarship of this kind has been an effort to situate translation and naming in post-conquest societies and so, often enough, to redescribe them as forms of power relations, a development that harmonizes well with efforts then commencing to view Romanization as a form of competitive performance among local elites. Exemplary studies of this kind include Alföldy 1985; M. Alföldi 1999, who issues the important caution that other aspects of cult—including ritual—were likewise subject to "interpretation"; and Derks 1991. It would, however, be a mistake to reduce translation solely to a function of power: "In this chapter and the next I want to say: (1) that translation is an art of recognition and response, both to another person and to another language; (2) that it carries the translator to a point between languages, between people (and between peoples), where the differences between them can be more fully seen and more nearly comprehended—differences that enable us to see in a new way what each one is, or, perhaps more properly, differences in which the meaning and identity of each resides; (3) that it involves an assertion of the self, and of one's language too, that is simultaneously a limiting of both; and (4) that in all these respects it is a model of law and justice, for these two are at their heart also ways of establishing right relations, both between one person and another and between a mind and the languages it confronts" (White 1990, 230).

have respected are the very different origins whence ancient evidence for the theory and practice of *interpretatio Romana* derives.[5] It is hardly a distortion to say that extant theoretical reflections on *interpretatio* are universally Roman, while the vast majority of evidence for its practice is provincial.[6] And while it might therefore be salutary to suggest that a certain caution is in order before aligning Roman theory with provincial practice, it is surely time that we placed Tacitus's remark in its Roman context and situated Roman theories of *interpretatio* alongside other Roman writings on religion, language, and knowledge.[7]

To start with, Tacitus's *interpretatio Romana* is perhaps most easily aligned with a glib but long-lived ancient tradition of remarking upon the names of gods (Cicero *Nat. deor.* 1.83–84):

> [83] Age et his vocabulis esse deos facimus quibus a nobis nominantur?
> [84] At primum, quot hominum linguae, tot nomina deorum; non enim ut tu, Velleius, quocumque veneris, sic idem in Italia Volcanus, idem in Africa, idem in Hispania.

> [83] Come now: Do we really think that the gods are everywhere called by the same names by which they are addressed by us? [84] But the gods have as many names as there are languages among humans. For it is not with the gods as with you: you are Velleius wherever you go, but Vulcan is not Vulcan in Italy and in Africa and in Spain.

Thus situated, Tacitus finds his place alongside Greeks from Herodotus to Ammianus and Romans from Caesar to . . . well, Ammianus, in rendering barbarian religions intelligible to the educated elite of the Mediterranean basin by, in effect, eliding problems of cultural and theological

---

5.   Another exception is Lund 1998, which attempts in part through philological argument to analyze in what sense Roman ethnographic writing was Romanocentric, and hence to estimate what evidentiary value it can have for students of the precolonial societies of the empire.

6.   Indeed, Wissowa 1916/19 is practically alone in recognizing in any systematic way how far modern inquiry into provincial forms of *interpretatio* has developed—indeed, has distanced itself from its theorizing at Rome. Note, e.g., 28: "Im allgemein darf man sagen, daß wir aus den *interpretationes Romanae* mehr für unsere Kenntnis römischen Denkens als für die der provinzialen Religionen gewinnen."

7.   There have been two attempts to consider *interpretatio Romana* in light of Roman writings on *interpretes,* neither terribly satisfactory: Girard 1980, 23–24; and Schenk 1989, 86, 92–93.

difference altogether.[8] (I say this despite some misgiving that Greeks and Romans based their practices of identifying and naming gods on very different grounds and gave them expression in very different arenas.)

This reading of Tacitus finds support in other uses of *interpretatio,* both within and without ethnographic literature. Pliny, for example, explained that the Druids held nothing more sacred than mistletoe and the tree on which it grows—provided that tree is an oak. Indeed, he says, the Druids perform no rite without the foliage of those trees, so that it might seem that the Druids did in fact get, or at least appear to have gotten, even their name *interpretatione Graeca.*[9] Presumably what Pliny meant is that the Druids got their name from δρῦς, Greek for "oak." More specific to religion and akin to its usage in Tacitus is the use of *interpretatio* by Varro, who denominates *interpretationes physicae* or *physiologicae* the allegorical identification of gods with natural forces that constitutes one important doctrine of so-called natural theology.[10]

But there is a further problem. It is not simply that words rarely map precisely the semantic fields of other words, even in the same language. The Romans knew that and remarked frequently upon it: the emperor Tiberius urged senators to speak only Latin in the *curia,* and himself apologized for using "monopoly"; on another occasion, he requested that the word ἔμβλημα be replaced in a *senatus consultum* either with a Latin equivalent, regardless whether that took one word or several, or with a periphrasis—I mean, circumlocution (which Suetonius calls an *ambitus verborum*).[11] Quintilian acknowledged this difficulty when writing about "rhetoric": the standard translations *oratoria* and *oratrix,* he complained, were no less ugly than the Plautine coinages *essentia* and *queentia;* what is worse, they were inexact.[12]

The problem is rather one of cultural difference, of which language

---

8. Richter 1906, 5–11; Wissowa 1916/19, 2–18; Pease 1955, 426–27. On Herodotus in particular see Harrison 2000, 251–64.

9. Pliny *Nat.* 16.249: *iam per se roborum eligunt lucos, nec ulla sacra sine earum fronde conficiunt, ut inde appellati quoque interpretatione Graeca possint Druidae videri* ("[The Druids] even choose groves of such oak for their own sake, nor do they perform any rite without the foliage of those trees, so that they could seem to have been named 'Druids' by *interpretatio Graeca*").

10. Augustine *Civ.* 7.5; see Varro *Ant. div.* fr. 225 Cardauns, and cf. frr. 206 and 23.

11. Suetonius *Tiberius* 71.

12. Quintilian 2.14.1–4.

difference is but one index. Polybius's narrative of the negotiations between the Aetolians and Manius Acilius Glabrio exemplifies the pitfalls that confronted Greeks in their early encounters with Roman magistrates, in which cultural differences were problematically masked by the apparent ease with which each side supposedly translated what the other was saying.[13] In 191 B.C.E. the Aetolians decided to ask the consul Glabrio for his pardon and resolved to commit themselves "to the faith of the Roman people" (εἰς τὴν Ῥωμαίων πίστιν), not knowing, as Polybius writes, the import (δύναμις) of the phrase. In fact, a Roman understood surrender *in fidem* as unconditional; the Aetolians, Polybius explains, were deceived by the word "faith" into believing that their action would obtain a more complete pardon (ὡς ἂν διὰ τοῦτο τελειοτέρου σφίσιν ἐλέους ὑπάρξοντος). After granting the Aetolians an audience, Glabrio began to dictate the terms under which they could act in the future. The Aetolians cried out in surprise: "What you demand is not Greek [Ἑλληνικόν]." Glabrio responded coldly: "Are you still going to run around acting Greek [ἔτι γὰρ ὑμεῖς ἑλληνοκοπεῖτε], even after you have given yourselves εἰς τὴν πίστιν? I will throw you all in chains if I want to."[14]

The jurist Gaius reflected rather more self-consciously on this issue when treating verbal obligations, which are created by formulas of question and response. The particular *verborum obligatio* "*Dari spondes? Spondeo*," "Do you promise conveyance? I promise," he writes, was peculiar to Roman citizens. Other obligations, he allows, are part of the *ius gentium*, and so are valid among all people, citizens and aliens alike. Did he mean that the one formula could be employed only by Roman citizens, and only in Latin, whereas all others were available to both citizens and aliens? And could those formulas be uttered in any language? And if Gaius indeed drew that distinction, on what basis did he do so? Gaius goes on to list Greek formulas valid between Roman citizens—provided they un-

13. For preliminary remarks on Roman attitudes to language difference in diplomatic and provincial contexts, see Dubuisson 1982 and Eck 2000; for some further remarks on dissonance between Greek and Latin political vocabularies and on the "effectiveness" of translation, see Ando 1999, 7–18.

14. Polybius 20.9–10. The accounts of this episode have generated an enormous bibliography that is not immediately relevant to my purposes here, since I cite this episode merely as an example of a larger phenomenon that is not itself in doubt. For bibliography and a thorough reading see Gruen 1982; on *fides* in international relations see Hölkeskamp 2000, esp. 234–48.

derstand Greek—and he concedes that Latin formulas are valid between aliens, provided they understand Latin. "But the verbal obligation *dari spondes? spondeo,* is so peculiar to Roman citizens that it cannot even be rendered in Greek in an accurate interpretation [*ut ne quidem in Graecum sermonem per interpretationem proprie transferri possit*], even though the word *spondeo* is said to derive from a Greek word."[15]

The specific connection here established between language and political identity merits further study; it is in many ways peculiar, and peculiarly Roman.[16] For now, I want to work my way back to religion and to Tacitus. For what Quintilian, Polybius, and Gaius draw our attention to is the contingent particularity and cultural specificity of concepts and the terms used to represent them. In other words, they draw our attention to translation as an historical problem, one we should seek to locate not simply in place and time, but from place to place, and time to time.

Within the sphere of religion, constructing an identity between gods through naming will have elided differences in iconography and theology that must have been negotiated at levels other than the language of prayer, for example. This much is already visible at moments when an *interpretatio* was contested. So, for example, Tacitus concludes an extended meditation on the origin of Serapis by allowing that (*Hist.* 4.84.5):

> deum ipsum multi Aesculapium, quod medeatur aegris corporibus, quidam Osirin, antiquissimum illis gentibus numen, plerique Iovem ut rerum omnium potentem, plurimi Ditem patrem insignibus, quae in ipso manifesta, aut per ambages coniectant.

> Many identify the god himself with Aesculapius, because he heals the sick; some with Osiris, a very ancient divinity of those peoples; many again identify him with Jupiter, for his power over all things; but most identify him with Dispater, from the emblems that are manifest in him, or through arcane reasoning.

We can perhaps trace something of the intellectual energy involved in these processes of identification in Pliny's remarks on the god who per-

15. Gaius *Inst.* 3.92–93.

16. For the present see Adams 2003 and Ando 2004, esp. 97–98.

mits the harvesting of cinnamon: for it can be culled only *non nisi per-miserit deus,* "if the god allows it." "Some *understand* [*intellegunt*] this god to be Jupiter; the Ethiopians call him Assabinus."[17] The identification apparently required more than merely instantaneous recognition.

The slippery nature of such identifications was never more evident than when those identifications were based on iconography, for the ancient world had itself already developed a sophisticated critical tradition on action and representation in the practice of cult.[18] This emerges with particular clarity—or particular complexity—in Lucian's remarkable ethnographic travelogue regarding the temple of Atargatis at Hieropolis. Of its inner chamber Lucian writes (*De dea Syriae* 31–32):

ἐν δὲ τῷδε εἴαται τὰ ἔδεα, ἥ τε Ἥρη καὶ τὸν αὐτοὶ Δία ἐόντα ἑτέρῳ οὐνόματι κληΐζουσιν ... Καὶ δῆτα τὸ μὲν τοῦ Διὸς ἄγαλμα ἐς Δία πάντα ὁρῇ καὶ κεφαλὴν καὶ εἵματα καὶ ἕδρην, καί μιν οὐδὲ ἐθέλων ἄλλως εἰκάσεις. ἡ δὲ Ἥρη σκοπέοντί τοι πολυειδέα μορφὴν ἐκφανέει· καὶ τὰ μὲν ξύμπαντα ἀτρεκέι λόγῳ Ἥρη ἐστίν, ἔχει δέ τι καὶ Ἀθηναίης καὶ Ἀφροδίτης καὶ Σεληναίης καὶ Ῥέης καὶ Ἀρτέμιδος καὶ Νεμέσιος καὶ Μοιρέων.

In it are two images, one Hera, the other Zeus, whom they call by another name. . . . Certainly the image of Zeus resembles Zeus in all respects—his head and cloak and throne—so that you would not willingly liken him to anyone else. But Hera will reveal to you as you look at her a form of diverse appearances. Taken all together, to be sure, she is Hera, but she also has something of Athena and Aphrodite and Selene and Rhea and Artemis and Nemesis and the Parcae.

Lucian's text is rife with such play on the identity of gods and statues. Here it is perhaps sufficient to note the irony that Hadad can be confidently identified as Zeus on the basis of iconography, despite the fact that the god was there addressed by another name, while the identity and name of Atargatis, or Hera, are not explicitly problematized, despite the enormous caveats Lucian must then issue about the form she assumes in the temple.[19] It is,

17   Pliny *Nat.* 12.89.

18.   See above, chapter 2, pp. 24–25.

19.   On this passage see Elsner 2001, 136–38; and Lightfoot 2003, 434–39.

however, precisely to the question of form or appearance that Gaius Aurelius Cotta addressed himself in his dismissal of Epicurean anthropomorphism at the end of *De natura deorum* 1:[20]

[82] What are you thinking? That Apis, that bull sacred to the Egyptians, does not seem to the Egyptians to be a god? He is as much a god to them, I'll wager, as that Sospita of yours is to you. Nor do you ever see her, even in your dreams, but that she is dressed in a goatskin with a spear, small shield, and little shoes turned up at the toe. But such is not Argive or Roman Juno. Therefore Juno has one form among the Argives, another among the Lanuvians. Indeed, the form of Jupiter is that of Capitolinus among us, but that of Ammon among the Africans.

The difficulties raised by Cotta, of sheer iconographic heterogeneity, on the one hand, and of the appearance of Roman gods in foreign lands on the other, were often discussed, and Cicero's comments deserve placement in that long tradition.[21] What demands our attention here is not, once again, the fact of any given correspondence. Rather, Cicero through Cotta dramatizes the dynamics of naming and interpretation in two ways.[22] First, as part of an overall assault on anthropomorphism, he draws attention to the paradoxical power and contingency of representations. Velleius *always* sees Juno as Juno Sospita, and yet others see Juno in radically different forms, and will, presumably, *always* see her in those forms. And yet, Cotta asks, must we believe that Jupiter himself always has a beard, or that Apollo is in fact beardless?[23]

The second problem to which Cicero draws our attention is that such

20.   Cicero *Nat. deor.* 1.82: "Quid igitur censes? Apim illum sanctum Aegyptiorum bovem nonne deum videri Aegyptiis? Tam hercle quam tibi illam vestram Sospitam. Quam tu numquam ne in somnis quidem vides nisi cum pelle caprina, cum hasta, cum scutulo, cum calceolis repandis. At non est talis Argia nec Romana Iuno. Ergo alia species Iunonis Argivis, alia Lanuinis. Et quidem alia nobis Capitolini, alia Afris Hammonis Iovis."

21.   See, e.g., Kleve 1963, 98 n. 2, suggesting that Cotta's argument might be an adaptation of a sophistic argument against belief in gods altogether.

22.   On the probability that Cotta distorts Epicurean disquiet about the naming of gods see Kleve 1963, 100–101; for a positive treatment of the Epicurean position see Obbink 1996, 427–29.

23.   Cicero *Nat. deor.* 1.83 (cf. 1.101–2): *Isto enim modo dicere licebit Iovem semper barbatum, Apollinem semper inberbem.*

identifications, once made, must be made to work in and over time. Having identified Ammon with Jupiter through *interpretatio Romana,* short of repudiating the identification, one would have the ongoing challenge of recognizing in Ammon with his horns—the essence? the person? of Jupiter brandishing his thunderbolt.[24] Hence what might have appeared a simple problem of translation stands revealed as but one moment in a complex nebula of personal accommodation and cross-cultural dialogue whose implications reach far beyond the merely lexical. At the level of cult, such accommodation will have hard-won and long-lived effects at the level of practice that are visible today almost exclusively in the material record.

Cicero and Varro's most attentive ancient reader did not fail to perceive the logical instability of this system, even at the level of cult within a single state. Writing about Jupiter, Augustine complained (*Civ.* 7.11):

> Dixerunt eum Victorem, Invictum, Opitulum, Inpulsorem, Statorem, Centumpedam, Supinalem, Tigillum, Almum, Ruminum et alia quae persequi longum est. Haec autem cognomina inposuerunt uni deo propter causas potestatesque diversas, non tamen propter tot res etiam tot deos eum esse coegerunt.

> They called him Victor, Invictus, Opitulus, Inpulsor, Stator, Centumpeda, Supinalis, Tigillus, Almus, Ruminus, and other names that it would take long to enumerate. They have assigned these *cognomina* to one god for different reasons, on account of different powers; nevertheless, they did not compel him to be as many gods as they had justifications for names.

We should be careful to observe first what Augustine for once does *not* seize upon, and that is the classical Roman tendency to atomize godheads

---

24. Cf. Lucan 9.511–14:

> Ventum erat ad templum, Libycis quod gentibus unum
> inculti Garamantes habent; stat sortiger illic
> Iuppiter, ut memorant, sed non aut fulmina vibrans
> aut similis nostro, sed tortis cornibus, Hammon.

> He arrived at the temple, which one alone for the races of Libya
> the uncivilized Garamentes maintain; the Dealer of Lots stands there,
> Jupiter, so they say, but neither brandishing lightning bolts
> nor as before us, but as Ammon, with twisted horns.

and individuate divine powers and personalities at the level of cult.[25] Indeed, the power of his critique here partially rests upon his magnanimous concession that gods normally have single powers and are known by virtue of them: in other words, that one can identify a god by the *vis* of its *numen*, to adopt the terminology of Tacitus.[26]

The object of Augustine's scrutiny here is thus not Varro's *Divine Antiquities*, but his *De lingua Latina*, a fact made clear by attention to the niceties of Augustine's diction.[27] In reading that work, we are, alas, constrained by the loss of its first four books, and especially of the second, third and fourth, in which Varro discussed the science of etymology in general, as well as arguments for and against it.[28] But beyond whatever he will have said there about etymology—he will, for example, have had to consider whether names are natural or arbitrary—he turns in his fifth book to case studies and there admits a further object of study, namely semantics. As he there asserts: "Every word has two innate features: from what thing and in what thing it is assigned as a name" (*Cum unius cuiusque verbi naturae sint duae, a qua re et in qua re vocabulum sit impositum*).[29]

Varro's first case study is the body of terms used to describe places and the things that are connected to them; his second subject is immortal and mortal things, which he discusses in such a way that he treats things concerning the gods first.[30] At an etymological level, some gods' names are

---

25.   Scheid 1999b (= Ando 2003b, 164–89); see also Ando 2003b, 141–46.

26.   Cf. Caesar *B. Gall.* 6.17: "Post hunc Apollinem et Martem et Iovem et Minervam. De his eandem fere, quam reliquae gentes, habent opinionem: Apollinem morbos depellere, Minervam operum atque artificiorum initia tradere, Iovem imperium caelestium tenere, Martem bella regere" ("After him, [they worship] Apollo and Mars and Jupiter and Minerva. Concerning them [the Gauls] have practically the same opinion as other races do: Apollo wards off disease; Minerva teaches the principles of works and crafts; Jupiter holds the rulership of the heavens, and Mars reigns in warfare")—a list of *potestates* if ever there was one. The problem of identifying gods by their *vires* is noted, if not theorized, by Girard 1980, 25, "Les identifications que fait l'*interpretatio Romana* ne sont pas, comme l'on dit aujourd'hui, génétiques, mais fonctionelles"; and M. Alföldi 1999, 597: "Konkret zu unserer Übersetzung mag man fragen, was soll 'die Kraft der Gottheit' besagen?"

27.   Cf. Varro *Ling.* 5.1 (*In his ad te scribam, a quibus rebus vocabula imposita sint in lingua Latina*), 5.58 (*Terra enim et Caelum, ut Samothracum initia docent, sunt dei magni, et hi quos dixi multis nominibus*), and 5.62 (*Utrique testis poesis, quod et Victoria et Venus dicitur caeligena*).

28.   Varro *Ling.* 5.1.

29.   *Ling.* 5.2 (translation after Kent).

30.   *Ling.* 5.10, 57.

clearly arbitrary, as others are natural: otherwise, they could not derive from their powers, as Saturn is from *satus*, "sowing"[31]; nor could their names or the names of their powers be specific to Latin.[32] It might then seem quite natural for Varro to supply foreign names for gods. But that task—which is not, I should acknowledge, a dominant feature of his project—involves more complicated problems of theology and language than it might seem at first glance to do.

Take, for example, the gods to whom he devotes the most space, Caelum and Terra (Heaven and Earth). These, it turns out, are also Serapis and Isis of Egypt, and Saturnus and Ops in Latium. Varro uses many different phrases to establish or describe these identities; indeed, he himself allows that he can call Heaven and Earth *multis nominibus*, by many names.[33] We may or may not, as ancient readers might or might not, find the arbitrary nature of gods' names troubling. But there is still a further difficulty, and that is one of semantics. It is not simply that as Varro allows Latin names to point to gods who are known by other names in other cultures, so he must also allow that gods' names are subject to the processes of coinage and borrowing and the vagaries of usage that he so meticulously documents regarding everyday words.[34] Among many examples, he cites the currency of Pollux, which not only derives from Greek, but is itself a departure from old Latin *Polluces*.[35]

Rather, the semantic problem rests with the naming of gods in the first place, and with the epistemic foundation upon which practices of naming must rely. For even as Varro refuses to qualify his equation of Caelum with Serapis with Saturn with Jupiter, he nevertheless debates the appropriateness of any given name. Ennius calls Jupiter *pater*, "Father," writes Varro, because Jupiter *patefacit*, "makes evident" the seed: "for then it is evident

31. *Ling.* 5.64.

32. I take the emphatic focus on *vocabulorum impositio in lingua Latina* at the start of book 5 to be decisive in this regard (*Ling.* 5.1).

33. *Ling.* 5.58. See also *Ling.* 5.57 (*Principes dei Caelum et Terra. Hi dei idem qui Aegypti Serapis et Isis. . . . Idem principes in Latio Saturnus et Ops*), 5.64 (*Quare quod caelum principium ab satu est dictus Saturnus, et quod ignis, Saturnalibus cerei superioribus mittuntur. Terra Ops, quod hic omne opus et hac opus ad vivendum, et ideo dicitur Ops mater, quod terra mater*), and 5.65 (Idem hi dei *Caelum et Terra Iupiter et Iuno*).

34. See the abstract discussion at *Ling.* 5.3 and 5.5–6.

35. *Ling.* 5.73–74.

that conception has taken place, when what is born comes out." "This same thing is shown more clearly by Jupiter's ancient name: for he once was called Diovis and Diespiter, which is to say, 'Father Day.'"[36] (I note in passing that Tacitus *Hist.* 4.84.5, cited above on p. 49, seems to reject precisely the identification of Jupiter and Dispater that Varro here assumes.)

If some names are more appropriate than others, and if naming normally proceeds from the perception of an exercise of power on the god's part, then both naming and identification must remain subject to the uncertainties inherent in any religious system that relies upon an empiricist epistemology. "*Luna,* Moon," we are told, "is so named because she alone shines at night."[37] And if one does not so neglect the stars? "Some call her Diana, just as they call *Sol* Apollo."[38] But why do those who do *not* call *Luna* Diana act as they do? Whom do they call Diana? What if the moon is not Diana? And what if she is?[39]

But here we must part company with Varro, or at least with Augustine's disingenuous reading of *De lingua Latina.* For if *interpretatio* were merely a matter of cataloguing names—if, that is, it consisted solely in *nominis pro nomine positio*[40]—then we might expect two things: a more extensive set of mappings than is attested, the vast majority of names of gods receiving no *interpretatio;* and near universal consensus on particular *interpretationes,* especially in later periods, and especially at particular cult sites, within, as it were, a specific linguistic or cultic community. But that we do not find. For what speaking thus of names as synonyms in fact ignores are two related factors essential to the unpacking of any trope, including *interpretatio*—and metonymy, for that matter: the capacities of in-

36. *Ling.* 5.65–66.

37. *Ling.* 5.68.

38. *Ling.* 5.68.

39. Cf. *Ling.* 5.69: *Quae ideo quoque videtur ab Latinis Iuno Lucina dicta, vel quod et Terra, ut physici dicunt, et lucet; vel quod ab luce eius qua quis conceptus est usque ad eam, qua partus quis in lucem, luna iuvat* ("She appears therefore to be called Juno Lucina by the Latins, either because she is also Earth, as natural scientists maintain, and shines [*lucet*]; or because from that light of hers in which someone is conceived, until that light in which someone is born into the light, the moon [*luna*] helps"). See also 5.71: To be sure, gods are named *a fontibus et fluminibus et ceteris aquis.* But how do the waters get their names, and what is the nature of the connection between god and river?

40. The phrase is Quintilian's, describing not *interpretatio,* nor, for that matter, translation, but metonymy (8.6.23).

dividual speakers and the microcontexts of their utterances, on the one hand, and the referents for their signs, on the other.[41] By referents, naturally, I intend the gods. But it is precisely the gods who even in antiquity were as elusive as their identification was essential (Varro *Ant. div.* fr. 3 Cardauns):

> eo modo nulli dubium esse . . . ita esse utilem cognitionem deorum, si sciatur quam quisque deus vim et facultatem ac potestatem cuiusque rei habeat. Ex eo enim poterimus . . . scire, quem cuiusque causa deum invocare atque advocare debeamus, ne faciamus, ut mimi solent, et optemus a Libero aquam, a Lymphis vinum.

> For this reason it should be doubtful to no one, how useful is knowledge of the gods, if one could know what power and skill and capacity each god has in any matter. For from this we would be able to know which god we ought to summon and to call upon for any particular reason, lest we should act like mimes are accustomed to do and wish for water from Liber, or wine from Lymphs.

The pronounced tendency of Romans in foreign lands to worship the gods of those lands by the names they held there, or even by such generic titles as *genius* or *praesides huius loci,* may thus be understood as the consequence of an epistemic problem and a theological conundrum: one needed to address the very god in a position to provide aid, but the naming of that god rested ultimately upon factors extralinguistic.[42] Nor, importantly, was that practice confined to Romans in foreign lands: in some years (but not all), the Arval Brethren at Ostia, too, included in their prayers an invocation of "the god or goddess, under whose protection lies this grove and place."[43] The problem may be simply stated, if not simply solved: one needed to know, and knowledge is hard to come by.

In light of these concerns, we should return to Varro's assertion of a simple identity between Terra and Isis and Ops and Juno, and Caelum and

41. Cf. Schofer and Rice 1977, 133–36.

42. See Ando 2003b 141–46; see also Scheid 1999b. On the worship of local gods, see, e.g., Saddington 1999.

43. Scheid, *CFA* no. 94 (183 C.E.), col. II lines. 3–4; and, in abbreviated form, no. 100a (218 C.E.), line 3. On these texts see Scheid 1999b (translated in Ando 2003b, 165–89).

Serapis and Saturn and Jupiter, for what Varro asserts about them is precisely what Cicero could not allow regarding Vulcan (*Nat. deor.* 1.84; above, p. 46). It is, of course, possible, even likely, that Cicero meant no more than that Vulcan was not *called* Vulcan in Africa or Spain; likewise, it is possible that Cicero meant no more than that Jupiter is not always *represented* as bearded, any more than Apollo is always *depicted* as beardless. But how would we know? We run afoul here of that tendency in ancient literature to refer to cult statues as though they *were* the gods whom they seem to represent.[44] I say "*seem* to represent" both because ancient theorists often deplored the representational capacity of plastic images and their power "over the affections of the miserable," and because what is at stake in Cicero's diction might not be representation at all.[45]

There remains in any event the problem that the identity of the gods turns out to be distressingly and disconcertingly labile. It is not simply their names and forms, but the gods themselves who are πολυειδεῖς and *multiplices*. On this point, cult practice diverges strongly from philosophical theology, for it was Plato who set the terms for virtually all traditions of Hellenistic theology, and they believed in gods whose identities were fixed and unchanging. The ontological presuppositions of cult were quite different. How should one then name a god? And how did one recognize another's god as identical to one's own, not least in light of their radical difference?

Gods were not alone in defying the reductive taxonomies of the semantic urge. Of the oak Pliny the Elder wrote: "It is not possible to dis-

---

44.   Gordon 1979. See further chapters 5 and 7 below. For a valuable survey on the representation of gods in cult see Funke 1981.

45.   See Augustine *En. Ps.* 113.2.6 (quoted and discussed in Ando 2001, 24–53):"But, it will be said, we have many instruments and vases made of materials of this kind or from metal, for use in celebrating the sacraments, which, being consecrated by this function, are called holy, in honor of Him who is worshipped for our salvation. And what are these instruments or vases, except the works of human hands? But do they have mouths, and not speak? Do they have eyes, and not see? Do we pray to them, because through them we pray to God? This is the chief cause of that impious insanity: the form resembling a living creature has such power over the affections of the miserable that it arouses prayers to itself, even though it is clear that it is not alive, so that it ought to be despised by the living. The images have more power to distract an unhappy soul because they have mouths, eyes, ears, noses, hands, and feet than they have power for correcting such a soul because they do not speak or see or hear or smell or argue or walk." Cf. Cicero, *Nat. deor.* 1.84, discussing the sheer multiplicity of gods.

tinguish the types of oak by their names, which are different in different places, for while we see the *robur* and *quercus* growing all over, we do not see the *aesculus* everywhere, while a fourth member of the oak family, which is called the *cerrus,* is unknown even to a large part of Italy. We will therefore distinguish them by their characteristic properties and natures and, when compelled, by their Greek names."[46] What then of the Druids, whose name, you may recall, Pliny not only proposed to derive from δρῦς, Greek for "oak"; he seems to have suspected that it might *actually* have come from Greek. But a Druid was not an oak, nor, it seems, did Pliny necessarily believe that Gallic oaks were, in fact, δρύες, to the extent that he associated that word with a specific kind of oak. In other words, *if* Druid did in fact derive from δρῦς by *interpretatio Graeca,* it did so despite being, in Varro's terms, etymologically and semantically untrue. In other words, if it is true, it is false.

Which returns us, at long last, to Tacitus. If the Alci *were* Castor and Pollux by *interpretatio Romana,* I do not know how to construe that identity. I suppose, in the words of William Jefferson Clinton, "it depends on what the meaning of 'is' is."

This much at least is clear. In its enigmatic status, *interpretatio Romana* resembles many of the other mechanisms with which Romans and their subjects negotiated cultural difference, translation among them; it is likewise emblematic of the myriad problems besetting the study of cross-cultural contact in the ancient world.

I will close by asking one more question that I cannot answer. I turn once again to Tacitus (*Germania* 43.4): "There are no images, no trace of any foreign superstition, but nevertheless, they worship these gods as brothers and young men." Foreign to whom?

46. Pliny *Nat.* 16.17.

4

RELIGION AND *IUS PUBLICUM*

The two great codifications of law undertaken in Christian late antiquity are often presented as novel interventions in the history of religion. As the first such codification since the Twelve Tables a thousand years before, we are told, the Theodosian Code did more than advertise the maturation of imperial government; it aggressively highlighted that government's adherence to Christianity. For Theodosius departed from the precedent of the Twelve Tables by including in his Code a book on religion—the sixteenth and last; while Justinian did him one better by placing his book on religion first.[1]

Even crediting their brevity, it is not possible to let these descriptions stand. Later in this chapter I shall attempt somewhat more precisely to describe the ambitions of the Codes and to distinguish them from each other. For now, let me point out two things. First, neither text cites the Twelve Tables as a precedent—though, oddly enough, each does cite precedents, and they not surprisingly differ in their practice in this regard. In light of their neglect, we ought eventually to seek the source of the privileged

An earlier version of this chapter appeared in Ando and Rüpke 2006, 126–45.

1.   Harries 1999, 14; Matthews 2000, 120, 290.

claim that the Twelve Tables have had on the scholarly imagination. Second, neither Code actually describes any of its books as devoted to "religion" in any catholic or totalizing sense of the word. Indeed, the Theodosian Code offers no titles for its books; the last *chapter* of book 16 is entitled *De religione,* "On religion"; that book's first chapter is entitled *De fide catholica,* "On the Catholic Faith."[2] The first chapter of the first book of Justinian's Code, on the other hand, bears the title *De summa trinitate et de fide catholica et ut nemo de ea publice contendere audeat,* "On the Highest Trinity and on the Catholic Faith and That No One Should Dare to Argue about It Publicly."[3] The logic of their language betrays a clear anxiety that forms of religiosity other than Catholicism should not be embraced by any global category such as our "religion."[4]

These concerns aside, the gathering, editing, and republication of laws on religion as part of corpora of law invite reflection on the place of religion within the concerns of law and government, as on the relationship between individual and corporate religious identities. What, for example, is the force of *publice,* "publicly," in the title of chapter 1, book 1, of Justinian's Code? What is more, the incorporation of religion within the law's sphere of interest, and the logic of that action, must have enabled and might well have mobilized particular interactions between the government and religious minorities, regardless wherein the novelty of either late antique codification might have lain.[5]

This chapter uses the evolving relationship between religion and law in classical and Christian Rome as a lens through which to investigate the social-theoretical postulates of classical and Christian religion. In particular, I ask what the law and legal theory might reveal about the metaphysical status that each tradition would extend to human institutions, not least the law itself. At issue are a number of questions, not least of which are these, namely on the basis of what sort of knowledge, and under what authority, did humans construct the institutions by which their societies were organized? Chapter 1 stressed the absence at Rome of aetiological myth, prescribing the form of rituals and authorizing forms of funda-

2.   *CTh* 16.1 and 11.

3.   *CJ* 1.1.

4.   On *religio* see above, chapter 1, pp. 2–5.

5.   On these and related questions see Ando and Rüpke 2006.

mentalism. In that chapter, as in chapter 3, I stressed both the importance and the fragility of Roman religious knowledge. In the late Republic, the regulation of that knowledge, as of the priesthoods that accumulated and adjudged it, were subordinated by intellectuals to systems of law. Those intellectuals described their projects as archaeologies or excavations, and their products were thereby endowed with complex histories retrojected into the remote past.[6] The relation at Rome between religion and law is thus double: conjoined in practice and politics from the beginning, they were subject in the late Republic to homologous systems of elaboration and rationalization. Each has much to say about the other.

That said, in our own inquiry we confront substantial problems of evidence, whose nature is perhaps clarified by recalling that the law of the Christian empire was essentially classical, regardless whether it served as basis or point of departure. How should we understand the massive secularity of the civil law as it is preserved for us, or the claims to novelty embedded in the Christian codifications? Are we to believe that religion had no place in classical jurisprudence? Can we really be expected to believe that Rome itself functioned for a thousand years without systematically codifying its laws or rationalizing its legal system, despite almost unimaginable growth in the scope of its responsibilities? However incredible, these postulates are the necessary presuppositions of the view of law and religion in the Christian empire with which I began. On their reasoning, we confront in the pagan Roman empire a society that regarded neither law nor religion as essential to the maintenance of order, whether we define that negatively as the absence of public violence and private criminality, or positively as the adherence to a particular ethical code. In that light, one ambition of this chapter consists in asking how, when, and why pagan and Christian Roman lawyers and legislators offered new theorizations of society and of the legal, social, and religious ties that bound it together.

We might start by analyzing the ways discovered by Theodosius and Justinian to express the specifically religious dimensions of their legislative programs. We should have first to confess that neither codification was justified as a body of Christian law. Their authors identified their novelty and need by reference rather to the state of confusion then ob-

6. Rüpke 2005, 1547–66; Scheid 2006.

taining in the courts and schools of law.[7] This is not to say that these were not Christian codifications, or that their Christian character was not flagged. Rather, I would emphasize how different were the means their authors adopted for inscribing their Christianity in their Codes. It would be easy—and, I think, it would be wrong—to argue that they had no precedent to follow: to argue, in other words, that they embarked on their projects de novo and that their codifications were, by virtue of being Christian, sui generis. One might as easily say that qua codifications of Roman law, the Codes merely collated a few hundred years of legislation, and that qua Roman codifications of law, the Codes of late antiquity had abundant precedent for accommodating religion within the interests of the law. I should like, moreover, to go one step further, and argue that the longevity and influence of codes of law rest very directly on the willingness and ability of their authors to make explicit the grounds of their normative power and on the contingent acceptance and appeal of those claims. The final section of this chapter will discuss the divergent fates of the Theodosian and Justinianic Codes from precisely this perspective.

The emperors Theodosius II and Valentinian III announced their intent to produce a new codification of law on 26 March 429, the first and third sentences of which decree read as follows (*CTh* 1.1.5.):

Ad similitudinem Gregoriani atque Hermogeniani codicis cunctas colligi constitutiones decernimus, quas Constantinus inclitus et post eum divi principes nosque tulimus, edictorum viribus aut sacra generalitate subnixas.

In imitation of the Gregorian and Hermogenian Codes, we order to be collected all the constitutions bearing the force of edicts or sacred general applicability, issued by the renowned Constantine and by the divine emperors after him and by ourselves.

Sed cum simplicius iustiusque sit praetermissis eis, quas posteriores infirmant, explicari solas, quas valere conveniet, hunc quidem codicem et priores diligentioribus conpositos cognoscamus, quorum scholasticae

---

7.   *CTh* 1.1.5 and 1.1.6.1; *NTh* 1.1–3; Justinian *De novo codice componendo* 2; idem *De Iustiniano codice confirmando* 1; and esp. Justinian *Dig. praef.* II (*Omnem rei publicae nostrae sanctionem*).

intentioni tribuitur nosse etiam illa, quae mandata silentio in desue-
tudinem abierunt, pro sui tantum temporis negotiis valitura.

Although it would be simpler and more legal to omit those constitutions that later ones have invalidated and to set forth only those that
remain valid, we recognize that even this Code, and the earlier ones
as well, are composed for more diligent men, to whose scholarly desire
it is granted to know those things, too, that, having been consigned to
silence, have passed into desuetude, having remained valid only for affairs
of their own time.

As a program, the ambitions of Theodosius and Valentinian for their Code
are fantastically circumscribed. That is true in spite of the enormity of the
editorial undertaking upon which, following this decree, Antiochus the chief
compiler and his collaborators embarked.[8] Two of the limitations speci-
fied here demand comment: first, the emperors recognized a very limited range of texts and institutions as proper sources of law—they excluded,
for example, the entire body of jurisprudential literature whose excerpts
fill Justinian's *Digest*—and, second, they tacitly rejected the legislative capacities of non-Christian emperors. Indeed, in their practice the editors
also excluded legislation authored by Constantine prior to 313—proof,
if any were needed, that he was understood in the ancient world to have
converted in response to his visions and dreams before and during his Italian campaign in fall 312.[9]

In contrast, Justinian's editors aspired to include all valid nonredundant
imperial constitutions then extant—the exception to this principle being
matters of religion, the focus of the first thirteen chapters of the Code's
first book.[10] For those sections the editors drew almost exclusively on legislation by Catholic emperors, the one exception being a rescript of Caracalla on the Jews of Antioch.[11] If those sections bear some passing resemblance to the corresponding chapters in the Theodosian Code, the

---

8. On their work see Matthews 2000.

9. For the chronological limits of *CTh* see Mommsen 1905, 1:xxix, ccix.

10. For materials prior to 438 the editors relied on "the three ancient *codices*," the Gregorian, Hermogenian, and Theodosian: *De novo codice componendo* 1; *De Iustiniano codice
confirmando* 1.

11. *CJ* 1.9.1.

overall impression made by Justinian's compilation is rather different. In significant measure this arises from that work's very different historical self-perception. Take, for example, the chapters that each devotes *De re militari*, "On Military Affairs." Theodosian Code 7.1 contains eighteen citations, the first from Constantine and a full seven from Valentinian and Valens. Justinian's Code 12.35 likewise contains eighteen citations, but they range widely, from Caracalla to Alexander Severus, Gordian, Philip, Constantine, Constans, Gratian, Valentinian, Theodosius, Arcadius, Honorius, Leo, Zeno, and Anastasius. But the historical pageant on display in this chapter is not simply more true to history in some simple way, for empires, like kingdoms, can renew themselves and begin their histories afresh. Rather, it conforms more strictly to an historically dominant principle of legitimation in Roman imperial ideology, namely its willingness, even eagerness, to record, publish, and abide by precedent.[12]

This engagement with the long history of the empire and partial, at least, realigning of the Christian empire's practical self-awareness with that history find expression also in the justification of Justinian's *Digest*. Justinian first announced work on that project in a constitution of 15 December 530, addressed to the officials charged with reading and editing the two thousand books of extant jurisprudential literature (*CJ* 1.17.1.5; translation after G. E. M. de Ste. Croix):

> Cumque haec materia summa numinis liberalitate collecta fuerit, oportet eam pulcherrimo opere extruere et quasi proprium et sanctissimum templum iustitiae consecrare et in libros quinquaginta et certos titulos totum ius digerere, tam secundum nostri constitutionum codicis quam edicti perpetui imitationem, prout hoc vobis commodius esse patuerit, ut nihil extra memoratam consummationem possit esse derelictum, sed his quinquaginta libris totum ius antiquum, per millesimum et quadringentesimum paene annum confusum et a nobis purgatum, quasi quodam muro vallatum nihil extra se habeat.

> Since this material will have been composed with the supreme indulgence of the Deity, we ought to set it out in a most handsome work, consecrating as it were a fitting and most holy temple of justice, and to distribute the whole of the law into fifty books and distinct titles,

12. See Ando 2000, 30–40; Ando 2006, 184–85.

in imitation both of our Code of Constitutions and of the Perpetual Edict, in such as a way as may seem convenient to you, such that nothing might be left out of the aforementioned compilation, but that in these fifty books the entire *ius antiquum,* ancient law—in a state of confusion for almost fourteen hundred years and rectified by us—might be defended, as it were, by a sort of wall and leave nothing outside itself.

The recovery and recuperation of *ius antiquum,* of ancient law, for the Christian empire reflects a profound ideological and intellectual adjustment of the editorial program designed by Theodosius and his advisors. On the one hand, it constitutes a recognition that the motivating bases of social order in late Roman society were multiple. What exactly this recuperation of classical jurisprudence and, indirectly, of classical social theory will have contributed to Byzantium, I hope in short order to clarify. At the very least, however, this invocation of the *Digest* is a reminder that Justinian's Code did not stand alone as a foundation of law in its day. On the contrary, his "twelve books of imperial constitutions" stood alongside his "four books of *Institutes* or *Elements* and fifty books of the *Digest* or *Pandects*" as the repository into which "the whole legal establishment of our *res publica* has been cleansed and ordered."[13] How do the religious chapters of Justinian's Code appear in that larger context?

At first glance, the distinctly classical books of the *Digest* and *Institutes* appear distinctly secular. But those works are not innocent or unproblematic mirrors of the concerns of classical law. We must first of all remember that the works of Justinian's corpus were intended to complement each other: for example, nothing "laid down in imperial constitutions" was in "any way allowed to appear" in the *Digest,* "a reading of the constitutions, as it were, being sufficient."[14] The secularity of the *ius civile* as it emerges in the *Digest* might therefore result not from some quality intrinsic to classical legal thought or even from the capacity of sixth-century Christian editors so to read and edit it. On the contrary, such concerns of pagan religiosity as were expressed in classical jurisprudence are likely to have been rigorously excluded, even as the principle of com-

13. *Dig. praef.* II, *pr.*
14. *CJ* 1.17.2.14.

plementarity will have urged readers seeking laws on religion to the chronologically, religiously, and doctrinally relevant chapters of the Code. The *Institutes* distinguishes itself from the Code on different grounds. In the words of its first book's first section, *De iustitia et iure,* "On Justice and Law" (*Inst.* 1.1.1, 4):

> Iuris prudentia est divinarum atque humanarum rerum notitia, iusti atque iniusti scientia. . . . Huius studii duae sunt positiones, publicum et privatum. publicum ius est, quod ad statum rei Romanae spectat, privatum, quod ad singulorum utilitatem pertinet. dicendum est igitur de iure privato, quod est tripertitum: collectum est enim ex naturalibus praeceptis aut gentium aut civilibus.

> Mastery of the law is knowledge of divine and human matters and understanding of justice and injustice. . . . There are two aspects to this subject, public and private. Public law is that which regards the condition of the Roman state; private law is that which relates to the well-being of individuals. We therefore speak here of private law, which has three parts: for it derives from natural precepts, from those of the nations, and those of the state.

As the first section of Justinian's Code had concerned itself with laws urging "that no one should dare to argue about <Catholicism> publicly," so, we are informed in the edict that authorized its publication, the Code represented the culmination of its author's efforts *ad prima communium rerum sustentationis semina,* "to provide for the maintenance of the common good."[15] However problematic the terms "public" and "common" are both individually and in their interconnections, we might nevertheless find in these passages authorization for ignoring the *Digest* and the *Institutes* in our inquiry into the relationship between religion and law in the Roman empire.

As it happens, it is precisely reading the *Digest* and *Institutes* together that forestalls any such easy dismissal of those texts. For what we then quickly learn is that Tribonian preceded the adaptation of Gaius that occupies much of Justinian's *Institutes* with an adroit paraphrase from the

15. *De Iustiniano codice confirmando, pr.*

opening book of the *Institutes* of Ulpian. A longer, continuous portion of that work opens the first book of the *Digest,* where the following definition of *ius* is, in Ciceronian terms, enumerated:[16]

> Huius studii duae sunt positiones, publicum et privatum. publicum ius est, quod ad statum rei Romanae spectat, privatum, quod ad singulorum utilitatem: sunt enim quaedam publice utilia, quaedam privatim. publicum ius in sacris, in sacerdotibus, in magistratibus constitit. privatum ius tripertitum est: collectum etenim est ex naturalibus praeceptis aut gentium aut civilibus.

> There are two aspects to this subject, public and private. Public law is that which regards the condition of the Roman state; private, that which regards the well-being of individuals. For some matters are of public and others of private interest. Public law consists in *sacra,* priests, and magistrates. Private law has three parts: for it derives from natural precepts, from those of the nations, and those of the state.

The continued presence of Ulpian's definition of *ius publicum,* of public law, in its programmatic position in the *Digest,* and the traces it has left in the *Institutes,* provoke several questions. We might first ask what influence it had on the shape of either work or, for that matter, on the Code. The *Institutes* are, as we have seen, avowedly concerned only with private law. The *Digest* and the *Code,* on the other hand, clearly reify in their individual arrangements the basic categories of Ulpian's definition, the former in part by what it lacks, the latter by what it contains.[17]

Furthermore, questions begged earlier about the sheer novelty of embracing religion within the sphere of the law, even religion in its public dimension, whatever that might be, can now be articulated and reframed. For neither the existence of laws on religious matters per se, nor their placement within Justinian's Code, at any rate, represented an innovation. The codifying of laws on religion does not, therefore, in itself suggest that Chris-

16.   Ulpian *Inst.* bk. 1 fr. 1908 (Lenel 1889, 2:926–27) = *Dig.* 1.1.1.2. Translation after D. N. MacCormick.

17.   For the titles of the chapters in *CJ* bk. 1, see Krueger 1954, xxi. The first book of the *Digest* lacks, of course, chapters on *sacra* and *sacerdotes,* but their absence is palpable.

tian legislation on religion constituted a new form of legislation, deriving from some new understanding of the nature and scope of government. Nor, it must be said, does it require that Christian legislation alone have been included merely because Christianity was somehow novel, such that Christian legislation against pagans and heretics was similar both in formulation and also in presuppositions to earlier pagan legislation against Christians—because, in other words, it was new, and the other was old.[18]

But the questions most insistently provoked by Ulpian's definition of *ius publicum* and its continued relevance are about its meaning, for Ulpian himself as for Justinian. For what its survival reveals more than anything is the continuity in language maintained by lawyers and legally trained social theorists between the high and late empires. Though we shall have presently to explore the prior history of Ulpian's terminology, we can even now point to the difficulty that its survival sets before us. How are we to assess and describe changes in the understanding of government, law, and religion, or their respective and mutually implicated roles in the constitution of society, if the terms devised by Romans in the classical period to articulate these fundamental truths passed without remark into the linguistic toolboxes of Christian lawyers in late antiquity?

We thus seek to identify and measure a gap, a difference, the evidence for which is provided by texts compelled to elide it.[19] Consider, for example, the authority invoked by Justinian to support his belief that the

---

18. The final phrase is an allusion to Arthur Darby Nock's famous definition of conversion: Nock 1933, 7.

19. See, for example, the following pieces of legislation, or references to legislation, on minority religions: Pliny *Ep.* 10.96.3: "Neque enim dubitabam . . . pertinaciam certe et inflexibilem obstinationem debere puniri"; Diocletian, *Edictum de Manichaeis* (*Mos. et Rom. leg. collatio*) 3: "unde pertinaciam pravae mentis nequissimorum hominum punire ingens nobis studium est"; Constantine to Celsus (Appendix VII to Optatus): "Eos, quos contra fas et religionem ipsam recognovero reosque violentes conpetentis venerationis deprehendero, sine ulla dubitatione insaniae suae obstinationisque temerariae faciam merita exitia persolvere"; Augustine, *De anima et eius origine* (*PL* 44.522) 3.15.23: "Nam haec si pertinaciter singula defendantur, tot haereses facere possunt, quot opiniones esse numerantur. Quocirca considera, quam sit horrendum ut omnes sint in uno homine, quae damnabiles essent in singulis singulae"; and *NTh* 3.8: "Hinc perspicit nostra clementia paganorum quoque et gentilis inmanitatis vigiliam nos debere sortiri, qui naturali vesania et licentia pertinaci verae religionis tramite discedentes nefarios sacrificiorum ritus et funestae superstitionis errores occultis exercere quodammodo solitudinibus dedignantur, nisi ad supernae maiestatis iniuriam et temporis nostri contemptum eorum scelera professionis genere publicentur."

ground on which consecrated buildings stood remains sacred even after the buildings themselves are demolished:[20]

> Sacra sunt, quae rite et per pontifices Deo consecrata sunt, veluti aedes sacrae et dona quae rite ad ministerium Dei dedicata sunt, quae etiam per nostram constitutionem alienari et obligari prohibuimus, excepta causa redemptionis captivorum. si quis vero auctoritate sua quasi sacrum sibi constituerit, sacrum non est, sed profanum. locus autem, in quo sacrae aedes aedificatae sunt, etiam diruto aedificio, adhuc sacer manet, ut et Papinianus scripsit.

> Sacred things are things that have been duly consecrated to God by the *pontifices,* for example, sacred buildings and gifts duly dedicated to the service of God; by our constitution, we have forbidden these things to be alienated or assigned as security, except for the ransoming of captives. If anyone should establish something as somehow sacred for himself, it is not sacred but profane. The ground on which sacred buildings are built remains sacred even after the building is torn down, as Papinian too wrote.

Setting aside for the moment the collapsing of polarities—Christian and pagan, public and private—imminent or under way in this text, let me remark for now only that Papinian cannot, it seems to me, have meant the same thing by a "sacred building" as Justinian did.[21] That one might conclude such a passage with so casual a remark, *ut et Papinianus scripsit,* demands explanation.

LEX EST RATIO SUMMA

We might start by framing a set of questions, or devising second-order categories, that permit us to get past the problematic formulations that Ulpian and Justinian shared. Bracketing for the moment Ulpian's troubling *sacra*—things belonging to, or actions performed for, the gods—

---

20. Justinian *Inst.* 2.1.8. Cf. Gaius *Inst.* 2.4–5: "Sacrae sunt quae *diis superis* consecratae sunt, religiosae quae *diis Manibus* relictae sunt. Sed sacrum quidem hoc solum existimatur quod ex auctoritate populi Romani consecratum est, veluti lege de ea re lata aut senatus-consulto facto."

21. On the sacralization of space in pagan and Christian Rome and Byzantium see below, chapters 5 and 7; and cf. Ando 2003b, 247–51.

and concentrating instead on the civic roles of persons encapsulated in his "priests and magistrates," we might proceed along two fronts, one anthropological, the other social-theoretic.

As regards the first, we should want to know what sort of anthropology conditioned their approaches to legislation on religion, and how that understanding was expressed in the language of the law. Consider, for example, the very different ambitions and expectations for the efficacy and reach of government action expressed by Theodosius in the fifth century of this era, and the praetor Cornelius Hispalus in the second of the last. In the constitution of 429 that announced his desire to publish a code of law, Theodosius projected the completion of a second volume, to follow the Code itself: the Code would collect the diversity of general constitutions then permitted to be cited in court, omitting only their "empty copiousness of words"; the later volume was to omit "all that diversity of law" and take up *magisterium vitae,* "the guidance of life," showing, in other words, *sequenda omnibus vitandaque,* "what should be pursued and what should be avoided by all."[22] In contrast, when, more than half a millennium earlier, Cornelius Hispalus took action against the Jews in Rome, his measures were limited to expelling them beyond the borders of the city and removing "their private altars from public spaces."[23] The dramatic change in the conception of individual religious identity in its public dimension illuminated by the ambitions of these men finds a disturbing parallel in the shifting aims of judicial and public torture in the Roman empire. For where once judicial torture in classical courtrooms had aimed to elicit true statements about a self or a self's knowledge, public torture in the Christian empire aimed to alter the self—in other words, to compel conversion.[24] In the last words of Augustine's only sermon on Luke's disturbing admonition "to compel them to enter":[25]

22. *CTh* 1.1.5.

23. Valerius Maximus 1.3.3, in the epitome of Nepotianus: *Iudeos quoque, qui Romanis tradere sacra sua conati erant, idem Hispalus urbe exterminavit arasque privatas e publicis locis abiecit.* On the import of this confrontation within a broader consideration of the categories Roman and alien, public and private, see Ando 2003b, 193–98; and Ando and Rüpke 2006, 7–13.

24. On judicial torture see Gleason 1999, 287–313. On religious coercion see Brown 1963, 283–305; and Kirwan 1989, 209–18.

25. Augustine *Serm.* 112.8. Augustine also cites and discusses Luke 14.21–23 at *Contra Gaudentium* 1.25.28 and *Ep.* 185.6.24. It is perhaps worth emphasizing, as regards Cornelius

Voluntate, inquiunt, nostra intremus. Non hoc Dominus imperavit:
Coge, inquit, intrare. Foris inveniatur necessitas, nascitur intus voluntas.

"Let us enter of our own will," they say. That is not what the Lord
commanded. "Compel them to enter," he said. Let compulsion be found
outside, and the will shall be born within.

At the level of social theory, we might inquire into the understanding of
social order and civil society that conditioned late Roman lawyers' views of
the scope and purpose of legislation. One approach lies with studying the
organizational principles at work in both the Theodosian and Justinianic
codifications and the use made in both works of the praetor's edict.[26] To
the extent that such a code of private law relies upon and itself reifies a particular vision of civil society, the reliance of both late antique codifications
on the *edictum perpetuum* testifies to the unwillingness or inability of their
compilers and the authors of their contents alike to imagine a wholesale
restructuring of the legal basis for social order. This is not to say, of course,
that legislation on particular issues did not come to reflect some new set of
"Christian priorities";[27] nor do I claim that it was impossible so to reimag-
ine the foundations of society. It is merely that government lawyers did not
do so, and that fact itself had important social-historical consequences.

Another avenue to pursue in this unpacking of social-theoretic postulates might seem to lie in the language of the Codes themselves, and particularly the Justinianic one. For when Justinian distinguished between *ius
civile* and *ius gentium,* he observed a distinction widely familiar to classical
lawyers;[28] and when he then located in an ontologically and ethically prior
position some "natural law," established by divine providence, he again

---

Hispalus, that I am *not* saying that he limited himself in acting as he did, as though he might
have done more. Rather, his understanding of religious identity and religious affiliation permitted no greater action; among other things, he could not have conceived of forcing someone to convert.

26. On the influence of the *edictum perpetuum* on bks. 2–4 of the Theodosian Code and
bks. 2–7 of Justinian's Code, see Mommsen 1905, 1:xiii–xviii; or Matthews 2000, 104–8
and 117–18. For its influence on Justinian's legal projects in general see also *CJ* 1.17.1.5.

27. See, e.g., MacCormack 1997, 644–73.

28. Justinian *Inst.* 1.2.1–2; Gaius *Inst.* 1.1; and cf. Cicero *Leg.* 1.17. For a recent survey see
Kaser 1993, 10–22, 40–59; and cf. Schiavone 2005.

used language familiar from Roman political and legal theory, at least since the absorption of Cicero's books *On the Laws*.[29] But such similarities in terminology and networks of allusion only return us to the position whence we began. When Justinian contrasts *naturalia iura,* natural laws "observed by all races equally and established by a certain divine providence," with "the laws that each civic community establishes for itself, which it is customary to change by tacit consent of the people or by legislation," and Cicero, for his part, contrasts the Law, "which is highest reason, rooted in nature," with the "laws by which states ought to be governed," and again with "the statutes and decrees of peoples that have actually been formulated and composed"—how are we to assess them, the one against the other? We need some apparatus outside the language of the law and legal philosophy with which to evaluate the gaps each posits between divine providence or nature, on the one hand, and the enactments of particular states, on the other. And then, *within* the language of the law, how might each have understood it to say of the *ius publicum* of his own state, that it consisted in *sacra,* priests, and magistrates?

IUS PUBLICUM: AN ARCHAEOLOGY

The debates to which Ulpian was party, and those that he influenced, both rested on and contributed to ongoing negotiations over the relationship between civic law, religion, and social order. Those negotiations were themselves implicated in cultural-historical changes of the most fundamental and far-reaching kind. To sketch their parameters we might begin by inquiring into *ius publicum* itself. That effort immediately reveals three things. First, for that phrase English, at any rate, has no equivalent:

29. See Justinian *Inst.* 1.2.11 ("Sed naturalia quidem iura, quae apud omnes gentes peraeque servantur, divina quadam providentia constituta, semper firma atque immutabilia permanent: ea vero quae ipsa sibi quaeque civitas constituit, saepe mutari solent vel tacito consensu populi vel alia postea lege lata"), to which compare Cicero *Leg.* 1.17–18 ("Natura enim iuris explicanda nobis est, eaque ab hominis repetenda natura, considerandae leges quibus ciuitates regi debeant; tum haec tractanda, quae conposita sunt et descripta iura et iussa populorum, in quibus ne nostri quidem populi latebunt quae uocantur iura ciuilia. . . . Igitur doctissimis uiris proficisci placuit a lege, haud scio an recte, si modo, ut idem definiunt, lex est ratio summa, insita in natura, quae iubet ea quae facienda sunt, prohibetque contraria. Eadem ratio, cum est in hominis mente confirmata et perfecta, lex est"), 2.10 and 13; and Gaius *Inst.* 1.1. On so-called reason and natural law see Moatti 1997, 163–73, and Dyck 2004 *ad loc.* Some of these passages are discussed further below.

neither "constitution," which has a common meaning, nor "public law," which does not, will do.[30] Second, Rome had no constitution, of whatever description—that is to say, we know of no authorized or circumscribed body of law, statutory, jurisprudential, or other, that comprised *ius publicum*. Third, despite the easy economy of Ulpian's apparently ostensive definition, *ius publicum* as a concept itself appears to have a foreshortened history. The authority of the jurist appears, on first examination, chimerical.

This is not to say that Republican and early imperial Rome did not have bodies of law, but rather that their internal heterogeneity and divergence as a group from the Codes of the high empire alike require analysis. The Twelve Tables, for example—the erstwhile antecedents for the Codes—dealt, so far as I can tell, exclusively with civil and criminal law and procedure; they contained nothing relevant to "*sacra,* priests, and magistrates."[31] Indeed, the surviving text that most clearly aspires to provide a statement of a Roman community's *ius publicum* deals not with Rome itself, but with the municipalities of Spain, the so-called *lex Flavia municipalis*. As its name implies, this text might accurately be described not only as a "constitution" or "charter," but a "statute" or "law," for it seems to have been the product of comitial lawmaking, as would have been its Augustan and Julian antecedents, such as they were, if they existed.[32] The structure of that law clearly anticipates Ulpian's schema: on any reasonable reconstruction, it opened with chapters treating *sacra* and priesthoods, before turning to magistrates, the subject of the first extant chapter—the nineteenth of ninety-seven.[33] And insofar as the Flavian

---

30. On this topic see Cloud 1994, 491–99. For an analysis focused not on the reception of classical law but on historiography about it see Thomas 1984.

31. For a text of the extant fragments, see now the edition by Humbert, Lewis, and Crawford 1996, *RS* no. 40. This seems to me an accurate characterization of the fragments, in spite of several ancient testimonia that suggest a much wider range of concerns for the Tables, the most explicit of which is Livy 3.34.6: "Even now, amidst an immense accumulation of statutes piled on statutes, the [original Ten] Tables are the *fons omnis publici privatique . . . iuris.*" Others, including Pomponius, regarded the Tables more narrowly as the source "whence the *ius civile* began to flow" (*Dig.* 1.2.2.6). On the secular character of the Tables see Magedelain 1986, one of many studies that subject the rather fragile evidence for the content of the Tables to linguistic-historical analysis—"Dans la Rome archaïque, le droit est un langage" (296)—with, it must be said, some considerable philological naïvete.

32. The *lex* is most easily read in González 1986, 147–243.

33. On the contents of the first eighteen chapters see Galsterer 1988, 79–82.

municipal law was written at Rome, it implicitly raises the question when and why *ius publicum* began there so to be conceived, not least in light of the Romans' persistent unwillingness or, perhaps, uninterest in codifying their own.

To answer this question properly, we should want to pose it on at least three levels: lexical, cultural-historical, and intellectual-historical. As regards the first, we might ask whether the indeterminacy of *ius publicum* corresponds in any way to the history of *ius*. If *ius* could designate a body of law, what did it mean to say of an action that it was not *ius?* A cultural historian should inquire into the history of bodies of law and ask how their history intertwines with that of theorizing law itself. What forces conspired to produce particular understandings of the purpose and sources of law? Finally, as a matter of the history of ideas, we might ask how the particular anthropological and theological postulates of any given culture found expression in its views on law and, in this case, in their codifications of law.

Although I concentrate in this chapter on the last of these questions, I should acknowledge that none can be fully answered in isolation from the others. So, for example, Cicero occasionally distinguished between *ius religionis* and *ius rei publicae,* between a "law of religion" and a "law of the state," glossing the latter as *ius publicum,* and then defining this last phrase by apposition as "the *leges,* the statutes used by this community of citizens."[34] Thus described, *ius rei publicae* and *ius publicum* bear a striking resemblance to the *ius civile* as defined by Cicero in the *Topica,* in an exercise in enumeration: "So, for example, one might define *ius civile* as made up of statutes, decrees of the Senate, judicial decisions, the authority of those learned in the law, the edicts of magistrates, custom, and equity."[35]

This lack of specificity or, better yet, this fluidity in the usage of *ius* is illustrative of two trends, both relevant here. On the one hand, it attests the cachet of law itself, and in particular of law as a system of knowledge

---

34. Cicero *Dom.* 32–33. See also Cicero *Har. resp.* 14–15: "Multae sunt domus in hac urbe, patres conscripti, atque haud scio an paene cunctae iure optimo, sed tamen iure privato, iure hereditario, iure auctoritatis, iure mancipi, iure nexi: nego esse ullam domum aliam privato eodem quo quae optima lege, publico vero omni praecipuo et humano et divino iure munitam; quae primum aedificatur ex auctoritate senatus pecunia publica, deinde contra vim nefariam huius gladiatoris tot senati consultis munita atque saepta est."

35. Cicero *Topica* 28.

or body of doctrine. The rise in the century before Cicero of a body of experts and corpus of texts on what Ulpian would later call *ius publicum* in itself testifies to broad-based and mutually implicated changes in attitudes to constitutional law and knowledge production.[36] Although these changes can be measured across the full span of contemporary intellectual activity,[37] and not least in theology and cultural geography,[38] what must be stressed here is that the range of disciplines whose erudition and ways of knowing were subordinated in the age of Cicero to the notion of *ius* was enormous, and that, crucially, among these disciplines were the regulations, principles, and bodies of knowledge that we follow Cicero and his contemporaries in denominating the *iura* of the *pontifices,* the augurs, and the fetials. Cicero himself remarked upon this sea change when in book 2 of his treatise *On the Laws* (*De legibus*) he invoked the Scaevolae, jurists and *pontifices* of the previous two generations, and asked why they wished to associate pontifical and civil law. "Through knowledge of the civil law, in fact you destroy in a sense pontifical law. For religious obligations are connected to money by the authority of the *pontifices,* not by statute. So, if you were only *pontifices,* pontifical authority would survive; but because you are most learned in civil law, you make a mockery of the one branch of learning through the other."[39]

Two features of Cicero's analysis merit attention now, before returning to the twin developments in classical theorizing about the law and bodies of law mentioned above: first, as a matter of historiography, the epistemic revolution that we have described in the abstract, Cicero as a classical intellectual conceived in biographical terms, and the agency behind broad-based cultural change he thus located in the aspirations and actions of two named individuals;[40] second, as a matter of history, Cicero gestured toward one essential feature of relations between law and religion in classical Rome, namely that where once the language of statutes had been deeply indebted to that of religion, the late Republic witnessed a profound reinscription of priestly knowledge and authority within and

36. On law, see Moatti 1991, 31–45.
37. See Moatti 1997.
38. On these see Beard 1986, 33–46; and Nicolet 1991.
39. Cicero *Leg.* 2.52 (trans. after James E. G. Zetzel).
40. Cf. Pocock 1996, 3–7.

under the overall authority of the Senate, which was itself then coming to be understood as an institution or apparatus of the state.[41]

This returns us to the second movement attested by the fluidity of *ius* in the age of Cicero. Situating this discourse about law properly in its historical context requires the asking of at least two questions, namely what made it necessary, and what made it possible. In replying to the first, we might point to the dramatic expansion of the Roman state over the long century between 167 and 51—namely between the decision *not* to annex the kingdom of Perseus of Macedon and the writing of Cicero's books *On the Laws*. Rome expanded over that span in two very different ways, in the sheer amount of territory embraced by its empire (perhaps quadrupling), and in the size and geographic spread of its citizen body (more than tripling in number). The range of peoples, language groups, and legal systems thus united will have been enormous, and the demands thereby placed upon Roman officials, operating within an ancient technological regime, staggering.[42] The Romans responded in practice largely by adapting mechanisms for negotiating across cultural and legal systems that they had developed—or told themselves they had developed—during the unification of Latium in the late fourth century. But the violence of the adaptation required in this period produced on the one hand a sundering of old assumptions about patriotism, language, ethnic affiliation, and their interconnections,[43] and on the other tremendous pressure to theorize anew the nature and variety of human communities: how they arise, how they cohere, and how they relate to one another.[44]

This brings us to the second question framed above, namely what made it possible for late Republican theorizing about human communities to assume the form it did. If the answer loosely must be the absorption across this same century of a Greek passion for abstraction, a more precise one

41.   On the language of the law see Thomas 1988. On priesthood, see Beard 1990; and Gordon 1990b, 179–98 (reprinted in Ando 2003b, 62–83). See also Rüpke 1996a and 2005.

42.   The most comprehensive history of this century remains Nicolet 1979; the most exciting analysis of nature of government in the mid-first century B.C.E., the same author's (1996) *Financial Documents and Geographical Knowledge in the Roman World*.

43.   On this topic see Thomas 1996.

44.   For some reflections on this topic see Ando 2002.

would focus on the reception of Peripatetic cultural historiography.[45] At the same time, at a theoretical level, the influence on the human sciences of an Aristotelian preference for elaborating theoretical constructs on the basis of empirical observations ultimately proved decisive. But despite the impulse provided by these currents, the theorizing of religion, law, and society then performed at Rome assumed very particular and idiosyncratically Roman forms. Take, for example, one of Cicero's many attempts to describe the forms and bases of human communities, that in book 1 of *On Duties* (*De officiis* 1.53; translation after E. M. Atkins):

> Gradus autem plures sunt societatis hominum. Ut enim ab illa infinita discedatur, proprior est eiusdem gentis nationis linguae, qua maxime homines coniunguntur. Interius etiam est eiusdem esse civitatis; multa enim sunt civibus inter se communia, forum fana porticus viae leges iura iudicia suffragia, consuetudines praeterea et familiaritates multisque cum multis res rationesque contractae. Artior vero conligatio est societatis propinquorum; ab illa enim immensa societate humani generis in exiguum angustumque concluditur.

> There are indeed several *gradus* of *societas,* degrees of fellowship, among humans. To proceed from the one that is unlimited, next there is a closer one of the same race, tribe, and language, through which humans are bound strongly to one another. More intimate still is that of common citizenship; for many are the things held in common by citizens between themselves: the forum, temples, porticoes, and roads; statutes and legal rights; legal judgments and political elections; and, besides these, acquaintances and companionships and those business and commercial transactions that many of them make with many others. A tie narrower still is that of the fellowship between relatives: moving up from the vast fellowship of the human race we end up in a confined and limited one.

Cicero's recourse here to the term *societas* betrays a distinct reliance, however analogical, on the Roman law of corporations, not simply for understanding the consensual and normative basis of *civitates,* communities of citizens, but for representing interpersonal relations in general; like-

45. On the arrival of Aristotle at Rome see J. Barnes 1997, 1–69.

wise Roman is his insistence on enumerating the *res communes,* both legal and abstract, and material and concrete, of communities of citizens, and the vocabulary he uses for them is stringently Latin.[46]

Within a specifically legal discursive tradition, this theorizing resulted in the drawing of two closely related distinctions, between natural law and civil law, on the one hand, and between the various civil law traditions of individual states, on the other. As regards the first, in Cicero's formulation, "that *ius,* that Law, is unitary by which the fellowship of humans is made fast, and it was established by a single *lex,* a single statute, which statute is correct reasoning in commanding and prohibiting."[47] "Therefore, just as that *divina mens,* that divine mind, is the *summa lex,* the highest statute, so, when it is brought to perfection in humans, <it resides> in the minds of the wise. The legislation that has been written down for nations in different ways and for particular occasions has the name 'statute' more as a matter of courtesy than of fact."[48] Cicero's interest in discussing this Law, this "highest statute," lay with assessing against it the "institutions and statutes of nations,"[49] and so in the theoretical sections of the first two books of *On the Laws* he argued principally about the ethical status of individual statutes, and he generally dealt in hypotheticals:[50]

> Quodsi populorum iussis, si principum decretis, si sententiis iudicum iura constituerentur, ius esset latrocinari, ius adulterare, ius testamenta falsa supponere, si haec suffragiis aut scitis multitudinis probarentur.

> If instantiations of this Law were really established through the decrees of nations or commands of kings or decisions of judges, then it would be lawful to commit brigandage or adultery or to suborn false testimony, so long as these things were approved by votes or decrees of the multitude.

---

46.   On this passage see Remy 1930; on the cross-pollination between legal and philosophical treatments of *societates* see Moatti 2001, 825–27. On the Romanness of late Republican political theory, see Ando 1999, 9–18; and cf. idem 2004, 95–98.

47.   Cicero *Leg.* 1.42: *est enim unum ius, quo devincta est hominum societas, et quod lex constituit una; quae lex est recta ratio imperandi atque prohibendi.*

48.   Cicero *Leg.* 2.11 (trans. after James E. G. Zetzel).

49.   Cicero *Leg.* 1.42.

50.   Cicero *Leg.* 1.43 and 2.13 (translation James E. G. Zetzel); cf. Cicero *Rep.* 1.39.1, on which see Macrobius *Somn.* 1.8.13.

Quid quod multa perniciose, multa pestifere sciscuntur in populis, quae non magis legis nomen adtingunt, quam si latrones aliqua consensu suo sanxerint? Nam neque medicorum praecepta dici vere possunt, si quae inscii inperitique pro salutaribus mortifera conscripserint, neque in populo lex, cuicuimodi fuerit illa, etiam si perniciosum aliquid populus acceperit. Ergo est lex iustorum iniustorumque distinctio, ad illam antiquissimam et rerum omnium principem expressa naturam, ad quam leges hominum diriguntur, quae supplicio inprobos adficiunt, defendunt ac tuentur bonos.

What of the fact that many things are approved by peoples that are damaging and destructive, which no more approach the name of law than whatever bandits have agreed upon among themselves? The instructions of doctors cannot truly be so called if in ignorance and inexperience they prescribe poisons in place of medicine; nor, even if the people approve it, will something harmful in a nation be a law of any kind. Law, therefore, is the distinction between just and unjust things, produced in accordance with nature, the most ancient and first of all things, in accordance with which human laws are constructed that punish the wicked while defending and protecting the good.

Despite Cicero's particular interest in the normative ethical status of laws of individual states, his reasoning might seem to permit the construal of *ius civile,* of civil law, as the product of historical and contingent human institution building; and thus it would seem to permit the assigning of like ontological status to all civil law traditions.

And that, at the level of theory, is precisely what subsequent jurists then maintained. So, for example, the sentence that now opens Gaius's *Institutes* asserts that "the *ius* that each people establishes for itself is peculiar to it and is called the *ius civile,* as being the law peculiar to that community of citizens; whereas the law that *naturalis ratio,* natural reason, has established among all humans is observed by all peoples equally and is called the law of nations, as being the law used by all nations."[51] When Gaius then came to trace the development of Roman law in his books on the Twelve Tables, he thus insisted that its history began *ab urbis initiis,* with

---

51. Gaius *Inst.* 1.1; translation after De Zulueta 1946, whose notes merit consultation throughout.

the foundation of the city.[52] Similarly, although Gaius's contemporary Pomponius opened his *Handbook* with the allowance that it was necessary for him "to go over the origin and development of *ipsius iuris,* of law itself," in point of fact his story opens *initio civitatis nostrae,* "at the beginning of our community of citizens," and traces its passage from an archaic condition without statutes or fixed legal rights through its growth to a condition wherein statute law was necessary.[53]

For his part, Justinian started the second chapter of the first book of his *Institutes* by quoting the opening of Gaius's work of that name, but upon Gaius's terse formulation he then offered a considerable elaboration (*Inst.* 1.2.2):

> A particular *ius civile* is named after an individual state, for example,
> the Athenians: for if someone wished to call the laws of Solon or Draco
> the *ius civile* of the Athenians, he would not err. So, too, we name the
> *ius civile* of the Romans that *ius* that the Roman populace uses, or the
> *ius Quiritium* that *ius* that the Quirites use, for the Romans are called
> Quirites from Quirinus. But when we add no word signifying the state
> whose law we discuss, we speak of our own *ius;* just as when we say "the
> poet" and add no name, among Greeks it is assumed that the excellent
> Homer is being named, but among us, Vergil.

Justinian returned from this digression to a discussion of the sources of law and the forms of Roman legal enactments, before closing the chapter by revisiting the problem of natural law, in a passage that alludes to both Cicero and Gaius (*Inst.* 1.2.11):

> Sed naturalia quidem iura, quae apud omnes gentes peraeque servantur,
> divina quadam providentia constituta, semper firma atque immutabilia
> permanent: ea vero quae ipsa sibi quaeque civitas constituit, saepe mutari
> solent vel tacito consensu populi vel alia postea lege lata.

> But natural laws, which are observed uniformly among all peoples,
> are established by a certain divine providence, and abide fixed and
> immutable; the laws that each community establishes for itself, on the

---

52. Gaius *Ad legem Duodecim Tabularum* bk. 1 fr. 418 (Lenel 1889, 1:242) = *Dig.* 1.2.1.
53. Pomponius *Enchiridion* fr. 178 (Lenel 1889, 2:44–45) = *Dig.* 1.2.2.*pr.*–3.

other hand, are accustomed to be changed often, either by the tacit consent of the people or by the passage of a new statute.

On this evidence, the Christian emperor seems to share with his classical forebears a sense that civil law traditions each potentially participate in, as well as depart from, some superior Law or laws, while figuring each of them as the product of historical actions on the part of their authoring communities.[54] Here, at least, Justinian evinces an openness of mind, a classical relativism, that substantially tempers the normative claims implicitly advanced in the act of sovereign lawgiving.

Cicero had, of course, advanced two different claims, of two different kinds, about the nature of law at the opening of book 2 of *On the Laws*. One, as we have seen, was metaphysical; it located the origin of law in nature, "the most ancient and first of all things." The second was descriptive: "Law," he wrote, "is the distinction between just and unjust things." This latter claim had a reception, too, one connected to the reception of the first by the etymological association of *ius,* "law," with *iustitia,* "justice." Roman lawyers and philosophers after Cicero followed him in exploiting and exploring through plays on words the potential divergence between law as contingent legal enactment and law as reification of a transcendent virtue. Ulpian, for one, did so at the very start of his *Institutes:*[55]

Iuri operam daturum prius nosse oportet, unde nomen iuris descendat. est autem a iustitia appellatum: nam, ut eleganter Celsus definit, ius est ars boni et aequi. Cuius merito quis nos sacerdotes appellet: iustitiam namque colimus et boni et aequi notitiam profitemur, aequum ab iniquo separantes, licitum ab illicito discernentes, bonos non solum metu poenarum, verum etiam praemiorum quoque exhortatione efficere cupientes, veram nisi fallor philosophiam, non simulatam affectantes.

54. It is in this context important to observe that the passages of Gaius and Pomponius treating the origins of (Roman) law open the chapter of the *Digest* entitled "De origine iuris et omnium magistratuum et successione prudentium" (On the Origin of Law and of All the Magistracies and the Succession of the Jurists).

55. Ulpian *Inst.* bk. 1 fr. 1908 (Lenel 1889, 2:926–27) = *Dig.* 1.1.1.*pr.*-1 (translation after D. N. MacCormick).

A law student at the outset of his studies ought first to know the derivation of the word *ius*. Its derivation is from *iustitia*. For, in terms of Celsus's elegant definition, *ius* is the art of goodness and fairness. Of that art we [jurists] are deservedly called the *sacerdotes,* the priests; for we cultivate *iustitia,* justice, and claim awareness of what is good and fair, discriminating between fair and unfair, distinguishing lawful from unlawful, aiming to make people good not only through fear of penalties but also indeed under allurement of rewards, and espousing a philosophy that, if I am not deceived, is genuine, not a sham.

Ulpian's slightly younger contemporary Paul connected Cicero's two claims in a digression on the meanings of *ius* in book 14 of his work *Ad Sabinum:*[56]

Ius pluribus modis dicitur: uno modo, cum id quod semper aequum ac bonum est ius dicitur, ut est ius naturale. altero modo, quod omnibus aut pluribus in quaque civitate utile est, ut est ius civile.

The term *ius* is used in several senses: in one sense, when it is used as meaning what is always fair and good, it is *ius naturale,* natural law. In the other, as meaning what is in the interest of everyone or a majority in each *civitas,* each community of citizens, it is *ius civile,* civil law.

When, three hundred years later, Justinian published his *Institutes,* he followed Ulpian in offering a definition of *ius* at the outset—in a chapter entitled *De iustitia et iure,* "On Justice and Law"—before turning to the different forms or meanings of *ius* in chapter 2, *De iure naturali et gentium et civili,* "On Natural Law, the Law of Nations, and Civil Law":[57]

Iustitia est constans et perpetua voluntas ius suum cuique tribuens. Iuris prudentia est divinarum atque humanarum rerum notitia, iusti atque iniusti scientia.

56. Paul *Ad Sabinum* bk. 14 fr. 1864 (Lenel 1889, 1:1287) = *Dig.* 1.1.11 (translation D. N. MacCormick).
57. Justinian *Inst.* 1.1.*pr.*-1 (translation after Peter Birks and Grant McLeod).

> Justice is the constant and unending desire to render to each his due. Learning in the law entails knowledge of divine and human matters and mastery of the just and unjust.

The last clause clearly invokes Cicero's description of law as *iustorum iniustorumque distinctio,* "the distinction between just and unjust things." Whence derived Justinian's interest in "divine and human matters," and what did it mean to say of them both that, like the law, they were knowable?

LAW AMONG HUMAN AND DIVINE MATTERS

Our first impulse might be to recall Ulpian's "*sacra,* priests, and magistrates," and then to despair that, once again, the Christian emperor's classicizing language has left us ill positioned to isolate and assess the distance legal theory traveled between the first, third, and sixth centuries. But Justinian's allusion is far more precise, and its unraveling offers, I believe, the heuristic device we have so far lacked. For he gestures, I would argue, not to Ulpian, nor, for that matter, to a jurist at all, but to Cicero's contemporary Varro, Rome's greatest cultural historian, and specifically to that author's *Antiquitates rerum humanarum et divinarum,* "The Antiquities of Human and Divine Matters." Varro's interest was not the law, of course; but he shared with Cicero a passion to articulate and respect the knowledge interests and historical postulates of what we might call a classical Roman anthropology. In Varro's work, together with Augustine's reaction to it, we have, I shall argue, a Christian reading of classical thought that parallels Justinian's use of Cicero and the jurists, but that voices its concerns in an entirely different language—precisely the apparatus we sought at the end of the section "*Lex Est Ratio Summa*" above.[58]

According to Augustine, "Varro wrote forty-one books of *Antiquities,* which he divided into human and divine affairs; to human affairs he apportioned twenty-five books, and to divine sixteen."[59] The positioning of divine affairs after human ones was deliberate and, indeed, Varro him-

---

58. Above, p. 72; see also chapter 1, pp. 15–18.
59. Augustine *Civ.* 6.3 = Varro *Ant. div.* fr. 4 Cardauns.

self both remarked upon and justified it (Augustine *Civ.* 6.4 = Varro *Ant. div.* fr. 5 Cardauns):

> Varro himself admits that he wrote about human affairs first, and then
> about divine affairs, because civil societies arose first, and subsequently
> the things established by them. "Just as a painter is prior to his painting,
> or a builder is prior to a building, so communities of citizens are prior
> to the things that are instituted by them."

In his reading of the *Antiquities,* Augustine poured the full force of his ire into a denunciation of what seems, on his reading, to have been Varro's central presupposition, namely the chronological priority of human communities over the practices and institutions established by them. But Augustine ultimately disputed more than the claim of chronological priority advanced by Varro on behalf of civil societies and, in doing so, he argued past and ultimately distorted him. For Augustine advanced his critique on the basis of a metaphysical postulate that was, for him, axiomatic: namely that God is both ontologically and chronologically prior to humans, and hence things established by God, or by humans on the basis of his Scripture, themselves have a claim to priority over the institutions of earthly cities. Moreover, precisely because Augustine regarded that claim as axiomatic, his response to Varro's defense of the structure of the *Antiquities* makes no attempt at sympathetic understanding, nor even at the articulation, of Varro's own presuppositions and the differences that lay between them (Augustine *Civ.* 6.4):

> But the true *religio* was not established by any terrestrial society; on the
> contrary, it was the true religion that established heavenly society. This
> in truth is revealed and taught by the true God, the giver of eternal life,
> to his true worshippers.

Within this argument, we can identify three crucial points of contention between Augustine and Varro, each in some way the product of the postulate described above. First, Augustine is concerned that *religio* be true; second, he posits religion as prior to both heavenly and earthly societies, of which the former was in fact "established" by religion; and third, some, or perhaps *the,* truth about these matters is communicated directly and unproblematically from Augustine's God to his worshippers.

There is the constant danger in reading Varro through Augustine—and there is, alas, no other way to read him—that the force and skill of Augustine's polemic will cause us to misrecognize the very different position whence Varro began. Sharing a notion of "religion" more in keeping with Augustine's *religio* than Varro's *res divinae,* modern readers have not unpacked the import of Varro's own description of his project.[60] That description is, alas, available to us only through Augustine's condescending attempt to co-opt Varro's critique of civic religion for his own purposes:[61]

> Does Varro not acknowledge that he does not of his own judgment uphold the things that he records the Roman *civitas* as having instituted? Does he hesitate to affirm that if he had been founding a new city, he would have given the gods and their names rather according to the rule of nature?

Indeed, Varro allowed that had he been writing *de omni natura deorum et hominum,* "about all the nature of the gods and humans," he would have written about divine matters first, and then about human matters. But as it was, "he wrote his books about human affairs not with respect to the entire world, but with respect to Rome alone."[62]

Varro clearly did not assign either chronological or ontological priority to humans over gods. Far from it. He departed from Augustine elsewhere. Crucially, Varro's gods—Roman gods—did not communicate directly with their worshippers. This is not to say that they were not present to the Romans in some fashion; on the contrary, as we have seen, the gods of Rome were residents and citizens of the city itself.[63] They were, moreover, held to communicate all the time, but with enormous indirection—so much so, that from a Roman perspective, the structure and complexity of the apparatus of state cult resulted precisely from the need to record and ad-

---

60. On *religio* and religion, see above, chapter 1, pp. 2–5.

61. Augustine *Civ.* 4.31 = Varro *Ant. div.* fr. 12 Cardauns; cf. Augustine *Civ.* 6.4.

62. Augustine *Civ.* 6.4 = Varro *Ant. div.* fr. 5 Cardauns.

63. Scheid 1985a; 1987/89, 125–36; and 2001, 47–76, esp. 69–76.

judge such information as the gods provided.[64] But the sort of expertise produced by the recording of hundreds of takings of auspices, for example, even together with a record of the success or failure of the action that followed, was at best not a knowing what to believe, but a knowing what to do.[65] The chronological priority of Varro's gods or, perhaps, his belief in their priority did not, therefore, produce for them a privileged role in his conception of the rise of human institutions. And institutions—that is, the institutions of religious worship—were Varro's topic, *not* "the nature of the gods" per se. This sundering of historical agency from the gods was thus the product of an epistemic position fundamentally different from Augustine's, visible not least in Varro's claims on behalf of theology: *theologia* was for him a *ratio, quae de diis explicatur,* a discursive system for explaining things about the gods. The various forms of theology were, in other words, merely branches of human wisdom, employed to elucidate something altogether ontologically distinct from themselves.[66]

Varro himself chose to write in the latter books of his *Antiquities* a theology of practice. Having divorced *res divinae* from any metaphysical claim that one might make on behalf of the gods, Varro could then argue that institutions of worship should not be differentiated from any other institution established by humans. Like Cicero's laws, Roman ways of worshipping the gods existed in such a worldview alongside many parallel ways of worshipping gods, and there were no a priori reasons for privileging any one set of ways over the others.

On the chronology advanced here, the easy simplicity of Ulpian's language reflects hard-won confidence. Indeed, the very lack of specificity in the notion of *ius publicum* in the late Republic reflects the tentative nature of the project on which Cicero and Varro were engaged. Roman magistrates and priests had, of course, long cooperated in the performance of rituals and the management of sacred properties, much as Roman legal writing and legal practice had always already been implicated in the language of sanctions and oaths. But Roman political action ultimately and,

---

64. See above, chapter 1, pp. 13–15.
65. Linder and Scheid 1993, 47–62 at 49–50; Gordon 1990a, 193–94 (= Ando 2003b, 77–78).
66. Varro *Ant. div.* frr. 7–11 Cardauns.

to a degree, inadvertently brought massive historical pressures to bear upon the theoretical constructs that had ordered social and religious life in the middle Republic. Historiography to one side, it became necessary to explain the situation of Rome in the world, and the systems of abstraction developed in the course of that undertaking found expression in cultural and legal theory in the promotion of *ius* and relativizing of *sacra*.

CLASSICAL SOCIAL THEORY
AND CHRISTIAN METAPHYSICS

In the chapter that Justinian devoted to *rerum divisio,* "the classification of things," he considered briefly how things come to be the property of private individuals. This happens in many ways, he wrote (*Inst.* 2.1.11):

> [Singulorum autem hominum multis modis res fiunt:] quarundam enim rerum dominium nanciscimur iure naturali, quod, sicut diximus, appellatur ius gentium, quarundam iure civili. commodius est itaque a vetustiore iure incipere. palam est autem, vetustius esse naturale ius, quod cum ipso genere humano rerum natura prodidit: civilia enim iura tunc coeperunt esse, cum et civitates condi et magistratus creari et leges scribi coeperunt.

> Ownership of some things arises from natural law, which, as we have said, is also called the law of nations; ownership of other things arises from *ius civile.* It is easier to begin from the older law. For it is clear that natural law is older, as nature produced it at the same time as the human race; but civil law traditions came into existence only when communities of citizens began to be established, and magistrates created, and statutes passed.

As it happens, Justinian borrowed extensive portions of this material from book 2 of Gaius's work *Quotidian or Golden Things:*[67]

> Quarundam rerum dominium nanciscimur iure gentium, quod ratione naturali inter omnes homines peraeque servatur, quarundam iure civili,

---

67. Gaius *Rerum cottidianarum* bk. 2 fr. 491 (Lenel 1889, 1:251) = *Dig.* 41.1.1.*pr.*

id est iure proprio civitatis nostrae. et quia antiquius ius gentium cum ipso genere humano proditum est, opus est, ut de hoc prius referendum sit.

Ownership of some things arises from the law of nations, which is observed in accordance with natural reason among all humans equally; ownership of other things arises from civil law: that is, from the law that is specific to our civitas. And since the older law of nations was produced together with the human race itself, it is necessary to treat of it first.

Justinian's brief remarks notably expand upon the cultural and historical ambitions of his exemplar, which is not to say that he wrote anything with which Gaius would have disagreed. But his slight alterations—the explicit recognition accorded other civil law traditions; the emphatic association of civil law with communities of citizens passing laws upon themselves—reflect an ecumenism and historical vision that are as humane as they are classical.

It is not that Justinian's view of the human past was necessarily incompatible with a Christian one. In the early chapter that he entitled "The Law of Nature, the Law of Nations, and Civil Law," whence I quoted his digression on the civil-law traditions specific to Athens and Rome, Justinian observed that "the law of nations," by contrast, "is common to the entire human race" (*Inst.* 1.2.2):

[Ius autem gentium omni humano generi commune est.] nam usu exigente et humanis necessitatibus gentes humanae quaedam sibi constituerunt: bella etenim orta sunt et captivitates secutae et servitutes, quae sunt iuri naturali contrariae; iure enim naturali ab initio omnes homines liberi nascebantur.

For pressing need and human necessities led such human peoples as there were to establish the law of nations for themselves. For wars arose and captives were taken, and slaves—whose condition is contrary to natural law, for by natural law all humans were initially born free.

Justinian's view of warfare here finds a close kin in two famous chapters on warfare in book 19 of Augustine's *City of God*. Augustine dedicated that book to an inquiry into happiness, and asked how or whether it might be found in earthly society. Having shown, as he imagined, the deplorable position of the judge within communities of citizens, compelled by *humana societas,* by human fellowship, to torture innocent people and render judgments in ignorance, Augustine moved on to the world (*Civ.* 19.7):

> After the *civitas* or city follows the world, in which they place the *tertium gradum . . . societatis humanae,* the third degree of human fellowship, starting from the household and then the city, and coming by progression to the world.

In that larger arena of human contact, Augustine maintained, people must first overcome language difference just to make each other's acquaintance, and even then, having made friends, they must worry "lest [their friends] be afflicted by hunger, by war, by sickness, by captivity, lest they suffer in slavery such things as we are not strong enough to imagine." Augustine then mourned two failings of friendships—that friends often cease to be friends, and that friends die. He who would avoid the sadness brought by the deaths of friends "must shun, if he can, friendly conversation, must forbid or destroy friendly affection, must disrupt with the ruthless violence of his mind *humanarum omnium necessitudinum vincula,* the bonds of all human relationships."[68]

The lexical coincidence between these passages to one side—following immediately upon the abstraction *usu,* "need," Justinian is likely to have intended *necessitates* as an abstraction, too; while Augustine clearly refers to human relationships—Augustine's terminology is in many respects no less classical than Justinian's. But as with his rejection of Varro's anthropology, here Augustine alludes to Cicero only to upend his classical Roman privileging of the *civitas,* the community of citizens. For Cicero did far more than devote the most space to the *gradus* of the *civitas* in his remarks on human fellowship in book 1 of *On Duties.* The authoring of *On the Laws* in itself testifies to the valuation he accorded the *civitas* as the supreme arena for the exercise of human virtue, to say nothing of the argument of *On the Republic.* We need only recall from those books his most remarkable and enduring achievement, namely his contention that the

---

68. Augustine *Civ.* 19.8.

bonds that united and sustained *civitates* were those that citizens made for themselves, namely their laws.[69] Augustine's rejection, however sorrowful, could not be more stark. Not only did he dismiss the *civitas* as an arena for the pursuit of happiness first, rather than last, among the degrees of fellowship, he did so on the grounds that not even a wise man could enforce its laws without guilt.

Augustine had the luxury of writing as an outsider, though he, too, tended a human community, or two of them—his church and his monastery. Theodosius, on the other hand, resembled Justinian in having the pragmatic concerns of an administrator. But his attempt to produce a Christian code of law by citing only laws written by Christian emperors failed to advance an explanation for how and why communities arise and cohere, and so failed to justify the place of law, even Christian law, within conceptions and systems of social order. The precariousness of its hold on the imagination of kings and scholars resulted directly from that fact.

The remarkable influence of Justinian's Corpus may thus be attributed in part to its recuperation of classical political and legal theory, and in this respect it stands alongside a much wider and more complicated revival of classical learning and classical beliefs in sixth-century Byzantium.[70] The sheer ambition of his project nevertheless merits still further reflection— for Justinian and his collaborators embarked on it not in order to return classical law to a West that had lost it, but to revive it for Christian Constantinople. Read with that fact in mind, Justinian's justification for producing the *Digest* shocks and amazes (*CJ* 1.17.1.1; translation after G. E. M. de Ste. Croix):

> Whereas, then, nothing in any sphere is found so worthy of study as the authority of law, which sets in good order both divine and human affairs and casts out all iniquity [*quae et divinas et humanas res bene disponit et omnem iniquitatem expellit*], yet we have found the whole stream of our laws, which has come down from the foundation of the city of Rome and the days of Romulus, to be so confused that it extends to

---

69. Cicero *Rep.* 1.39.1: *Est igitur, inquit Africanus, res publica res populi, populus autem non omnis hominum coetus quoquo modo congregatus, sed coetus multitudinis iuris consensu et utilitatis communione sociatus.*

70. Cf. chapter 7, below.

an inordinate length and is beyond the comprehension of any human nature.

We might have expected Justinian to acknowledge some other rank-ordering between law and *res divinas,* or to recognize the strands within Christianity that claimed to transcend the contingent political boundaries of empires, or even to look beyond the foundation of Rome to those prior ages whose history functioned, for Augustine, at least, to diminish the historical and metaphysical claims of the city of Romulus.[71] What we find instead is, once again, a polite reversal of Varro's categories and the modest claim, quoted from Salvius Julianus, "that other *civitates* ought to follow the *consuetudo* of Rome, and not Rome those of other *civitates.*"[72]

There is one place in his theorizing on law where Justinian did declare an adherence to a Christian view of government, and it falls, curiously enough, in the constitution that authorized the *Digest* (*CJ* 1.17.2.18; translation after G. E. M. de Ste. Croix):

> Now things divine are entirely perfect, but the character of human law is always to hasten onward, and there is nothing in it that can abide forever, since nature hastens eager to produce many new forms. We therefore do not cease to expect that matters will henceforth arise that are not secured in legal bonds. Consequently, if any such case arises, let a remedy be sought from the Augustus, since in truth God has set the imperial function over human affairs, so that it should be able, whenever a new contingency arises, to correct and settle it and to subject it to suitable procedures and regulations. We are not the first to say this. It is of ancient descent, since Julian himself, that most acute author of legal writings and of the Perpetual Edict, set it down in his works that if anything defective should be found, the want should be supplied by imperial legislation. Indeed, not he alone, but also the deified Hadrian, in the composition of the Edict and the *senatus consultum* that followed it, laid down in the clearest terms that if anything were found to be not stated in the Edict, later authority could settle this in accordance with its rules and opinions and by closely following these.

71. A topic taken up briefly below in chapter 7, pp. 178–80.
72. *CJ* 1.17.1.10.

Here, oddly enough, at a moment when Justinian explicitly cited a classical precedent, he departed violently from it. For Julian, and Hadrian, too, will have located the power of the emperor to make law in the *lex* that the people passed, transferring to him and into him its power of command and legislative authority.[73] Justinian recognized no such earthly source of his power: *Deo auctore*.[74]

---

73. Cf. Ulpian *Inst.* bk. 1 fr. 1916 (Lenel 1889, 2:928) = *Dig.* 1.4.1.*pr.*

74. *CJ.* 1.17.1.*pr.*: *Deo auctore gubernantes imperium, quod nobis a caelesti maiestate traditum est.*

PART II

GODS OF THE
FAR-FLUNG EMPIRE

5

A RELIGION FOR THE EMPIRE

The Flavian municipal law has been called remarkable for what it omits: the extant chapters make no allusion to priests and no reference to the concrete actions of the provincial governor or the emperor.[1] It is also remarkable for what it takes for granted. Consider, for example, the oath stipulated for town magistrates. Each was to swear openly "in an assembly by Jupiter, the divine Augustus, the divine Claudius, the divine Vespasian Augustus, the divine Titus Augustus, the *genius* of Imperator Caesar Domitian Augustus and the *dei Penates*" that he would act in accordance with the law and in the best interest of the town.[2] Similarly, while the law almost undoubtedly allowed decurions to establish their city's official calendar anew each year, it presumes that among the *feriae*, holidays, of each city will be days set aside *propter venerationem domus Augustae*, "for the veneration of the imperial house."[3] These clauses have analogs in earlier municipal legislation, and so they have a place in the history of Roman governance, both in its extension into municipal life and in its acculturative

---

1. Galsterer 1987, 79–80 and 87.

2. *Lex Irnitana* 26; cf. chapters G, 59, 69, and 73. I cite the *Lex Irnitana* and the *Lex Malacitana* from González 1986. On the relationship of extant laws to a postulated *lex Flavia municipalis* see Galsterer 1987 and Galsterer 1988, 83.

3. *Lex Irnitana* 31; cf. chapters 79, 90, and 92. Rüpke 1995, 544–55; Scheid 1999a, 390–93.

effects.[4] But the presence of Jupiter and the *dei Penates* in Irni, Malaca, and Salpensa also presents a theological problem, for these were cities of Latin status, and if the Romans knew anything about the *dei Penates*, it was that they were worshipped at Lavinium, where they themselves had chosen to reside.[5]

The list of gods charged with superintending the magistrates of Flavian municipalities should surprise us at least as much as the presence of the Capitoline triad at the Roman colony at Urso. But the presence of Roman gods and Roman cults in the two locations, each with its own status in public law, has not, in fact, occasioned much notice. For historically it has not been the spread of Roman cults—their reduplication in multiple civic contexts—that has been deemed worthy of comment. On the contrary, the empire has been found wanting precisely because it did not in any systematic way establish a *Reichsreligion,* a religion of and for the empire. The forms of analysis leading to this judgment have rested largely on two assumptions: first, that what religions do is spread, or better yet, that what the religious do is proselytize; and second, that empires must have projects, whose furtherance and indeed whose legitimacy should properly rest upon the establishment among conquered populations of the religion of the metropole.[6]

4. For control of the calendar at Urso see *lex coloniae Genetivae* chapters 70–71 and 128; for the oath and the location in which it should be administered see *lex coloniae Genetivae* 81 and *Tabula Bantina* lines 17–18 and 24, and cf. Thomas 1990, 146 n. 19. On the social-historical and religious-historical importance of municipal legislation see Galsterer 1987 and 1988; Scheid 1999a; and Rüpke 2006.

5. Valerius Maximus 1.8.7: "Referam nunc quod suo saeculo cognitum manauit ad posteros, penetrales deos Aeneam Troia aduectos Lauini conlocasse: inde ab Ascanio filio eius Albam, quam ipse condiderat, translatos pristinum sacrarium repetisse, et quia id humana manu factum existimari poterat, relatos Albam voluntatem suam altero transitu significasse" ("I will now relate something known in its own time, which has been passed down the generations: Aeneas settled at Lavinium the *deos penetrales* that he had brought from Troy; then, when they had been moved to Alba by Ascanius his son, who founded that city, they sought out their ancient repository; since it was considered possible that this had been the work of human hands, they were carried back to Alba and displayed their will by a second return"). For the connection of the *dei penetrales* to the *dei Penates* see Dionysius of Halicarnassus 1.67.1–3, the Scholia Vetustiora on Juvenal 4.60 (and cf. on 12.70); Servius *ad Aen.* 1.270 and 3.12, and *Origo gentis Romanae* 17.2–3. On the Penates in general see Dubourdieu 1989; on their worship at Lavinium see ibid. 219–29 and 319–61, and esp. Thomas 1990.

6. I have taken up this problem in religious historiography at greater length in Ando 2007a. That essay focuses on the reduplication of strictly Roman cults in Roman colonies.

Part 2 of this book attempts to turn this literature on its head. Its conclusion as regards the pursuit of an imperial religion might be summed up as follows: a religious system that conceived the spread of cults as occurring through the transfer of specific cult objects from one place to another was in fact ill equipped to conceive the imposition of a single cult and endless reproduction of its apparatus throughout the empire. The chapters below pursue this insight along several lines, but each attempts above all to take ancient literature seriously as religious literature and to unpack its theological postulates. I concentrate on two bodies of evidence: first, the bodies of religious law or, rather, those references to religious law concerned with geographic aspects of priestly action and authority, and second, Roman historical accounts of their own attempts to move cults. Such actions were often described, as we shall see, as attempts to move the god himself or herself; their success is therefore seen as contingent upon the willingness of the god to move and, often enough, concurrently to accept not just any, but quite particular new worshippers. However we might wish to redescribe those concerns in light of our own theoretical predilections, the framework within which Romans conceived the spread of cults and adhesion of individuals to them is clearly radically different from our own.

In point of fact, while the spread of peculiarly Roman cults has long been studied as one part of the formation of Roman *Reichsreligion,* scholars have generally argued that it was not Jupiter or the Penates, but the emperor who provided the empire with its only shared deity.[7] Arguments of this kind have generally involved one or the other or both of two subsidiary claims. First, Roman cult of the late Republic was devoid of true— read "personal"—religious significance, and its effective domain was that of politics. Hence Roman paganism survived and flourished under the empire *as* imperial cult only because it had long since abandoned its agricultural, domestic roots and become a formal, secular *Loyalitätsreligion.*[8] Second, Graeco-Roman religion was properly the religion of the polis, and the structures and concerns of any particular religion—its priesthoods, participants, and liturgies—were homologous with the social and politi-

---

7.   Fears 1981 is an important exception; Goodman 1994, 20–37, is one of the few attempts to explain this in religious—albeit Christian religious—terms.

8.   Warde Fowler 1911; Beaujeu 1955, 28–29; Latte 1967, 25–26 and 31–32. Scheid 1985b, 95–127, is perhaps the most sophisticated essay of this kind.

cal structures of its city-state.[9] But the fit between these claims and the religious and political structures of the empire is doubly problematic. On the one hand, the binarisms inherent in them, between public and private and center and periphery, necessarily situate diaspora cults and imperial cult in competition with or in opposition to traditional religion.[10] And on the other, their relevance to the nascent political and religious reality of a united Mediterranean is far from obvious, not least because the nature and function of cities and conduct of municipal life under a universal empire were hotly contested issues already in antiquity.[11]

In point of fact, it is just this tension between Roman center and peripheral municipalities at the level of law, affection, and political philosophy that we might exploit in attempting to unfold the history of Roman religion as an imperial religion. It is not simply that the strain caused by imperial expansion elsewhere in Roman life had analogs in religious thought and practice, although within a limited and limiting analytic framework, in which the spheres of religion and politics operate autonomously from each other, one might say just that. Indeed, within such a framework, self-consciously constructed, it is precisely at this point of rupture that the explanatory power of polis religion might best be tested.[12]

9. Gordon 1990b, 1990c; Frankfurter 1998, 33–36 (and cf. 97–144); Woolf 1997, 71–77 (reprinted in Ando 2003b, 39–54); Sourvinou-Inwood 2000a, 2000b.

10. North 1992 and Rives 1995, 173–249, attempt to explain the gradual demise of polis religion in the larger community of the empire: religious identity became less politically charged just as increasingly cosmopolitan societies atomized individuals and presented them with more choices to which to adhere. The argument, both in the North's model and Rives's application, begs serious questions. Gordon 1990b and 1990c provide a powerful argument for the continued vitality of civic religion under the empire and, therefore, for the continuing usefulness of the polis religion model.

11. There are, of course, other ways to unpack the history of histories of Roman religion: Smith 1990, 1–53, concentrates on the Protestant Christian roots of religious studies; Scheid 1987 traces interdependence of hostility to polytheism and charges of formalism; while Durand and Scheid 1994 and Bremmer 1998 discuss the influence of late nineteenth-century anthropology on twentieth-century studies of Graeco-Roman paganism. There have been few studies of Roman religion, and fewer still of imperial cult, that have not been loosely functionalist.

12. Cities in political life and thought under the empire: Ando 1999 and 2000, 406–12, summarizing a long argument. For a very different view of the effectiveness of ancient communicative practice see Bendlin 1997, 38–44. On Roman interference in local religious life see Bendlin 1997, 54–63; Frateantonio 1997; Beard, North, and Price 1998, 1:211–44; and Cazanove 2000b.

Rather, one must also acknowledge that at the levels of both practice and discourse, religion was a principal arena for debate among Romans regarding the nature of their imperial project. On one level, those debates focused on questions of what we might call imperial politics—how one might integrate or further disjoin the peoples of the empire; whether to assimilate the institutions of civic life in the myriad provincial communities to those of Rome, or further codify (but also homogenize) patterns of differentiation across those same communities.[13] One mechanism among several to achieve this latter goal lay in the official enjoining by Rome of an obligation upon subject communities that they should sustain their ancestral cults as they had received them.

On another level, these debates concerned the very nature of the Roman community, again on two levels, that of the (political) subject and that of the community. To mention only two examples discussed further below, the cultivation of the cults of Lavinium and the body of myth that surrounded them allowed for the elaboration in ritual action of the new realities of Roman identity in this period—that most citizens of Rome had their *origo,* their origin as a matter of law, elsewhere.[14] Inquiry into the history of fetial law by late Republican antiquarians, on the other hand, constituted a debate on the very structure of the Roman polity. For when they posited that fetial law had not been shared by communities outside Latium, and furthermore that it required substantial revision in the age of transmarine warfare, they wrote on the one hand a religious anthropology of their empire, and on other recognized that the institutions of an archaic city-state—which is to say, of their own archaic past—were not suited to the present that those very institutions had brought into being.

This chapter puts these questions to ancient theorists of polis religion, as it were, and considers the challenges that confronted their theoretical and theological presuppositions as the social and political structures of the Roman city evolved in the larger ecumenical community of the early empire. Chapters 6 and 7 then study specific aspects of this broader topic. Chapter 6 pursues the history of *evocatio,* "summoning forth," a ritual where-

13. On Roman interaction with foreign religions see Wissowa 1912, 38–60, who perhaps overestimates the historical value of late Republican theological taxonomies that were even then inscribed in religious-historical narratives. See also Wissowa 1916/19; Scheid 1995 and 1998b; and Cancik 1999.

14. See below, pp. 108–9 and 138–48.

by Roman generals invited the tutelary deities of hostile cities to desert their charges and move to Rome. It diagnoses Roman histories of the ritual as metonymic upon the Roman imperial project writ large; at the same time, as I have already suggested, the ritual reveals the insufficiency of Roman religion for the broader task of universalizing any specifically Roman cult for the empire as a whole. Chapter 7 then pursues the history of attempts to establish a sacred center for the empire from fourth-century Rome to sixth-century Constantinople, paying particular attention to the role that classical Roman thought regarding the sacrality of objects and placement of the gods continued to play, in altered form, well into Christian late antiquity.

THE ROMAN PEACE AND THE DIASPORA CULTS

The Mediterranean world of the high Roman empire was integrated as never before.[15] This can be studied in a number of ways: trade, migration, communication, and, as a special example of the latter two, the spread of diaspora cults. In each of these areas we must observe and attempt to control the bias of our literary sources. Aelius Aristides, for example, praised Rome for its receipt of all the goods of the world, as though all trade passed to the capital likes the spokes of a wheel.[16] The elder Pliny, on the other hand, considered the empire-wide trade in medicinal plants one of the crowning glories of the Roman achievement: thanks to the *immensa Romanae pacis maiestate,* the "immense majesty of Roman peace," such plants are transported *ultro citroque humanae saluti in toto orbe,* "here and there throughout the world, for the health of humankind." "Thus do the gods seem to have given the Romans to human affairs, like a second sun" (Pliny *Nat.* 27.2–3: *adeo Romanos velut alteram lucem dedisse rebus humanis videtur).*[17] The actual dynamics of early imperial trade were far more complex.[18]

---

15. Shaw 2000, whose investigation presupposes a notionally unified empire; cf. Ando 2000, 131–74 and 303–35.

16. Aristides *Or.* 26.11.

17. Pliny *Nat.* 27.2–3: *adeo Romanos velut alteram lucem dedisse rebus humanis videtur.* See also *Nat.* 14.2. On this aspect of the Roman achievement in ancient thought see Ando 2000, 54, 347–48, and 389.

18. Andreau 2000, 784–86, and Harris 2000, 710–31, both citing earlier work.

The same bias bedevils the study of migration, travel, and tourism.[19] Not only do most testimonia concern the flow of Eastern migrants into Rome; they deplore it. Juvenal's famous lament that "the Syrian Orontes flows into the Tiber and dumps therein its language and customs, its badly strung harps, horns, and foreign drums, and the girls who sell themselves by the Circus" is but one voice in a chorus that grew more shrill as the tide rose and won.[20] The fluidic metaphor was a common one. In the same generation, for example, Tacitus wrote of Rome that "every sort of crime and disgraceful activity flows from everywhere else into the city and is practiced there."[21] The wild variety of populations that came to Rome, together with their languages, customs, and gods, clearly bewildered, and must have presented an experience both awesome and overwhelming.[22] To Roman conservatives—as for example the emperor Augustus, who was reputed to have warned his countrymen not to free too many slaves lest they dilute the Roman name—the experience was clearly disturbing. To others, like the Egyptian Athenaeus, the capital was "an encapsulation of the world" (τὴν Ῥώμην πόλιν ἐπιτομὴν τῆς οἰκουμένης) precisely because one could count so many individual cities within the οὐρανόπολις, "the heavenly city" of Rome, where ὅλα ἔθνη, "entire nations" settled, each in its own place.[23]

That said, we would do well to remember that not all migrants were voluntary, nor did they all travel to Rome.[24] The resolution of the Jewish War produced ninety-seven thousand slaves, who carried their religion into servitude.[25] Their cult, and with it those of Egypt, were regular objects of scrutiny in periods of xenophobia. To speak only of the Princi-

19. On migration see Cracco Ruggini 1980a; Frier 2000, 808–11; Noy 2000; and esp. Moatti 2004. On tourism see Foertmeyer 1989.

20. Juvenal *Sat.* 3.62–65.

21. Tacitus *Ann.* 15.44.3: *cuncta undique atrocia aut pudenda confluunt celebranturque.* Cf. Seneca *Dial.* 6.2–4, also employing a compound of *fluo.*

22. Dionysius of Halicarnassus 2.18.2–19.3: καίπερ μυρίων ὅσων εἰς τὴν πόλιν ἐληλυθότων ἐθνῶν, οἷς πολλὴ ἀνάγκη σέβειν τοὺς πατρίους θεοὺς τοῖς οἴκοθεν νομίμοις, οὐδενὸς εἰς ζῆλον ἐλήλυθε τῶν ξενικῶν ἐπιτηδευμάτων ἡ πόλις δημοσίᾳ. (Although innumerable races have immigrated to the city, each of which must worship its ancestral gods according to the customs of their native lands, the city itself has avoided adopting publicly any of these foreign rites).

23. Athenaeus 1.20c–d. On immigrant communities in early imperial Rome see Cracco Ruggini 1980a; MacMullen 1993; and cf. Camodeca 2006.

24. Harris 1980; Andreau 2000, 721–22.

25. Josephus *Bell. Iud.* 6.420.

pate, already under Tiberius the Senate had sent to Sardinia some four thousand slaves "infected" with Jewish and Egyptian superstitions, and two generations later, under Nero, Cassius Longinus would claim that Roman households contained *nationes in familiis . . . , in quibus diuersi ritus, externa sacra aut nulla sunt,* "entire nations of slaves, practicing diverse cults and foreign rites, or none at all."[26]

The political stability and social order that allowed migration and trade to reach new heights also supported the spread of cults, most famously those of Eastern origin: Cybele, Isis, Atargatis, Mithras, Jupiter Dolichenus, and Christ. This, too, became a topos of imperial literature. Lucian's Menippus, for example, flew to heaven only to find himself seated next to Pan, the Corybantes, Attis, and Sabazius, "foreign and dubious gods," while his Momus found the council of the gods attended by Attis, Corybas, Sabazius, Mithras, Anubis, and Apis.[27] Their astonishment was matched only by their dismay. Christians took a more positive view: according to one significant strand of Christian literature, widely influential in later eschatology, Christ had appeared in the reign of Augustus, even as the empire was established, so that his worship might spread more rapidly through a unified world.[28]

The importance of the diaspora cults would be easy to overestimate. They once loomed large in histories of imperial religion. Looking for precursors to Christianity, scholars postulated a category of "Oriental" or "mystery" cults that commingled soteriological messages with private, personal initiations.[29] As scholars have studied them in greater detail, their similarities have faded, and their significance as a category has correspondingly diminished.[30] What is more, these cults traveled with immigrants and so moved largely through shipping lanes; their worship was largely confined to cities and was far more common in Italy than elsewhere in the West.[31] But their dispersion, however quantitatively or ge-

26. Tacitus *Ann.* 2.85.4 and 14.44.3. A. Linder 1987 catalogues Roman legislation on the Jews.

27. Lucian *Icar.* 27 and *Deor. conc.* 9–10.

28. Ando 2000, 48 n. 148.

29. Burkert 1987, 1–3; Smith 1990, 31–33, 43–45, and esp. 55–84.

30. Smith 1990, 116–43; Turcan 1996, 3–9; cf. Burkert 1987, 30–53.

31. See Malaise 1972, 159–70 and 255–354, and Malaise 1984 on Egyptian cults in Italy and the western provinces; Stark 1996, 129–45, on Christianity. Turcan 1996 discusses the spread

ographically limited, nevertheless makes them the other to the locative cults of Graeco-Roman city-states. We need not be surprised that the diffusion of the mystery cults exhibits a pattern, nor is the pattern itself unexpected. It is the mere fact of their diffusion, in a world of poleis and polis religions, that requires explanation.[32]

For a cult to spread, several factors must converge.[33] First, the relationship between its god or goddess and material reality, in the form of both landscape and cult object, must be of a kind that permits him or her to be in many places at once. In other words, a cult needs to presuppose theories of materiality, representation, and immanence that allow worship to have meaning even for practitioners aware of the potential—and perhaps of the real—simultaneous replication of their liturgy in multiple locations. Extant narratives of the arrival of Cybele in Rome, as we have seen, stress that the Romans brought from Pessinus "the stone that the natives said *was* the goddess."[34] If the *baitulos* that arrived in Rome in 204 B.C.E. in some irreducible and exclusive way was the goddess, Cybele's precinct at Pessinus should have closed or, at least, diminished in importance. It did neither. To explain why it did not, chapter 2 suggested that worshippers of Cybele at Pessinus and Rome might well have understood that Cybele somehow was, and yet was not, coextensive with their black stone, and so acknowledged that in some way she might also have been, but not been, identical with other black stones. What limits there may have been to the duplication of gods and sacred objects—whether excessive geographic dispersal ultimately brought mere attenuation—is an important theoretical problem, but one not strictly relevant here.

A second factor necessary for a cult to spread lies with the god or god-

---

of each cult he surveys, relying (as do all) on the data collected and published in the series *Études préliminaires aux religions orientales dans l'empire romain* edited by Maarten Vermaseren.

32. I observe as an aside that so long as modern religious historiography follows ecclesiastical historians in adopting martial metaphors, *some* utopian cult will always emerge victorious, for locative cults by definition do not spread.

33. I set aside two problems. First, that of "choice," which has been central to much recent English-language literature on imperial religion, as though the only precondition for the spread of a cult were the appeal of its practices and doctrines. This seems to me conceptually at best a secondary concern. Then, of far greater theoretical interest, the willingness of gods to accept new worshippers: the ancient world knew cults whose members dispersed but whose god did not desire new worshippers.

34. Livy 29.11.7, on which passage see above, chapter 2, p. 25.

dess, who must be willing to be known and worshipped by previously unfamiliar individuals, either without mediation or through the intervention of individuals chosen by the god himself or goddess herself.[35] The institutional structures of such a cult need not be heterologous with the social and political structures of the poleis in which they are practiced, but its epistemological basis will be quite different from that underpinning polis religions. At Rome, the selection of priests by an electorate composed of citizens, the authority of those priests within their bailiwick, and the power of the Senate in religious life presume the gods' willingness that humans and the institutions that humans establish should determine, for well or ill, the shape and structure of their worship. We are returned to the problems of metaphysics and agency raised by Augustine's critique of Varro, and in particular to its focus on the ontological status and epistemic bases of religious institutions.[36] Hence, as a participant in, and theorist of, one particular polis religion, Varro understood its institutions to be the product of Romans, past, present, and future, striving after *cognitio deorum,* "knowledge of the gods" (*Ant. div.* fr. 3 Cardauns).[37] The sources of knowledge and lines of authority between god, goddess, priest, and initiate in any religion that had a mystery—and the

35. Consider Apuleius *Met.* 11.1–5: Lucius prays in ignorance of the identity of the *regina caeli,* and it is Isis who chooses to reveal herself, to offer instruction, and to accept Lucius as an acolyte. In the words of the priest, Lucius should henceforth "devote himself to the obedience of our *religio* and subordinate his will to the yoke of priestly office" (*Met.* 11.15: *teque iam nunc obsequio religionis nostrae dedica et ministerii iugum subi uoluntarium*). In contrast to most literature on this passage, which considers the perspective of the human and asks whether he "converted" (e.g. Bradley 1998, citing much earlier work), I would emphasize the agency of Isis.

36. See above, chapter 1, pp. 15–18, and chapter 4, pp. 83–86, treating Augustine *Civ.* 6.4 and Varro *Ant. div.* fr. 2a Cardauns. For Augustine's distortion through selective quotation of the epistemological concerns voiced by Varro, see *Ant. div.* frr. 204 and 228 Cardauns, quoted from the openings of books 14 and 15.

37. Compare the religious epistemologies of Balbus and Cotta in *De natura deorum:* what they appreciate is not simply that knowledge of the gods is acquired historically and incrementally, nor that increasing knowledge affects the performance of cult, but that the historical events become paradigmatic—are read as the actions of the divine in the world—only through the authoritative, interpretive powers of the Senate. Consider, too, Valerius Maximus 1.1.1b: the zeal of "our ancestors" not simply for preserving but also for expanding efficacious cult (*non solum servandae sed etiam amplificandae religionis*) was so great that the then flourishing city officially sent the scions of ten leading families to Etruria in order to learn the science of their rites (*percipiendae sacrorum disciplinae gratia*).

diaspora cults of the Hellenistic and Roman worlds share this feature, at least—were fundamentally different.[38] If it is true that Christianity as an "organization" ultimately came "to overthrow and eliminate" the "polis system," that process must be explained not simply in social and political terms.[39] The one religion's "organization" and the other's "system" expressed something fundamental about the way their gods existed in the world, and it is to the gods in Rome that we now turn.

ROMAN THEORISTS OF ROMAN RELIGION

Before expressing surprise that the imperial city did not impose or export its religion on or to its provinces, we would do well to ask what its religion was. According to Cotta the pontiff, speaking in book 3 of Cicero's *On the Nature of the Gods (Nat. deor.* 3.5):[40]

> Cumque omnis populi Romani religio in sacra et in auspicia divisa sit, tertium adiunctum sit si quid praedictionis causa ex portentis et monstris Sibyllae interpretes haruspicesve monuerunt, harum ego religionum nullam umquam contemnendam putavi mihique ita persuasi Romulum auspiciis, Numam sacris constitutis fundamenta iecisse nostra civitatis, quae numquam profecto sine summa placatione deorum inmortalium tanta esse potuisset.

> The entirety of the *religio* of the Roman people is divided into rites and auspices, to which is added a third thing, namely whatever warnings the interpreters of the Sibylline books or *haruspices* issue for the sake of foreknowledge on the basis of portents and omens. I hold that none of these *religiones* should ever be neglected, and I have persuaded myself that Romulus and Numa laid the foundations of our state by establishing the auspices and rites, respectively, and that our state could never have become so great without the greatest appeasement of the immortal gods.

---

38.   On the mysteries of mystery cults, see esp. Burkert 1987, 2–3 and 66–88, arguing that their similarities derive not from their putative, 'Oriental' origins, but from Greece. See also Smith 1990,121–25, distinguishing between locative and utopian mystery-religions: Eleusis is an example of the former, and Cybele, always ideologically foreign, an example of the latter.

39.   Burkert 1987, 51.

40.   On this passage see Pease 1958, 984–86.

Dividing his *Divine Antiquities* into five triads, Varro devoted the first triad *ad homines,* "to men," and employed within it a threefold division similar to that advocated by Cotta: one book treated the pontifices, another the augurs, and the last the *quindecimviri sacrorum.*[41] In adopting this definition of *religio,* Cotta the pontiff—and Cicero the augur—decisively rejected the premise from which Velleius the Epicurean and Lucilius the Stoic began—namely that religion originates with the impression left by the gods in the minds of all humans[42]—and they did so for the same reason that Varro treated human matters before divine ones: *quod prius extiterint civitates, deinde ab eis haec instituta sint,* "because communities arose first, and then the things instituted by them." And since Varro was not inquiring into "the entirety of the nature of gods and humans," he investigated human and divine affairs *non quantum ad orbem terrarum, sed quantum ad solam Romam pertinet,* "not with reference to the entire world, but only as far as pertained to Rome alone."[43] Varro and Cicero thus divorced the *religio* of the city, both in its praxis and its theology, from the naturalist theologies then in vogue in philosophical discourse.[44]

The separation between *religio* as praxis—even praxis with attendant theological presuppositions—and theological speculation, what Cicero calls the *quaestio de natura deorum,* the "inquiry into the nature of the gods," found expression elsewhere in the regulation of religion, not least in the boundaries drawn in theory and law between public, private, and foreign cults.[45] To label something private or foreign was not necessar-

41. Varro *Ant. div.* fr. 4 Cardauns. The odd man out in this tradition is Valerius Maximus 1.1.1a, which passage is translated and discussed above in chapter 1, pp. 1–2.

42. Cicero *Nat. deor.* 1.43 and 2.5.

43. *Ant. div.* fr. 5 Cardauns.

44. See, for example, *Nat. deor.* 1.1: the *quaestio de natura deorum* is necessary *ad moderandam religionem,* "for the regulation of religion," but it is not itself *religio.* The most famous and influential way of distinguishing types of religion and religious discourse was Scaevola's "tripartite theology" (Augustine *Civ.* 4.27); note Varro's insistence that the third kind of theology, the civic, *accommodata est ad urbem,* "is appropriate for civic life" (*Ant. div.* frr. 7–10 Cardauns). On the tripartite theology see Pépin 1956; Lieberg 1973 and 1982. On the development of a Roman theological discourse see Beard 1986; for attempts to situate Varro and Cicero in an era of rampant religious speculation see Jocelyn 1982 and Momigliano 1987, 58–73 (reprinted in Ando 2003b, 147–63). For a fascinating attempt to situate that religious speculation in its political, imperialist context, see Cancik 1999.

45. See also Festus s.v. *sacrum* (424L): "Gallus Aelius ait sacrum esse, quocumque modo atque instituto civitatis consecratum sit, sive aedis, sive ara, sive signum, sive locus, sive pecunia,

ily to stigmatize it. These categories existed within official taxonomies of religious institutions, and they served not least to differentiate obligations to the gods on the part of aliens, individual citizens, and the citizen body itself, and likewise to delimit, as also to affirm, the authority of state priests in their proper sphere.[46] So, for example, the Bacchanalia may have been *peregrina sacra,* but they were abolished only when their conduct *ad perniciosam uaesaniam iret,* "passed into pernicious madness."[47] Likewise, the Senate did not impugn Fortuna of Praeneste when it forbade Lutatius Cerco to consult her: it simply decided *auspiciis patriis, non aliengenis rem publicam administrari . . . oportere,* "that the *res publica* should be administered under ancestral and not foreign auspices."[48] The banishing of the Jews by Cornelius Hispalus thus found its most characteristically Roman expression in the removal of their *aras privatas e publicis locis,* "of their private altars from public spaces," for what was at stake was the implication of the Roman people in alien rites, which problem might be solved by the removal of their cult and its apparatus to private soil.[49] In that light, Dionysius of Halicarnassus can be understood to have observed a Roman habit of mind when he separated the *religio* of the state and the religions of Rome's immigrants and confessed τὴν Ῥωμαίων μᾶλλον ἀποδέχομαι θεολογίαν, "I prefer to accept the theology of the Romans" (2.20.2; cf. 2.19.3).

Dionysius praised the Senate for policing the moral boundaries of the

---

sive quid aliud, quod dis dedicatum atque consecratum sit; quod autem privatis suae religionis causa aliquid earum rerum deo dedicent, id pontifices Romanos non existimare sacrum. At si sua qua sacra privata succepta sunt, quae ex instituto pontificum stato die aut certo loco facienda sint, ea sacra appellari, tamquam sacrificium; ille locus, ubi ea sacra privata facienda sunt, vix videtur sacer esse" ("Aelius Gallus says that those things are sacred which are consecrated according to the custom and law of the city, whether a building or altar or statue or site or money or anything else which is dedicated and consecrated to the gods; whatever private individuals dedicate to a god out of religious scruple, that the Roman *pontifices* do not consider sacred. But any private rite that must be performed on a particular day or at a particular site in accordance with pontifical law is nevertheless called sacred, like an offering; the site, where those private rites must be performed, scarcely seems to be sacred"). Cf. Gaius *Inst.* 2.5 and Ulpian at *Dig.* 1.8.9, quoted below in n. 85 and on p. 112, respectively.

46. On this topic see Ando and Rüpke 2006, 7–13.

47. Valerius Maximus 1.3.1; trans. Shackleton Bailey.

48. Valerius Maximus 1.3.2.

49. Valerius Maximus 1.3.3; see also Livy 25.1.12, but cf. Cicero *Leg.* 2.25.

religion of the Roman people.[50] But the potential for Roman religion to spread will have depended on the maintaining of boundaries of many different kinds, on the situation of the gods in the Roman landscape, and on the consequent parsing of that landscape along several axes: temporal, political, juridical, and ontological. This feature of Roman religion is at some level well known and much researched.[51] But the principles underlying this system of mapping the world placed enormous obstacles before any attempt to export the *sacra populi Romani*. Put in different terms, Roman religion and theology lagged far behind the political and cultural developments engendered by the imperial project. Between the polarities of importing gods through *evocatio* and sanctioning the continuation of a conquered city's particular cults lay an enormous range of possibilities for which *ius pontificale*, "pontifical law," could not account and of which it could not conceive.

THE PENATES AT LAVINIUM

According to an oft-related myth, Aeneas settled in Lavinium the gods that he had brought from Troy. When Ascanius subsequently founded Alba, he moved his ancestral gods to the new city of his people. The very next day, the gods were discovered back in their former *sacrarium*. "Since it was considered possible that this had been the work of human hands," the gods were moved again. "They made their will apparent by removing themselves a second time."[52] This tradition existed alongside the presence on the Velia in Rome of a residence for the Penates, attested already in Varro's list of the *Sacraria Argeiorum* and known to Dionysius and Livy.[53]

---

50. *Ant. Rom.* 2.19.5; cf. 2.19.2–3.

51. This is the major theme of Beard, North, and Price 1998, vol. 1. See also Catalano 1978; Linderski 1986; Scheid 1995, 1996, and 1999b.

52. See above, n. 5. Compare *CIL* X 797: Sp. Turranius Proculus Gellianus was *praefectus pro praetore iure dicundo in urbe Lavinio, pater patratus populi Laurentis foederis ex libris Sibullinis percutiendi cum populo Romano, sacrorum principiorum populi Romani Quiritium nominis Latini, quai apud Laurentis coluntur*. On the treaty and *pater patratus* see Livy 1.24 and Servius *ad Aen.* 9.52, together with Ogilvie 1965, 110–11 and 127–29, and Thomas 1990.

53. Varro *Ling.* 5.54; Dionysius of Halicarnassus 1.68.1–2; Livy 3.7.11, 5.30.6, and 45.6.5; but cf. Varro *Ling.* 5.144 and *Ant. div.*, appendix ad librum XV, frr. a, b Cardauns, as well as Livy 5.52.8 and Macrobius *Sat.* 3.4.11. On the coexistence of Penates at Lavinium and Rome see Thomas 1990, and on their association with Vesta see Thomas 1996, 147–48 and 150.

The myth does not recognize that temple. Within its narrative, the Romans accede to the *voluntas*, the "will" of the gods, and so continue throughout their history to travel to Lavinium to worship their ancestral gods in the city where they had chosen to reside.[54]

Lavinium was one among several sites at which "the thirty peoples of the Latin name" came together for common rites,[55] and scholars have long explained the existence of these multiple sites by suggesting that as hegemony over the cities of Latium passed from one city to another, so did the locus of its common festivals.[56] Yet the underlying assumption that the sacred and political topographies of Latium should be homologous fails, not least because it cannot explain why cults and rites were not moved as social, political, and economic energy shifted from city to city. The Roman explanation for the location of the Penates, on the other hand, centered on the *voluntas* of the gods themselves, and on the expression of that will through their presence in the world. Of course, the myth may have evolved to explain a seeming anachronism; if so, we should confess that the myth was current and effective in the early empire and beyond. Indeed, the anachronism must appear all the more violent if we accept the force of Yan Thomas's demonstration that the centrality of Lavinium in Roman myth and cult was a late development, and that "Lavinium" existed under the empire as an elaborate fiction: it was no more and no less than a *religiosa civitas* with magistrates and priests but no citizens, a constructed and complex ancestor and double for Rome itself.[57]

The Penates' immanence in Lavinium was not transitory; rather, it was expressed through an identity with their images so complete that the nar-

54.   See, e.g., Asconius *Sc.* 19 (p. 21 Clark); Livy 5.52.8; *ILS* 5004 and *CIL* X 797; Servius *ad Aen.* 2.296 and 3.12; and Macrobius *Sat.* 3.4.11. On the sacrifice of magistrates at Lavinium see also Scheid 1981, 168–71, esp. 171, and Dubourdieu 1989, 339–61.

55.   Livy 2.18.3; Dionysius of Halicarnassus 5.12.3; cf. Festus s.v. *prisci Latini* (253L), and Pliny *Nat.* 3.69, listing the *populi Albenses*.

56.   Momigliano 1989, 65 and 85; Cornell 1989, 264–69, discussing earlier work, and 1995, 71–72. Oakley 1998, 538–71, surveys settlement of Latin relations with Rome after the Latin war. On Lavinium in particular and the history of its interactions with Rome in the late Republic and empire see esp. Wissowa 1915, 21–33, as well as Oakley 1998, 506–8, 513, and 560–61; and Cooley 2000b.

57.   Thomas 1990; Scheid 1993 (translated in Ando 2003b, 117–38). For the phrase *religiosa civitas*, see Symmachus *Ep.* 1.71.

ratives of this episode paradoxically employ the gods in metonymy for their idols. But to analyze the language in these terms is to evade a profound ontological and metaphysical problem by labeling it one of representation.[58] As Greeks and Romans knew of races that worshipped aniconic objects, so they knew of races whose gods did not live in their cities. Citing Xerxes' famous complaint that the Greeks trapped their gods within walls, Cicero affirmed Greek and Roman practice: wishing to increase piety toward the gods, the Greeks and Romans *easdem illos urbis quas nos incolere voluerunt,* "desired that the gods should inhabit the same cities that they did."[59] To that end, the Romans consecrated *aedes sacrae,* sacred buildings, for the gods, whose actual *sedes,* whose "residences," were the inner rooms. The confounding of problems of agency, materiality, and representation that inheres in so much of Roman writing about religion is visible in miniature in explanations that Romans gave for the terms attached to temples. If the use of *aedis,* "domicile," could be taken emphasize the agency of the god in taking up residence, the derivation of *delubrum* offered by Varro stressed rather the agency of the humans in placing the god therein: "A *delubrum,* a shrine, . . . is a place in which an image of a god has been dedicated: so, just as the object to which people attach *candela,* candles, is called a *candelabrum,* a candelabrum, so they name a *delubrum* that place in which they put a *deum,* a god."[60]

The Romans acknowledged and negotiated the place of the gods in the landscape through religious laws, which oversaw the use and management of space, the organization of time, and the performance of ritual. The intimate connection between these categories emerges with particular clarity in the speech of Camillus that closes Livy's book 5 (5.52.2):[61]

Urbem auspicato inauguratoque conditam habemus; nullus locus in ea non religionum deorumque est plenus; sacrificiis sollemnibus non dies magis stati quam loca sunt in quibus fiant.

---

58. Gordon 1979, 7–8.

59. Cicero *Leg.* 2.26.

60. Varro *Ant. div.* fr. 70 Cardauns: *delubrum esse . . . aut in quo loco dei dicatum sit simulacrum, ut, <sicut> in quo figunt candelam, candelabrum appellat, sic in quo deum ponunt, delubrum dicant.* See also idem *Ling.* 5.160. On the translation of *aedes* as "residences" see Festus s.v. *aedis* (12L). Cf. Dubourdieu and Scheid 2000.

61. On the founding of cities, see Servius *ad Aen.* 1.466 and 4.212.

We inhabit a city founded after auspices were taken and rites of inaugu-
ration were performed; no place in it is not full of religious associations
and of gods; as many days are fixed for solemn rites as there are places in
which they are performed.

Camillus's argument against the Romans' decamping to Veii suggests that
Rome is not "full of gods" merely because the Romans invited them to
dwell there. On the contrary, the gods act both in the world and in time,
and Roman myth merely concretizes in narrative a concern for topography, for the timely and timeless presence of the divine in the material
world, that finds expression elsewhere in Roman thought in the use of
sacra (things consecrated to a god, and so belonging to or performed for
that god) as a substantive to designate both objects and actions.[62]

This apparent blurring within religious thought of ontological distinctions that contemporaneous philosophers would have dogmatically
maintained is paralleled in Roman law on the sacralization of space. According to Livy, the *pontifices* fleeing the Gauls buried some sacred objects
on the Capitol;[63] this legend is likely to be connected to the presence on
the Capitol of chambers and underground cisterns in which ancient consecrated objects were stored when they were no longer to be displayed
or, in the case of decorative statuary, when they had fallen from the temple they once adorned.[64] The sacrality of these objects required that their
disposal be conducted with due reverence, and their presence even when
buried sacralized the land. Yet these objects had been consecrated through
human ritual action; they were not gifts of a god, like Vesta's fire or the
Salian shields. About the latter category of objects, Camillus argued that
a god's act of giving in itself sacralized the site in which it took place:
"Here is Vesta's fire, here the sacred shields fell from the sky, here all the
gods are favorably disposed to you, so long as you remain."[65] On this the-

62. Roman myths as myths of place: MacCormack 1990, 9–13; Woolf 1997, 78. *Sacra:* see
Livy 5.51.9, where they are buried in the earth, and 5.52.4, where Camillus urges that *gentilicia* and *publica sacra* not interrupted by war not be interrupted in peace.

63. Livy 5.40.7–8, and see Plutarch *Camillus* 20.3–6

64. Varro *Ant. div., appendix ad librum* VII, fr. b Cardauns = Gellius 2.10. See also Thomas
1990, 150. On the continued reverence accorded sacred objects see Bouma 1993, treating
Etruscan terracottas, and Glinister 2000.

65. Livy 5.54.7: *hic Vestae ignes, hic ancilia caelo demissa, hic omnes propitii manentibus vobis di.*

ory, myth narrates the history of the presence of the gods in the world, and that presence, however transitory in its impression on the sense perception of contemporaries, revealed the gods' abiding interest in, or attachment to, particular landscapes.[66]

The continued power of Varro's *signa vetera* implies a still more profound and nuanced appreciation for the relationship between gods and objects. It reflects, among other things, Roman belief that humans should take cognizance of gods' attachments, and that man's primary vehicle for doing so was ritual action, properly performed. In this context, what is worth emphasizing is not the scruple with which Romans performed their rites and observed procedure, though the Romans themselves often reflected upon this aspect of their religiosity.[67] Rather, we should heed Pliny's confession that the efficacy of prayers, correctly recited in a ritual context, is much more than evidence merely that "the power of omens is under our control." On the contrary: there exists "no greater evidence of divine indulgence" than that the gods allow our words and actions such authority.[68] Roman law on the consecration of space, and on the limits of priestly power in that arena, reflects a similar respect for the ontological and metaphysical hierarchies inherent in the world (Ulpian at *Dig.* 1.8.9.*pr.*–2):

Sacra loca ea sunt, quae publice sunt dedicata, sive in civitate sint sive in agro. [1] Sciendum est locum publicum tunc sacrum fieri posse, cum princeps eum dedicavit vel dedicandi dedit potestatem. [2] Illud notandum est aliud esse sacrum locum, aliud sacrarium. sacer locus est locus consecratus, sacrarium est locus, in quo sacra reponuntur, quod etiam in aedificio privato esse potest, et solent, qui liberare eum locum religione volunt, sacra inde evocare.

Sacred places are those that have been publicly dedicated, whether in the city or in the country. [1] It must be understood that a public place can become sacred only if the emperor has dedicated it or has granted the power of dedicating it. [2] It should also be observed that a sacred

66. Cf. Lane Fox 1987, 102–67, a wide-ranging treatment of epiphany, esp. 127–41, on place.
67. See, e.g., Varro *Ling.* 7.88: *Quod est in versu 'alcyonis ritu,' id est eius instituto, ut cum haruspex praecipit, ut suo quique ritu sacrificium faciat, et nos dicimus VIviros Graeco ritu sacra, non Romano facere. Quod enim fit rite, id ratum ac rectum est.* See also Livy 5.52.5–12; Pliny *Nat.* 28.10.
68. Pliny *Nat.* 28.17.

place is one thing, a *sacrarium* another. A sacred place is a place that has been consecrated, but a *sacrarium* is a place in which *sacra* have been deposited. This could even be in a private building, and it is customary for those who wish to free such a place from its religious scruple to call forth the *sacra*.

The terminological precision inherited and maintained by Ulpian, devised to honor the polarity of public and private so central to Roman religion, was understood to reflect, and perhaps to be, a human institution, one that must yield before the possible presence of a god in unconsecrated sacred objects.[69] Furthermore, it must have been the potential identity of object and god, however conceptualized, that justified the implied attempt to address a religious formula to an inanimate object.

The use of *evocatio* to desacralize a *sacrarium* in itself breaks down the boundary between public and private, not least because the power of sacralizing or desacralizing belonged to the domain of the *pontifices*. That ritual is surely most famous for its use in "calling forth" the gods of besieged cities and inviting them to dwell in Rome, a topic taken up at length in chapter 6. The success of any given performance depended on two crucial things: the god or goddess had to be willing to move, and the Romans seemingly had to transport the cult statue of the god in question from its native city to its new home in Rome. To transfer the statue was to transfer the god: Livy, for example, believed not simply that Camillus promised a new temple to Juno, and that the Veientines failed to understand that Rome had promised new *sedes,* homes, to their other gods;[70] his narrative of Juno's actual removal elides entirely the fact that the soldiers were (presumably) carrying not the goddess but her statue.[71] And the emphasis laid on Juno's assenting to the move, with both gesture and voice, is correlative to the *voluntas* of the Penates: if *evocatio* looks for all the world like an antiquarian theological justification for imperialism, the decision of the Penates to remain in Lavinium suggests the limitations on human agency and human will

69. Cf. Gaius *Inst.* 2.5–7 (quoted below), allowing that provincial soil not properly *religiosus* or *sacer* is nevertheless *pro religioso* or *pro sacro habetur;* cf. Livy 1.55.4, quoted below.

70. Livy 5.21.

71. Livy 5.22.5–7; a similar pattern is visible at Dionysius of Halicarnassus 13.3.

inherent in the epistemological framework and metaphysics of power in Roman religion.[72]

ROME, ITALY, AND EMPIRE

Evocatio helped to explain the centrality of Rome in the sacred topography of its empire, and it did so by placing the gods in Rome, in accordance with their express desire.[73] But the need to situate the gods within the landscapes of Rome, Latium, and Italy that *evocatio* satisfied scarcely permitted the exportation of gods to Italy and the provinces; nor, indeed, is it obvious how or why a Roman committed to a theology of presence would have explained or justified interfering in the conduct of cults outside the locus of Rome itself. As we have seen, the colonial and municipal charters of the Julio-Claudian and Flavian periods negotiate this problem with a brevity that bespeaks a common understanding. Whence might it have arisen, and how would it have been expressed?

The city of Rome had its own Latin temple and cult, corresponding to those of the Penates at Lavinium and of Jupiter Latiaris at Alba. According to Roman legend, Servius Tullius established the temple of Diana on the Aventine *commune Latinorum,* "for the Latin people to have in common."[74] Servius reportedly himself wrote the law of the temple, which listed the cities it encompassed, their mutual rights, and the regulations of the cult. Dionysius of Halicarnassus saw an ancient copy of this law, and it subsequently served as a paradigm for the regulation of Roman-

---

72   Compare the tradition that develops around Tarquin's effort to *exaugurare,* to desacralize, the Capitol: Festus s.v. *nequitum* (160L: *Cato Originum lib. 1 "Fana in eo loco conpluria fuere: ea exauguravit, praeterquam quod Termino fanum fuit; id nequitum exaugurari,"* "there were many shrines in that area; he desacralized them, except the shrine of Terminus; that could not be desacralized"); Livy 1.55.4 (the refusal of Terminus to move even when summoned forth, *evocari,* was taken as an omen); Dionysius of Halicarnassus 3.69:3–6 (the augurs were supposed to find out ἐὰν παραχωρῶσιν οἱ θεοί, "whether the gods would move"). See also Ovid *Fasti* 2.667–70 and Servius *ad Aen.* 9.446: when it was discovered that the Tarpeian Hill was littered with the houses of the gods, it was decided to summon the gods forth (*evocare*) to new temples; Terminus alone did not want to move (*discedere noluit*) and so remained. On a similar problem in Roman religious epistemology, namely the formula *sive deus sive dea, in cuius tutela hic lucus locusve est,* see Scheid 1999b, 198–200.

73   On *evocatio* see below, chapter 6 *passim,* and chapter 7, pp. 181–85.

74   Varro *Ling.* 5.43; see also Cato *Origines* fr. 58 Peter, Dionysius of Halicarnassus 4.26.4–5 and 4.49, and Livy 1.45.2.

izing cults in provincial colonies.[75] At Narbo in 12 C.E., for example, the people of Gallia Narbonensis dedicated an altar to Augustus. Having listed a few specific regulations, they allowed that *ceterae leges huic arae eaedem sunto, quae sunt arae Dianae in Aventino*, "the other laws for this altar shall be the same as those for the altar of Diana on the Aventine."[76] The paradigmatic value of this law no doubt derived from its status as an ancient text governing a shared cult. About the original foundation we could ask, Why Diana?[77] We should also ask, Why the Aventine? The answer undoubtedly is that the Aventine lay outside the *pomerium*, the boundary established by the augurs that marked the limit of the urban auspices.[78] The importance of the *pomerium* as a ritually established boundary would be impossible to overstate: implicated in it were a host of binarisms central to the conduct of Roman public life—urban and rural, civil and military, Roman and foreign—whose divisions were precisely drawn and rigidly observed, for all the difficulty of their reconstruction.[79] The temple to Diana, founded as a site of intercity cult, had been deliberately situated outside the city of Rome as it was ritually and religiously defined, and it was its placement in that space that endowed its *lex* with continuing relevance.

The expansion of Rome and extension of the franchise taxed this metaphysical geography in a variety of ways, and the Romans devised a number of ways to accommodate those pressures. As Livy understood, even if through antiquarian reconstruction, the ritual of the *fetiales* originated in a period when Rome fought wars of purely local significance.[80] Polybius implies that the *fetiales* played little role in declaring war in the mid-second century B.C.E.; their importance had been revived by the time

---

75.   Dionysius of Halicarnassus 4.26.5; cf. Festus s.v. *nesi* (164L); Wissowa 1912, 39.

76.   *ILS* 112, side B, lines 20–22; similar wording is used on *ILS* 4907 and *CIL* 11.361. On the *leges* of altars see Wissowa 1912, 473–75.

77.   Romans cited the paradigm of the *fanum Dianae* at Ephesus: Livy 1.45.2 and *De viris illustribus* 7.9.

78.   Gellius 13.14.1–4 and Varro *Ling.* 5.143.

79.   Catalano 1978, 479–82, and Beard, North, and Price 1998, 1:177–81, offer brief surveys of the issues involved; on the role of the augurs in maintaining the *pomerium* see esp. Linderski 1986, 2156–57.

80.   Livy 1.32.6–14; cf. Servius *ad Aen.* 9.52. On the evolution and import of fetial ritual, see Wissowa 1912, 550–54, Ogilvie 1965, 127–36, and Rüpke 1990, 97–117. See also below, chapter 6, pp. 127–28; and Ando forthcoming a.

Octavian declared war on Cleopatra, if not before.[81] According to a tradition first attested only obliquely under Augustus, the war against Pyrrhus forced the Romans to adapt the ritual to the realities of transmarine warfare: "The Romans could not find a place where they could perform through the *fetiales* this ritual of declaring war" (*nec invenirent locum, ubi hanc sollemnitatem per fetiales indicendi belli celebrarent*), so they forced a captured soldier to buy a plot in the Circus Flaminius adjacent to the temple of Bellona, outside the *pomerium,* and satisfied the law of declaring war *quasi in hostili loco,* "as if in hostile territory."[82] This ritual had an essential correlative in the Romans' symbolic seizure of some piece of an enemy's land on which to place their camp and take the auspices: "Varro in his *Calenus* says that generals, when about to enter an enemy's territory, out of religious scruple would first throw a spear into that territory, in order to seize a place for a camp."[83]

The distinction between Roman and hostile territory formed part of a sacred topography determined by augural law and developed, like the ritual of the *fetiales,* in an early stage of Rome's expansion: "According to our *augures publici,*" wrote Varro, "there are five kinds of land: Roman, Gabine, peregrine, hostile, and indeterminate" (Varro *Ling.* 5.33: *Ut nostri augures publici disserunt, agrorum sunt genera quinque: Romanus, Gabinus, peregrinus, hosticus, incertus*).[84] In ossifying a taxonomy relevant to the earliest stages of Roman history, these categories obviously reveal an inherent conservatism; they also concretize, once again, an essential recognition of human epistemological limitations. This mapping within augural law was paralleled in pontifical law by a distinction between Roman and provincial *solum,* "soil." When Pliny wrote to Trajan asking whether he could safely move a temple of the Great Mother in Nicomedia, he attributed his hesitation to the lack of a *lex* for the temple, "as the method of consecration" (*morem ded-*

81.   Polybius 13.3.7, Dio 50.4.4–5.

82.   Servius *ad Aen.* 9.52; cf. Ovid *Fasti* 6.203–8, Suetonius *Claudius* 25.5, and Festus s.v. *Vellona* (30L). Compare the practice of the Senate, which met with returning generals and foreign embassies in the temple of Bellona, precisely because it lay outside the *pomerium:* see, e.g., Livy 26.21.1, 28.9.5, 30.21.12.

83.   Varro *Calenus* (*Logistorici* fr. 2 Semi = Servius *ad Aen.* 9.52): *Varro in Caleno ita ait duces cum primum hostilem agrum introituri erant, ominis causa prius hastam in eum agrum mittebant, ut castris locum caperent.*

84.   On these categories see Catalano 1978, 491–98.

icationis) practiced in Nicomedia was *alium apud nos,* "different from that practiced among us." Trajan responded that Pliny could be *sine sollicitudine religionis,* "without fear of violating religious scruple," as the *solum peregrinae civitatis capax non sit dedicationis, quae fit nostro iure,* "as the soil of a peregrine city cannot receive consecration as it is performed according to our law."[85]

Roman law was not static, nor did Rome's priestly colleges speak with a single voice. The interdependence of the sacred and political emerges with particular clarity in the definition of *municipalia sacra* preserved by Festus: "Those *sacra* are called *municipalia* that a people had from its origin, before receiving Roman citizenship, and that the *pontifices* wanted them to continue to observe and perform in the way in which they had been accustomed to perform them from antiquity."[86] The extension of the franchise necessarily extended and fundamentally altered the *pontifices'* domain. So, under Tiberius, the *equites Romani* wished to dedicate a statue to Fortuna Equestris but were unable to find a temple to that goddess in Rome; they did find one in Antium. *Repertum est,* "it was discovered," that all the rites, temples, and idols of the gods in the towns of Italy were *iuris atque imperii Romani,* "under the law and power of Rome."[87] This as-

85. Pliny *Ep.* 10.49–50. Cf. Gaius *Inst.* 2.5–7: "[5] Sed sacrum quidem hoc solum existimatur, quod ex auctoritate populi Romani consecratum est, ueluti lege de ea re lata aut senatusconsulto facto. [6] Religiosum vero nostra voluntate facimus mortuum inferentes in locum nostrum. [7] Sed in prouinciali solo placet plerisque solum religiosum non fieri, quia in eo solo dominium populi Romani est uel Caesaris, nos autem possessionem tantum vel usumfructum habere uidemur. utique tamen, etiamsi non sit religiosum, pro religioso habetur. [7a] Item quod in prouinciis non ex auctoritate populi Romani consecratum est, proprie sacrum non est, tamen pro sacro habetur" (That alone is thought to be sacred, which is consecrated on the authority of the Roman people, either by law or by decree of the Senate. We make things *religiosum* in private actions by bearing our dead to particular sites. But on provincial soil it is generally agreed that the soil cannot be *religiosum,* since there ownership rests with the Roman people or with Caesar, while we seem to have only possession or use. Nevertheless, even if it is not *religiosum,* it is treated as though it were *religiosum.* Similarly, whatever in the provinces is not consecrated on authority of the Roman people is properly not sacred, but it is nevertheless treated as though it were sacred).

86. Festus s.v. *municipalia sacra* (146L): *Municipalia sacra vocantur, quae ab initio habuerunt ante civitatem Romanam acceptam; quae observare eos voluerunt pontifices, et eo more facere, quo adsuessent antiquitus.* Cf. Livy 26.34.12, from the plebiscite passed before the capture of Capua: the pontifices were ordered to adjudicate which of the idols and statues captured from the enemy were sacred and which profane.

87. Tacitus *Ann.* 3.71.1.

sertion harmonizes so naturally with developments in politics, law, and culture that its rupture with the sacred topographies and theological bases of Roman Republican religion easily go unnoticed. It seems thus both intelligible and striking that it was the antiquarian emperor Claudius who enclosed the Aventine within the *pomerium*.[88]

THE MOST MANIFEST GOD

The emergent realities of political culture in the early empire did more than bring the Penates to Irni. The continued creation of colonies of Latin status, like the imposition of the *lex Flavia municipalis* on preexisting towns, testifies to a gradual development whose nodal points can be plotted in the ideology of colonization itself.[89] Domitian did not found Irni *contra suspicionem periculi . . . ut propugnaculum imperii,* "against the suspicion of danger, as a bulwark of empire," as Cicero in 63 B.C.E. had described the purpose of citizen colonies founded by "our ancestors."[90] The juridical status of its citizens, on the other hand, suggests that Domitian did not envision Irni as an *effigies parva simulacrumque quoddam,* as a "small representation and kind of reflection," of Rome itself, to quote the emperor Hadrian's characterization of citizen colonies two centuries later.[91] Even so, the creation of Latins in Spain, through the use of juridical categories devised in a very different geographic reality, however idiosyncratically Roman, will have raised religious and legal issues whose contours have hopefully now been clarified.

After the death of Augustus, the colony of Tarraco built a temple for him and so provided an example for all the provinces.[92] Other cities presumably learned of Tarraco's action in the same way that they learned of Mytilene's festival for Augustus: Tarraco told them about it.[93] What made it possible for these cities to share the emperor, and for the cult of the

88. Gellius 13.14.7.

89. On the religion of Roman colonies see above, n. 6.

90. Cicero *Agr.* 2.73.

91. Gellius 16.13.9.

92. Tacitus *Ann.* 1.78.1.

93. On Mytilene's publication of the decree establishing the festival see Ando 2000, 173–74; on similar advertising campaigns in the Hellenistic world, see Edmondson 1999, 78 and 85–86.

emperor to endure longer and spread farther than those of the Penates or the Capitoline triad?[94]

Let us return to the Penates in Lavinium. A long and complicated tradition identified them with the Great Gods.[95] Why were they called "Great?" "Because, having been moved from Lavinium to Rome, they twice returned to their place; because generals about to go to the provinces sacrificed first before them;[96] because no one knows their names; because they are felt to be *praesentissimi,* most present."[97] This last quality, that of immanence, of being present, is one the Penates seem to share with Isis: her first words to Lucius were *En adsum,* "Behold! I am present."[98] But the Penates were present only in Lavinium, whereas Isis revealed herself to Lucius where he was. The failure of any Roman cult to become a religion for and of the empire should therefore not surprise us. The gods of the capital made their homes there, and they became attached to its soil.[99] In the end, Rome gave to the empire as a whole two very different gods, who shared one essential quality. So long as his power endured, the emperor's immanence in his ubiquitous portraits made him ἐπιφανέστατος, "the most manifest," of the numinous powers of this world.[100] His chief rival, who became his chief patron, was likewise present everywhere in potentiality and promise: *Ubi enim sunt duo vel tres congregati in nomine meo, ibi sum in medio eorum.* "Wherever two or three of you are gathered in my name, there I am in their midst" (Matthew 18.20).

94. On Capitolia outside Rome see Barton 1982 and Ando 2000, 208.

95. Dionysius of Halicarnassus 1.67.3–4, citing Timaeus *FGrH* 566 F 59; Cassius *Hemina* fr. 6 Peter; Varro *Ling.* 5.58, *Curio de cultu deorum* fr. 1, *Ant. hum.* fr. VIII Mirsch, and *Ant. div., appendix ad librum* XV, frr. a, b Cardauns; Macrobius *Sat.* 3.4.6–10.

96. Cf. Wissowa 1912, 164 n. 6.

97. Servius *ad Aen.* 3.12: *quod de Lavinio translati Romam bis in locum suum redierint: quod imperatores in provincias ituri apud eos primum immolarint: quod eorum nomina nemo sciat: quod praesentissimi sentiantur.*

98. Apuleius *Met.* 11.5.

99. Wissowa 1912, 86–87; and cf. 408.

100. Mitthof 1993; Ando 2000, 232–53, 268–69, 295–96, 394–95, and 407.

6

RELIGION AND IMPERIALISM
AT ROME

RELIGION AND WAR IN THE ANCIENT WORLD

Killing is a serious business. The unleashing of fatal violence demands regard for the more-than-human. This is true regardless whether that violence is exercised privately or publicly, and never more so than in war. The religious communities of the ancient Mediterranean produced some of their most remarkable literature in grappling with the horrors of war and the sack of cities. Indeed, we cannot appreciate the resolutions they devised to these crises of meaning unless we recall how easy it was, in a world in which cultures and ethnic groups were imagined to be bounded by what we now call city-states, to conceive the destruction of the totality of a civilization. But those resolutions differed strikingly, one from another, in both their ethical and their theological components; and cultures and communities produced widely divergent resolutions across space and time.

It is, for example, perhaps the most remarkable achievement of early Greek literature that this work of imagination was performed above all by retelling the story of Troy. In other words, Greek poets and their audiences came to contemplate the meaning of loss, as well as of victory in warfare, through a process that aligned their subjectivity with that of their foreign victims. This was more than a narratological move, some trick of focalization. It required the conclusion that the violence wreaked upon Troy—the violence necessary to destroy an entire civilization—could not be mitigated or explained away by some originary crime. And so, in Aeschylus's telling, it is Zeus who drives the Atreïdae to Troy, and likewise Zeus again who punishes Agamemnon for his victory. "The gods fail not to mark those who have killed many; the black Furies, stalking the man fortunate beyond all right, wrench back again the set of his life and drop him in darkness."[1] Within a generation of the Persian wars, the Greeks lost this capacity to see themselves in their victims, and so came to find other—and to my mind less satisfactory—solutions to the ineluctable problems of guilt and grief in war.

We are in a different world in the book of Deuteronomy. There the Israelites receive instruction not to fear their enemies, though they be numerous, because their god goes with them and fights for them. Thus they should excuse from battle those who have recently built houses, or planted vineyards, or acquired wives, but have yet to enjoy them; and even those who are merely afraid are to be excused. As for their enemies, those who are far away are to be offered tributary status; if they refuse, every male in their city is to be killed, and the women and children enslaved. But the cities of those peoples inhabiting the land promised to Israel—the Hittites and Amorites and Canaanites and Perizzites and Hivvites and Yevusites—those the Jews are to destroy utterly, killing in them everything that breathes, and sparing only the fruit-bearing trees.[2]

The involvement of gods in war and affairs of state had more than merely ethical ramifications. *Est etiam theologica ratio,* as Servius says of Venus's removal of the cloud that obscured Aeneas's mortal sight at the sack of Troy.[3] For insofar as the peoples of the ancient Mediterranean each had their own gods—or were understood to do so—the confrontation of peoples in war implicated each party's gods, in their relations with their people and each other. In Tertullian's memorable words:[4]

> Unless I am mistaken, all kingship or empire is sought in war and
> extended by victory. Wars and victories depend on the capture and
> generally the overthrow of cities. That business cannot take place

1. Aeschylus *Agamemnon* 461–68 (trans. Lattimore).
2. Deuteronomy 20.
3. Servius *ad Aen.* 2.604.
4. Tertullian *Apol.* 25.14–16; cf. Minucius Felix *Octavius* 25.5–7.

without injury to the gods. The same destruction embraces walls and temples; the same slaughter citizens and priests; nor is there a different plundering of sacred and profane wealth. The sacrileges of the Romans are thus as many as their trophies; their triumphs over gods as many as those over nations; their booty as great as the number of surviving statues of captive gods. And yet these same undertake to be worshipped by their enemies and decree for them "empire without end!"

These multiple confrontations could issue in any number of outcomes, and were subject to different traditions of theology and representation. In Vergil's description of the battle of Actium, for example, the action on earth is mirrored by a struggle in the heavens, where "monstrous gods of every kind and barking Anubis draw down against Neptune and Venus and against Minerva."[5] The victory of Augustus and the West might therefore be understood as a victory of one set of gods—one set of anthropomorphic gods—over the bestial gods of their enemies: as Servius dryly notes, "Vergil says 'monstrous' because the Romans under Augustus had not yet taken up the rites of Egypt."[6]

In the narrative of Exodus and the injunctions of Deuteronomy, the departure of the Israelites from Egypt and their arrival in the Promised Land explicitly involve precisely those themes of theomachy and adhesion raised by Vergil. For God had promised Moses that even as he struck down all the firstborn of Egypt, "from man to beast," so he would "render judgment on all the gods of Egypt"—a promise taken by the Israelites as fulfilled when they asked of their god, "Who is like you among the gods?" and by Jethro, who responded to Moses' narrative saying, "Now I know, yes, Yahweh is greater than all gods."[7] But the attention of mortals is short, and so the Israelites were told, when entering the Promised Land,

> to demolish, yes, demolish all the places where the nations you are dispossessing served their gods, on the high hills and on the mountains

5. Vergil *Aen.* 8.698–700.

6. Servius *ad Aen.* 8.698.

7. Exodus 12.12, 15.11 and 18.11, from *The Schocken Bible*, vol. 1 (New York : Schocken, 1995), translated by Everett Fox.

and beneath every luxuriant tree; you are to wreck their slaughter sites; you are to smash their standing pillars; their Asherot you are to burn with fire; and the carved images of their gods you are to cut to shreds, so that you cause their name to perish from this place!

This wholesale destruction was justified by the need to prevent the Israelites from "inquiring about the gods of those destroyed from before them, saying, 'How do these nations serve their gods? I will do thus, I, too!'"[8]

In this chapter I discuss two aspects of Roman experience in their encounters with foreign cults: first, their practices in respecting, maintaining, or transforming those cults, insofar as we can now unpack them, and second, the ways in which that experience was understood and those understandings were deployed in apologetic and historiography under the empire. The ambitions of the chapter may be circumscribed in light of three interrelated concerns, each mentioned earlier in this volume but now converging. First, over the last twenty years or so, students of Roman religion have taken up the banner of "place" and sought to describe Roman religion as a local religion. But the shift *toward* place has also been a shift *away* from something, and that something was *Reichsreligion;* the search, once fashionable, for a religion of and for the empire—a cult, whether of the Capitoline triad or the emperor, whose deliberate spread could form part of that imperial project that the Romans, as Europe's originary imperialists, bequeathed to their expansionist progeny. The shift toward place lends both an urgency and, at least potentially, a new theoretical sophistication to inquiries into the relationship between religion and imperialism under both Republic and Principate.

Second, if all religions were local religions—if all cities, in Tertullian's memorable language, had their own *deos decuriones,* whose worship was circumscribed by their city's walls[9]—they were not therefore all equivalent, at least in Roman orderings of the world. Consider, for example, the

8. Deuteronomy 12.2–3 and 29–30; see also 7.16.

9. Tertullian *Nat.* 2.8.7: "Satis rideo etiam deos decuriones cuiusque municipii, quibus honor intra muros suos determinatur." See also Minucius Felix *Octavius* 6.1: "Inde adeo per universa imperia, provincias oppida videmus singulos sacrorum ritus gentiles habere et deos colere municipes, ut Eleusinios Cererem, Phrygas Matrem, Epidaurios Aesculapium, Chaldaeos Belum, Astarten Syros, Dianam Tauros, Gallos Mercurium, universa Romanos."

gods invoked by Decius at his *devotio:* "Janus, Jupiter, Father Mars, Quirinus, Bellona, Lares, divine *Novensiles, di Indigetes,* deities in whose power
are we and our enemies, and *di Manes,* I pray to you and worship you."[10]
One could not in the age of Actium number Anubis among those gods
quorum est potestas nostrorum hostiumque. The expansion of the empire
brought the Romans into ever more contact with peoples whose gods they
did not share and whose rites they could only misconstrue. The history
of my topic is thus part of a larger story about the expansion of Rome's
cultural and anthropological awareness.

My third motivation follows directly on the second: it is my sense that
debates about religion—in particular, debates about the history of cult
and bodies of religious law—were a principal mechanism for negotiating the nature and future of the empire as a political community. The
claim by Christians that divine providence had facilitated the founding of
the empire to prepare the world for the coming of Christ thus had Roman analogs and antecedents, but they were a product of the early and
high empire, and not the age of expansion. Their story, I will argue, provides one thread by which to unravel the decline of that polite and powerful empire.

PROBLEMS OF EVIDENCE

Within those parameters, Vergil's language in the ecphrasis of the shield
of Aeneas draws perhaps uncomfortable attention to the quixotic nature
of my quest: for though texts from Vergil's lifetime constitute our closest sources for religious actions under the Republic, Vergil's ecphrasis—
and his epic—were modeled on Homeric exemplars; and, as Servius points
out, the battle of the gods at Actium itself imitates Homer, "who says
that the gods had a contest among themselves, on behalf of the different
sides."[11] But to point that out is merely to acknowledge the impact on
literature of the cross-cultural contact that imperial expansion inevitably
compelled. What is more, to describe my project as the disentangling of
some purely Roman set of thoughts and actions from within a body of

10. Livy 8.9.6: *Iane, Iuppiter, Mars pater, Quirine, Bellona, Lares, divi Novensiles, di Indigetes,
divi quorum est potestas nostrorum hostiumque, dique Manes, vos precor veneror.*
11. Servius *ad Aen.* 8.699.

late, corrupt, and Hellenizing literature would be to align it with precisely the sort of inquiry whose methodological and historical assumptions came under such withering scrutiny in the last quarter of the last century.[12]

But my aim is rather more limited than that. I concentrate here on state actions: that is to say, on actions taken by magistrates or the Senate or the people as a sovereign body, in consultation with one or more bodies of priestly experts. The history of foreign religions in private worship at Rome unfolds rather differently, and if I had time and expertise, I should tell part of that story alongside my own. That said, the structures of thought and governing institutions of Roman religion differed in highly particularized ways from those of Israel or Athens, and consideration of those must precede any detailed inquiry into specific rites or traditions.

First, Roman gods did not speak to priests or magistrates in the course of ritual action, and very, very rarely outside it. As far as state cult was concerned, verbal communication from the gods was more or less restricted to the enigmatic prophecies in Greek verse contained in the officially sanctioned Sibylline books. The Romans signaled their appreciation for the only significant exception to this rule in the name they gave the god who spoke aloud, in Latin, in 391 B.C.E., to warn that the Gauls were coming: Aius Locutius, "Speaker Sayer." As Cicero happily pointed out to his brother in book 2 of his dialogue *On Divination (De divinatione)*, having acquired a temple, an altar, and a name, Speaker never spoke again.[13]

Partially, no doubt, as a result of this difficulty, the Romans could not receive from any god a promise of "empire without end," nor, indeed, could they consult the gods about matters of long-term state policy. Rather, magistrates sought through the taking of auspices to know whether a given action was likely to turn out well or ill, and the answer they obtained was good for one day. They might and did derive from a long-term pattern of successful actions two conclusions: first, that they had isolated an appropriate method for consulting the gods, and second, that they had somehow persuaded the gods to approve their actions more consistently than the gods did those of their opponents. (What they did not conclude was that their

---

12. Feeney 1998.

13. Livy 5.32.6–7 and 50.5; Cicero *Div.* 1.101 and 2.69; see also Varro *Ant. div.* fr. 107 Cardauns (Gellius 16.17.1). Valerius Maximus provides further examples (1.8.3–5), but Livy explicitly casts doubt on one of those.

gods were stronger than their opponents'.) It was thus an empiricist system: as Marcus Valerius Messalla informed the city of Teos in 193 B.C.E., the data were there for all to see (*RDGE* 34 [*SIG* 601], lines 11–17):

καὶ ὅτι μὲν διόλου πλεῖστον λόγον ποιούμενοι διατελοῦμεν τῆς πρὸς τοὺς θεοὺς εὐσεβείας, μάλιστ᾽ ἄν τις στοχάζοιτο ἐκ τῆς συναντωμένης ἡμεῖν εὐμενείας διὰ ταῦτα παρὰ τοῦ δαιμονίου· οὐ μὴν ἀλλὰ καί ἄλλων πλειόνων πεπείσμεθα συμφανῆ πᾶσι γεγονέναι τὴν ἡμετέραν εἰς τὸ θεῖον προτιμίαν.

That we have wholly and constantly attached the highest importance to piety toward the gods one can estimate particularly from the goodwill that we have experienced on this account from the divine. Not only that, but for many other reasons we are convinced that our own high respect for the godhead has become manifest to everyone.

And in the century and a half before Vergil declared Rome's *artes* to be those of dominion, the central claim of Roman orators was of superior piety: "In spite of how much we love ourselves," wrote Cicero, "we must confess that we do not surpass the Spaniards in number nor the Gauls in strength nor the Carthaginians in versatility nor the Greeks in craft, nor, finally, the Italians or Latins in the native and natural sense of this race and land; but in piety and religious scruple and in that particular wisdom that consists in the recognition that everything is ruled and governed by the divinity of the gods, we surpass all peoples and nations."[14]

Piety at Rome consisted principally in the observance of *religio,* religious scruple, which Cicero elsewhere glossed as *cultus deorum,* the proper performance of rites in veneration of the gods.[15] But the language used to describe the aim of such action is telling: in the words given by Cicero to Cotta in book 3 of *On the Nature of the Gods* (*Nat. deor.* 3.5): "I have persuaded myself that Romulus and Numa laid the foundations of our state by establishing the auspices and rites, respectively, and that our state could never have become so great without the greatest appeasement of the immortal gods." *Placatio,* placation, appeasement, was the chief aim

14. Cicero *Har. resp.* 19. See also Cicero *Nat. deor.* 2.8 and Horace *Carm.* 3.6.1–8; Pease 1958, 566–67, lists further parallels.

15. Cicero *Nat. deor.* 2.8. On *cultus* see above, chapter 1, pp. 4–5.

of state cult, and perhaps the most one could hope for from figures whose power was so great and will so enigmatic that their exercise could not but seem arbitrary.[16] The theoretical circumscription of the gods within a community of law, of which the most compact expression is perhaps Varro's equation of *numen*, "godhead," with *imperium*, the legitimate power to command Roman citizens, is thus characteristic not simply of Roman attitudes toward law and citizenship, but also of Roman conceptions of divinity as power.[17] It is in that light that we must read Pliny's allowance that "in the teaching of the augurs it is a fundamental principle that neither evil omens nor any auspices affect those who at the outset of an undertaking declare that they take no notice of them; no greater instance of divine mercy could be found than this."[18]

Finally, any inquiry into Roman religion must confront not simply the limits of our data, but the processes of selection and transmission that have brought those data to us. What do patterns and absences in our data actually mean? As it happens, for a pious nation, the Romans had a rather remarkable habit of forgetting to perform rites (and, famously, of allowing priesthoods to lapse). Let me give two examples, one pertinent to the theme of appeasement, the other to war. First, in 49 C.E., it was decided to revive the rite of *salutis augurium* after an omission of twenty-five years.[19] As Cassius Dio describes the rite in his narrative of 63 B.C.E., this was a sort of divination or augury in which one kind of asked the god whether one might ask for health for the people; but insofar as one couldn't perform the rite unless the state were at peace, it seemed to Dio, at any rate, as if the Romans felt it was unholy even to ask for such health unless permission had already been granted.[20] Dio seems to find the rite about as silly in itself as was its performance in the year of the Catilinarian conspiracy. But what are we to make of its irregular performances, in 63 and 29 B.C.E. and 24 and 49 C.E.?

Or what, for that matter, are we to make of the chaotic evidence for

---

16. On placation, see Livy 5.13.4–8, 7.2.2, and Arnobius 3.42.4–5.

17. Varro *Ling.* 7.85: *Numen dicunt esse imperium, dictum ab nutu, <quod cuius nutu> omnia sunt, eius imperium maximum esse videatur.*

18. Pliny *Nat.* 28.17.

19. Tacitus *Ann.* 12.23.1.

20. Dio 37.24.1–2. On the rite, see Wissowa 1912, 133 and 526; for the ancient data, see Pease 1963, 288 (on Cicero *Div.* 1.105).

the role of the fetials between the war against Pyrrhus and the battle of Actium?[21] According to authors of the late Republic, the fetials supervised Roman adherence to the *iura belli,* the laws of war. How, then, should we interpret the silence with respect to the fetials of Polybius, the central concern of whose history was Roman imperialism, but who mentions the fetials not even once? Servius tells us that their rites were transformed by Rome's need to fight an enemy across the sea, namely Pyrrhus of Epirus—but we cannot test that information even against Livy, whose narrative for the third century B.C.E. is lost until 219. Did anyone believe Varro that the fetials still played a role in the striking of treaties before they turned up striking a treaty in a triumviral *senatus consultum* inscribed at Aphrodisias?[22] What then of the supposed revival of their role in declaring war, instigated by Augustus for the war against Cleopatra? Was it a revival at all? Or had there been a revival earlier, as a result of antiquarian research in the seventh decade of the second century B.C.E.? Or multiple revivals? From similar or different motivations? Or no lapse at all?

EVOCATIO IN PRACTICE

The methodological aspect of those questions might be addressed by a case study. I turn therefore to the ritual of *evocatio,* "summoning forth," by which a Roman commander would invite the tutelary deity of a city to abandon his or her charge and accept equivalent or greater worship at Rome.[23] Only two lengthy accounts of the rite survive from antiquity: that of Livy, writing in the 20s B.C.E. about the sack of Veii in the first decade of the fourth century; and that of Macrobius, writing in the late 420s C.E. about the sack of Carthage 560 years earlier.

Before considering the history of *evocatio* in detail, I should observe that the Romans had many other options available to them in their encounters

21. I discuss late Republican literature on the fetials at some length in Ando forthcoming a. On the fetials after Pyrrhus see Giovannini 2000; and Zack 2001, 75–87.

22. J. Reynolds, *Aphrodisias and Rome,* JRS Monographs, 1 (London: Society for the Promotion of Roman Studies, 1982), no. 8, line 85.

23. On *evocatio* see Gustafsson 2000, a thorough study of the historical data and the modern literature. The aim of this chapter largely complements her work, as I am concerned above all to explicate the ideological and religious-historical significance of ancient historiography on the ritual.

with foreign gods. For example, regarding Juno of Carthage, Servius informs us that she was "beseeched" in the second Punic war, but summoned forth in the third.[24] This is, so far as I know, the only surviving reference to a ritual of *exoratio;* and it is not clear what it could have involved other than inviting Juno to abandon her city temporarily, to some deserved punishment.[25] But it would make sense for such a ritual to exist: the Romans did place enormous emphasis on the use of fetial ritual to insure that their wars were just, at least in the eyes of their gods; and Servius does say that the Romans summoned forth the gods of their enemies *propter vitanda sacrilegia,* "to avoid committing sacrilege."[26] The situation of Fregellae in Strabo's day may reflect one possible outcome of this desire. A Latin colony established in 328 where the Liris emerges from the Apennines into the plain, Fregellae revolted under mysterious circumstances in 125 B.C.E.[27] According to Strabo, Fregellae in his day was "just a village, but it [had once been] a noteworthy city, which held in attribution many of the surrounding cities": "Now those cities come together at Fregellae, to hold markets and perform certain rites."[28] The cults of Fregellae may thus constitute an extreme variant upon what Festus calls *municipalia sacra,* "municipal rites": religious observances associated with a particular place, which the Romans required its new inhabitants, or its newly constituted community, to con-

24. Servius *ad Aen.* 12.12.841: MENTEM LAETATA RETORSIT *iste quidem hoc dicit; sed constat bello Punico secundo exoratam Iunonem, tertio vero bello a Scipione sacris quibusdam etiam Romam esse translatam.*

25. For what it's worth, *exorare* does not seem to have any technical meaning in ritual. The passages that come closest to revealing such are Suetonius *Nero* 34.4 (*Quin et facto per Magos sacro evocare Manes et exorare temptavit*) and Petronius *Sat.* 44 (*Antea stolatae ibant nudis pedibus in clivum, passis capillis, mentibus puris, et Iovem aquam exorabant*), which seem to me to point rather in the opposite direction.

26. Servius *ad Aen.* 2.351. On the punishment that follows on a general's committing sacrilege, see Cicero *Pis.* 85: "A te Iovis Urii fanum antiquissimum barbarorum sanctissimumque direptum est. Tua scelera di immortales in nostros milites expiaverunt; qui cum novo genere morbi adfligerentur neque se recreare quisquam posset, qui semel incidisset, dubitabat nemo quin violati hospites, legati necati, pacati atque socii nefario bello lacessiti, fana vexata hanc tantam efficerent vastitatem."

27. For the foundation, see Livy 8.22.2. Evidence for the revolt and punishment is sparse: Cicero *Inv.* 2.105 and *Fin.* 5.62; Livy *Per.* 60; Asconius p. 17.17–22 Clark; *De viris illustribus* 65.2.

28. Strabo 5.3.10: ἔτι δὲ Φρεγέλλαι... νῦν μὲν κώμη, πόλις δέ ποτε γεγονυῖα ἀξιόλογος καὶ τὰς πολλὰς τῶν ἄρτι λεχθεισῶν περιοικίδας πρότερον ἐσχηκυῖα, αἳ νῦν εἰς αὐτὴν συνέρχονται, ἀγοράς τε ποιούμεναι καὶ ἱεροποιίας τινάς · κατεσκάφη δ᾽ ὑπὸ Ῥωμαίων ἀποστᾶσα.

tinue to observe in their traditional form.[29] Finally, having summoned forth the gods of a city, the Romans could merely sack it, or else "devote" it to destruction. Availing oneself of the latter option required a further ritual beyond the *evocatio,* namely the *devotio,* by which one requested the gods to fill one's enemy with flight, panic, and terror, and to deprive of the light of the day not only those who would bear arms against the legions and army of the Roman people, but also their people, cities, and lands, and all who dwelled within those places and territories, fields, and cities.[30]

Evocatio has obvious appeal: employing it, a general could avoid sacrilege even as he convinced his own troops that success was virtually guaranteed. Even in the abstract, however, it raised several problems. First, what if you didn't know the name of the god who protected any given city? In Robert Maxwell Ogilvie's memorable dictum, "Gods, like dogs, will only answer to their names."[31] The writers under the empire who treat *evocatio* all connect it with a "tradition," such as it was, that Rome had a secret name, or a tutelary deity, or both, which the *pontifices* had to keep secret to prevent an enemy from subjecting Rome, too, to an *evocatio.*[32] What is more, in Livy's account of the *evocatio* performed by Camillus at Veii, the dictator's prayer makes specific reference to Juno Regina.[33] But why shouldn't other cities have followed Rome's lead and kept secret the identity of their patron deity? In point of fact, Macrobius purports to give the exact words of the prayer performed at the *evocatio* at the sack of Carthage—transmitted, he says, in book 5 of *Secret Matters,* by the obscure Serenus Sammonicus, who drew upon the work of one Furius[34]— and that prayer names no specific god whatsoever (Macrobius *Sat.* 3.9.7–8):

---

29. Festus s.v. *municipalia sacra* (146L): "Municipalia sacra vocantur, quae ab initio habuerunt ante civitatem Romanam acceptam; quae observare eos voluerunt pontifices, et eo more facere, quo adsuessent antiquitus." See also Festus s.v. *peregrina sacra* (268L: "Peregrina sacra appellantur, quae aut evocatis dis in oppugnandis urbibus Romam sunt †conata†, aut quae ob quasdam religiones per pacem sunt petita, ut ex Phrygia Matris Magae, ex Graecia Cereris, Epidauro Aesculapi: quae coluntur eorum more, a quibus sunt accepta") and s.v. *peregrinus ager* (284L: "Peregrinus ager est, quae neque Romanus, neque †hostilius† habetur").

30. Macrobius *Sat.* 3.9.10.

31. Ogilvie 1969, 24.

32. Pliny *Nat.* 28.18; Plutarch *Questiones Romanae* 61; Servius *ad Aen.* 2.351; Macrobius *Sat.* 3.9.2–5.

33. Livy 5.21.2–3.

34. Macrobius *Sat.* 3.9.6.

Si deus, si dea est, cui populus civitasque Carthaginiensis est in tutela, teque maxime, ille qui urbis huius populique tutelam recepisti, precor venerorque veniamque a nobis peto ut vos populum civitatemque Carthaginiensem deseratis, loca templa sacra urbemque eorum relinquatis; absque his abdeatis eique populo civitati metum formidinem oblivionem iniciatis, proditique Romam ad me meosque veniatis, nostraque vobis loca templa sacra urbs acceptior probatiorque sit, mihique populoque Romano militibusque meis praepositi sitis ut sciamus intellegamusque. Si ita feceritis, voveo vobis templa ludosque facturum.

To whatever god or goddess there may be, under whose protection are the people and state of Carthage, and to you especially, who have accepted the guardianship of this city, I pray and offer worship, and I ask and seek from you that you should desert the people and state of Carthage and abandon their places, temples, rites, and city and depart therefrom; and that you should cast upon that people and state fear, terror, and oblivion; and, having set out, that you should come to Rome, to me and my people; and that our places temples, rites, and city should be more acceptable and more pleasing to you; and that you should take charge of me and the Roman people and my soldiers, such that we know and understand it. If you do this, I vow to make for you temples and festivals.

Some have accused the credulity of Macrobius and denied the authenticity of this prayer and, indeed, the facticity of the *evocatio* at Carthage altogether.[35] But in the language of its invocation, it now has a seeming parallel in an inscription from Isauria published in 1974:[36]

Serueilius C(aii) f(ilius) imperator, hostibus uicteis, Isaura Vetere capta, captiueis venum dateis, sei deus seiue deast, quoius in tutela oppidum uetus Isaura fuit, [. . .] soluit.

Servilius, son of Gaius, general, having conquered the enemy, captured Isaura Vetus, and sold many captives, to whatever god or goddess, in whose guardianship the town of Isaura Vetus was, . . . fulfilled his vow.

---

35. Most significantly, Wissowa, *RE* s.v. *evocatio* (vol. 6, col. 1152); Wissowa 1912, 313. The case for authenticity on purely philological grounds is perhaps best made by Frankel 1957, 237–38.

36. *AÉ* 1977, 816. For more on the invocation of gods whose names one does not know see above, chapter 3, p. 56.

The full name of Servilius son of Gaius is Publius Servilius Vatia, who took the cognomen Isauricus on the basis of this conquest, which can be safely dated to his promagistracy in Cilicia in 75 B.C.E., and he just happens to have been a pontifex. More about that, and how we know it, in a moment.

A second theoretical concern raised by *evocatio* was surely when to perform it. Consciously or subconsciously, one wanted rites to succeed; one also wanted rites that conduced success. As it happens, imperial accounts of *evocatio* satisfy both desires: according to Pliny, the ritual was performed *ante omnia,* before anything else, at the start of a siege; according to Macrobius, the ritual was performed "when they were besieging a city of the enemy and now felt confident that it could be captured."[37]

The attractions of *evocatio* to an imperial power, not least one that fancied itself preeminent in piety toward all manifestations of the divine, seem obvious. But if we turn now to the actual evidence for gods called forth to worship at Rome, we find a rather spectacular dearth of gods so summoned.[38] Gods explicitly identified as the objects of an *evocatio*—or even presumed to be such—include Juno Regina of Veii, summoned in 396 B.C.E.;[39] Vertumnus, summoned from Volsinii at its sack in 264 B.C.E.;[40] Juno Curitis and possibly Minerva Capta, summoned from Falerii Veteres in 241 B.C.E.;[41]; Juno Caelestis, summoned from Carthage in 146 B.C.E.;[42] and, possibly, the god of Servilius Vatia in 75 B.C.E. I say "possibly" because I am not entirely persuaded that Vatia performed an *evocatio*. For one thing, I would have expected him to record the fulfillment of his vow on the new temple he will have dedicated to the god at Rome—and not, that is, at Isaura.

On the basis of these data, the ritual was performed five times: three times before Etruscan cities; three times for goddesses named Juno—but the Junos are not all Etruscan.[43] If we exclude the sack of Isaura Vetus, the ratios become all the more striking. What to make of this pattern?

---

37.   Pliny *Nat.* 28.18; Macrobius *Sat.* 3.9.2.

38.   Fuller discussion of the data for the events listed below may be found in Gustafsson 2000.

39.   Livy 5.21–22.

40.   Propertius 4.2.1–4; cf. Pliny *Nat.* 34.34.

41.   Ovid *Fasti* 3.843–4, 6.49–50.

42.   Macrobius *Sat.* 3.9.

43.   On these patterns see also Ogilvie 1965, 674–75.

Was the ritual Etruscan in origin? Was its performance at Carthage the result of an antiquarian revival—like the consultation of the fetials regarding the surrender of Hostilius Mancinus to Numantia in the next decade?[44] Was its further performance by Servilius Vatia the result of another revival, by someone in a position to know, as it were? If so, how would such a revival take place? And how do we know further *evocationes* were not performed?

In seeking to answer these questions, we must beware the temptation to make all our data meaningful, to require, in other words, the devising of explanations—or even a single explanation—for all outliers: the non-Junos, the non-Etruscan cities, the seemingly late. For what is an outlier, anyhow, among a set of five events scattered across 325 years, in Italy, Africa, and Asia? On the other hand, the date for the dedication of Juno Regina's temple—1 September 392 B.C.E.—is widely preserved,[45] and basic information about the origin of new cults is precisely the sort of data one would expect to have been transmitted in pontifical records and also to have been available on dedicatory inscriptions.[46] We lack, of course, verbatim quotations from the yearbooks of the priestly colleges, though they seem to have contained lists of the members of the colleges, each ordered according to the relative date when a given member joined. We surmise that not because we have explicit evidence for it, but because two lists of *pontifices* preserved in literary texts and one list of augurs preserved on stone are so ordered.[47] It is, by the way, from one such list that we know that Servilius Vatia was a pontifex, and that he must have joined the college prior to his campaigns in Cilicia and Isauria. There is little reason to believe that the pontifical *annales* contained anything other than raw data about actions taken, chronologically ordered; and some reason to believe that such data as they did contain

44. For religious revivals and antiquarian learning in the second century B.C.E. see Rawson 1973 and 1974, reprinted in Rawson 1991 as chapters 5 and 8, respectively.

45. Wissowa 1912, 188.

46. That said, the case of the temple to Capitoline Jupiter provides a caution: for reasons both ideological and practical, the Romans wanted it to have been dedicated in the first year of the Republic, but that was not the case, and some few were willing to admit as much. For the data, treated as less tendentious than would be my own inclination, see Ogilvie 1965, 253–54.

47. Taylor 1942; Vaahtera 2002; Rüpke 2005, 1476–1528.

received little discursive elaboration. The so-called books of the augurs, cited by Varro, may have observed different principles of ordering and inclusion.[48]

Regarding the objects of *evocationes*, there is some reason to believe that the *di evocati*—the summoned gods—remained ideologically foreign, and so were numbered among the *sacra peregrina,* the "foreign rites": according to Festus, "so-called foreign rites are those performed for gods summoned to Rome during the sacking of cities, or those sought out in peacetime out of some religious scruple, such as those for Magna Mater from Phrygia, or Ceres from Greece, or Aesculapius from Epidaurus. They are worshipped according to the custom of those from whom they are received."[49] And it may be significant that Juno Regina, Vortumnus, and Minerva all received temples on the Aventine, outside the *pomerium,* and so outside the religious boundary of Rome itself—but that was not true of Magna Mater or Ceres or Aesculapius or, for that matter, Juno Curitis.[50]

And, frankly, it is no easier to make sense of the *sacra peregrina* than the *di evocati;* the latter phrase has no particular authority, but Festus, who must here follow Verrius Flaccus, clearly felt *sacra peregrina* did. But as it turns out, *sacra peregrina* is just one of many overlapping categories devised by writers of the late Republic and early empire, seemingly to make sense of the wildly variegated religious landscape of imperial Rome, often on the basis of the slimmest authority. Perhaps the oddest such list may be found in the *Rules* of pseudo-Ulpian, who tells us that one might institute as an heir only those gods to whom that right has been conceded by the Senate or the emperors, namely Tarpeian Jove, Didymaean Apollo of Miletus, Mars in Gaul, Ilian Minerva, Hercules of Gades, Diana of Ephesus, Cybele the Mother of the Gods, Nemesis—the one worshipped at Smyrna—and Caelestis of Carthage.[51] We can sometimes guess at the basis for such orderings of information. It was, for example, presumably from data like Livy's aside that Etruscan custom permitted only priests from a certain clan to touch the statue of Juno Regina, or his reference, through Camillus, to *sacra gentilicia,* that Arnobius concluded that the Romans dis-

48. Giovannini 1998.
49. Festus s.v. *peregrina sacra* (268L).
50. For the data, see Wissowa 1912, appendix 1.
51. Pseudo-Ulpian *Regulae* 22.6.

tributed some of the cults of gods of conquered cities privately to particular *gentes* and consecrated others publicly.[52] The particular example is unimportant; Arnobius's claim has little authority. Rather, what is worth stressing here is that in discovering such a pattern, extrapolating from it a rule, and positing that rule as an article of law, Arnobius declares himself not so much a Christian polemicist as an expert student of Roman religion. But on the whole, the religious landscape of Rome was too old, and its languages and gods were too complex, to submit to the Linnaean impulse of imperial theologians. Indeed, the inability of Romans of the classical period to explain just who were the *di Indigetes* and *di Novensiles* caused Christian apologists no end of amusement, and the whole project of classifying gods was denounced by Tertullian in a question: "Shall I run through them individually, as many as they are, and as great: the new, the old, the barbarian, the Greek, Roman, foreign, captive, adopted, private, public, male, female, rustic, urban, naval, and military?"[53]

EVOCATIO IN HISTORY

As the preservation among priests and historians of the date for the foundation of Juno Regina's temple suggests, the classification of gods was but one among many undertakings through which scholars of history and religion sought to make sense of their world. Above all, it points us toward their desire to explain their taxonomies as the products of historical action, the result not so much of encounters contingent upon the spread of Roman arms and the willful decisions of individual magistrates, but of a piety ordered and expressed by principles of religious law. In such efforts, *evocatio* came to occupy a central role in the historical imagination, kindred in the scholarly enterprise to the syncretism performed in the scholarly imagination by what we now call *interpretatio Romana*.

We get our first hint of the new prominence granted *evocatio* in Pliny the Elder's chapters on the power of language in prayer and magic. There he describes the Augustan polymath Verrius Flaccus as having cited "authorities by whom it was believed that in sieges, before everything else, it was *customary* for Roman priests to summon forth the god in whose

52. Arnobius 3.38.
53. Tertullian *Apol.* 10.5; Arnobius 3.38; Wissowa 1904, 175–91.

guardianship the city lay and to promise him the same or greater cult among the Romans."[54] But it is in the *Octavius* of Minucius Felix, in the remarkable and moving defense of Roman paganism voiced there by Caecilius, that the new role of *evocatio* in the history of Roman cult receives full elaboration. There, Caecilius is allowed to adapt the traditional argument that Roman rule was founded upon an exceptional piety—"they have deserved their rule, insofar as they have acknowledged and supported the rites of all nations"[55]—by expanding exponentially not only the appetite of Romans for new forms of the divine, but their efforts to relocate and ultimately to domesticate their worship (*Octavius* 6.1–2):

> Thus we see through all empires, provinces and cities that each people has its own sacred rites and worships its municipal gods: the Eleusinians worship Ceres, the Phrygians the Mother of the gods, the Epidaurians Aesculapius, the Chaldaeans Belus, the Syrians Astarte, the Taurians Diana, the Gauls Mercury; the Romans, all gods. And so their power and authority have occupied the circuit of the entire world; thus they have advanced their empire beyond the paths of the sun and limits of the ocean . . . for even amid the capture of a hostile city, with victory still raging, they worship the conquered gods [*numina victa*]; everywhere they seek out the gods of strangers and make them their own; and they build altars even to unknown gods and to the Manes.

I need scarcely point out that the category *numina victa* was not a Roman one: it was, rather, an invention of Christian polemic, and as such a favored object of ridicule by everyone from Tertullian and Minucius Felix to Augustine and Prudentius.[56] Grant that these *dei minuscularii* are in fact gods, they would say: What good would it do to place one's trust in them, who were already conquered? What power had they shown, to protect even themselves?

But the march of historical research went on regardless, and reaches its climax in the pagan literature of the fourth and early fifth centuries, in

54. Pliny *Nat.* 28.18.

55. Minucius Felix *Octavius* 6.3.

56. See, e.g., Tertullian *Apol.* 25.14–19 (on *dei captivi*); Minucius Felix *Octavius* 25.6–12 (on gods captured and conquered); Augustine *Civ.* 1.2–4, 7.4, 7.11; Prudentius *Symm.* 2.347–69.

the attempts by writers of that era to defend the centrality of Rome in the sacred topography of the late empire. Hence in the chapter of the *Saturnalia* that Macrobius devoted to *evocatio,* the pontifex Vettius Agorius Praetextatus concludes his exegesis of the rite with a list of the towns subjected to *evocatio* and "devotion":[57]

> I have found in works of ancient literature that the following towns were devoted: Stonii, Fregellae, Gabii, Veii, and Fidenae—these are all in Italy—and also Carthage and Corinth, as well as many enemy armies and towns of the Gauls, Spaniards, Africans, Moors, and other peoples of whom the ancient annals speak.

It was presumably on the basis of similar logic that Ammianus Marcellinus defended the decision by Constantine to remove from Heliopolis in Egypt to Rome a great obelisk, dedicated there to the Sun: "Constantine paid little heed to its prior dedication but tore it from its foundation, rightly thinking that he was violating no religious scruple if, having removed this marvel from one temple, he consecrated it at Rome—that is, in the *templum totius mundi,* the temple of the entire world."[58]

On this telling, the role of *evocatio* in early and high imperial histories of Roman religion thus respects many of the traditions—philosophical, theological, and historical—operative in the development of the empire from its earliest stages, and our own history of its use constitutes one important index of that story. From a rite practiced by a small city-state against similarly ordered cities of central Italy, it was redeployed in new contexts, in which it served the Romans' interests by explaining to them and to their enemies a particular Roman ordering of the world; it also facilitated a certain form of integration by domesticating the gods and rites of their far-flung empire. But it was a problematic legacy. The world of politics and power moved on. In the late fourth century C.E., in a plea to Christian emperors to permit the continuance of pagan rites and the pro-

---

57. Macrobius *Sat.* 3.9.13: "In antiquitatibus autem haec oppida inveni devota: Stonios, Fregellas, Gavios, Veios, Fidenas; haec intra Italiam, praeterea Carthaginem et Corinthum, sed et multos exercitus oppidaque hostium Gallorum Hispanorum Afrorum Maurorum aliarumque gentium quas prisci loquuntur annales."

58. Ammianus 17.4.13.

tection of pagan temples, the orator Libanius of Antioch directed their attention to the varied immanence of the gods in their world (*Or.* 30.33–34; trans. after A. F. Norman):

> But if the security of the empire rests upon the sacrifices performed at Rome, we must also believe that sacrifice everywhere operates to our advantage. Granted, οἵ ἐν Ῥώμῃ δαίμονες, the gods in Rome, give greater blessings; those in the countryside and the other cities give lesser ones; but any sensible person would accept even those. In an army, not everyone's contribution is equivalent; but in battle, everyone contributes *something.*

A quarter-century later, when Rome itself was sacked, it must have been hard to deny that "the gods in Rome"—the *numina victa*—had failed once again to protect not only their city, but even themselves.

EVOCATIO AND EMPIRE

Set thus against a backdrop of Jewish and Greek meditations on the connection between religion and war, *evocatio* emerges as an effort to grapple with a major religious and ethical problem, one largely left pending in Deuteronomy and the literatures of classical Greece. That situation may have been satisfactory when one allowed oneself to view pure conquest or victory alone as the issue, as in the conquest of Palestine or ultimately in the sack of Troy. But for the Romans, who came to view themselves as responsible—in different ways, at different times and places—not only for themselves, but for their empire, that is, for the ongoing life of conquered places and societies, a very different theology was required. Above all, they had to find ways, within their own religious and anthropological awareness, to conceive the existence of other gods and to permit, even encourage, the continuance of their worship within their communities. The legal and topographic arrangements devised to govern the cults of Latium in the late fourth century B.C.E. display remarkable sophistication of precisely this kind, as do the simultaneous dissolution of Fregellae's institutions of government and maintenance of its local cults.[59] It is im-

---

59. On the cults of Latium see Wissowa 1915.

portant in this context to observe that when Caecilius in Minucius Felix's *Octavius* allows that the Romans deserved their rule, insofar as they supported the rites of all nations, he refers at that moment to the continuance of cults in their ancestral locations, among subject peoples. The early imperial (re)creation of the cults of Lavinium was another expression of this role for religion and religious law, as mechanisms for debating the nature and future of Rome's imperial project. The centerpiece of this effort was a set of rituals by which the extra-Roman origins of Rome were not only acknowledged, but celebrated, in the form of the continued—or renewed—existence of a city that might have been Rome itself. This was, certainly, a virtuoso display of religious antiquarianism; it was also a remarkable attempt to create a religious framework that could articulate the now double nature of Roman identity, at a time when most Romans traced their origins to cities in Italy or the provinces, but their citizenship to Rome itself.[60]

Viewed in this light, the attacks by Christians like Tertullian, Arnobius, and Augustine upon the conquered gods struck at the very heart of what the empire was.[61] For their undoing of this theology would strike asunder one of the complex webs by which communities that might be—and had often once been—religiously, politically, and culturally autonomous were nevertheless bound together, to each other and to Rome. Many of these same writers also subscribed to the view that the empire was a tool of divine providence; I suspect that they cannot have reflected too critically upon the material facts of empire, in working as they did to dissolve it. For what it is worth, Augustine, who unlike those men saw in his final years the overthrow of the empire in potential reality, came to hold far more complex views about the role of divine providence in the foundation of empires and the importance of Rome in the maintenance of civil society.

That said, the empire as a network of cities, each with its own gods, did fall; and among the many factors contributing to this outcome the collapse of the civic compromise looms large. This was in part the result of Christian attacks upon it; but the brilliance of their polemic is not in itself sufficient to explain its demise. It was also, I contend, collapsing from

---

60. On Lavinium see Thomas 1996, 133—79; Scheid 1993 (translated in Ando 2003b, 117–38).
61. Cf. Gordon 1990b and 1990c.

within. *Evocatio* was either too effective, or insufficient. Wherein did its vulnerability lie?

Although I concentrate here upon themes connected with *evocatio,* and within that sphere upon the fate of the theology to which it contributed, *evocatio* is naturally not the only cipher one might use to unlock the history of religion and empire at Rome. The self-conscious maintenance into the Principate of religio-juridical taxonomies of land that steadfastly disjoined, rather than united, Roman, Italian, and provincial soil deserves similar investigation.[62] It would likewise be useful to consider the extent to which historiography, and specifically the history of practice, might be regarded as the exegetical mode not simply most characteristic of Roman religion, but even constitutive of it. For the Romans understood their religious practices to have changed over time—indeed, to have evolved— and knowledge of *emendationes sacrificiorum,* alterations to rites, as also of their causes, was far more essential to contemporary practice than an antiquarian search for aetiology.[63] Instead, let me focus upon two related issues, the first being the particular investment in materiality that underlay the cult acts whereby gods were relocated from Veii or Epidaurus or Pessinus to Rome; and second, upon what we might call the disadvantages of paganism for a universal state.[64]

To accomplish these tasks, we must take the theological underpinnings of classical Roman paganism seriously. This is no simple matter. To show what I mean by this, I return to a comparison I have adduced before, between texts that take us rather far from religion and war, but to the heart of gods and place, namely the openings of Genesis 22 and book 11 of Apuleius's *Metamorphoses.*[65] In the first, God summons Abraham (Gen. 22.1):

quae postquam gesta sunt
temptavit Deus Abraham et dixit ad eum
Abraham ille respondit adsum.

62. See above, chapter 5, pp. 110–14, and Ando forthcoming a.
63. Macrobius *Sat.* 1.7.36. On this topic see above, chapter 1, p. 15.
64. Cf. A. Momigliano, "The Disadvantages of Monotheism for a Universal State," *CPh* 81 (1986) 285–97 (= Momigliano 1987, 142–58).
65. See above, p. 26.

After these things were done
God tested Abraham and said to him,
"Abraham." He responded, "I am here."

Here, the narrative opens with a deliberate rejection of place and even of time: all that matters is the metaphysical relationship illustrated and perhaps established by the interpellation of man by God. In the *Metamorphoses,* it is the mortal who speaks first—Lucius, still in the form of an ass—who prays on the beach at Cenchreae, washed by the Aegean and Saronic seas, at the start of the first watch of evening, under the white light of an emergent full moon.[66] And in the *Metamorphoses,* it is the mortal, Lucius, who summons the god—his fulsome appellation alone takes more than a hundred words—and it is the god, Isis, who responds: "*En adsum,* Behold, I am here."[67] Now at one level these episodes present a challenge, resisting as they do our own taxonomic endeavors—the two Eastern, Oriental mystery cults, the one clearly utopian, the other more nearly locative. But they also recall two distinct problems involved in *evocatio,* and these are, first, the movement of the gods as such, from one distinct location to another, on each of which their favor is uniquely dispensed, and second, the insistence within our narratives that those transfers occur—in? through? as?—the transfer of their cult objects.

Here it might be tempting to invoke some episode from classical Roman literature, and through its explication to describe—or, rather, to isolate—some essential difference between Roman and Semitic cults, in their theological and philosophical postulates. We might, for example, quote Aulus Gellius's version (6.1.6) of the story that Scipio Africanus

used often to go to the Capitolium in the latter part of the night, before the break of day, give orders that the shrine of Jupiter be opened, and remain there a long time alone, apparently consulting Jupiter about matters of state; and the guardians of the temple were often amazed at his coming to the Capitolium alone at such an hour, yet the dogs, which flew at all other intruders, neither barked at him nor molested him.

66. Apuleius *Met.* 10.35 and 11.1.
67. Apuleius *Met.* 11.5.

And of it we might ask why Scipio could not have consulted Jupiter at home. But we should have also to confront other tellings of that story—like Livy's, in which Scipio is described as "going to the Capitol, entering the building, and taking a seat, often alone, and spending time there, in the recesses of the temple"[68]—and then, impelled by their differences, redescribe them not as narrations, but as exegeses of a practice. How then we should talk about the one, which involves a man conversing with a god, in a building in which we might perceive only its statue, and the other, which respects some ontological distance between the two, is a problem to which I shall return, albeit obliquely.

For now, let me set alongside these anecdotes another, the legend of Gaius Fabius Dorsuo. That outstanding young man chose during the Gallic sack of Rome in 390 B.C.E. to complete a sacrifice, established within his clan, whose efficacy depended on its being performed on the Quirinal. Dorsuo therefore dressed for the rite and departed the Capitol—the only one of the seven hills not controlled by the Gauls—walked fearlessly through the Gallic army, performed the rite, and returned.[69] This act, narrated in Livy's history, is then subjected to analysis later in the same book, in the speech delivered by the dictator Camillus in opposition to the proposal that the Romans should abandon the ruins of their city and decamp to Veii, whence, earlier in the very same book, Camillus as consul had summoned forth the first of our Etruscan Junos. Among several arguments, he suggests that it would be sacrilegious for the *flamen Dialis* or Vestal Virgins to leave the city and live on foreign soil. For the *flamen Dialis,* to leave the city would constitute a violation of pontifical law. But regarding the Vestals, whose power to fix the feet of runaway slaves to the ground was bounded by the *pomerium,* Camillus addresses Vesta herself: "Will your Vestals desert you, Vesta?"[70] Likewise, regarding the performance of cult, Camillus points to rituals that the Romans of his day, as also of Livy's, continued to perform on the Alban Mount and at Lavinium, sacred sites of ancient Latium: "If it was a matter of scruple that these rites not be moved to Rome, to us, from the cities of our enemies, shall we now transfer them without guilt hence to Veii, to the city of our en-

68. Livy 26.19.5.
69. Livy 5.46.2–3.
70. Livy 5.52.13. On the Vestals and the feet of slaves see Pliny *Nat.* 28.13.

emies?"[71] Alongside such public rites, Camillus proffered the example of Fabius Dorsuo, as illustrating one among many *sacra gentilicia* practiced at Rome and tied there to particular locales.

What Livy points to throughout book 5—in narrating the sack of Veii, the sack of Rome, and the speech of Camillus—is the need to respect the location of the gods, their desire to reside in particular locales, and the need to bring worship to them there. But so to speak is merely to describe one fact about some Roman gods in terms that a Roman would have found obvious. As satisfying as that might be—and proper historicism in religious history is not so easily achieved—it turns out not to get us terribly far. For the Romans also said things about religion that we find rather hard to understand, and it is in any event not clear what it would mean to claim or even to capture an insider's knowledge, or to use an insider's language. For not only do we lack the means to test that claim, but in adopting that position I would deliberately decline the effort at translation that would make this understanding intelligible to those outside my own linguistic community. Perhaps we should ask what the Romans believed about their gods that made these stories intelligible. About the narratives of *evocatio* in particular we might ask what the proper framework is, within which to analyze their confounding of gods and statues, in both language and ritual. Is it a problem of theology? Materiality? Representation? To answer those questions, let us turn to one final ingredient in attested evocations that I have not considered thus far, namely that they were all successful. All the summoned gods consented to come.

How did the Romans know that they had consented? How would they have known if they had declined? One necessary but not in itself sufficient indication of assent was surely the taking of the city, just as failure in that endeavor could be construed as evidence that the god had declined, for the day, at least, but it need not be so construed. In Livy's narrative, for example, the actual removal of Juno is preceded by a soldier's asking her whether she wished to come—this, after the dictator's performance of the ritual and sack of city.[72] And the Romans certainly had experience of unsuccessful rituals in the removal of gods. To illustrate their attachment to particular locales, Camillus himself cited the

71. Livy 5.52.8.
72. Livy 5.22.3–7.

gods Iuventus and Terminus, who famously declined *exaugurationes* from the Capitol.[73] But his mention of rites that the Romans performed at Lavinium rather than at Rome alludes to an equally famous expression of will on the part of the gods, this time on the part of the *dei Penates,* the household gods of Aeneas. In the version related by Valerius Maximus (1.8.7):

> Aeneas settled at Lavinium the *deos penetrales* that he had brought from Troy; then, when they had been moved to Alba by Ascanius his son, who founded that city, they sought out their ancient repository; since it was considered possible that this had been the work of human hands, they were carried back to Alba and displayed their will by a second return.

Two points bearing upon our concerns emerge from these stories. There is first the need to test the gods—a feature, if ever there was one, of the empiricism of Roman religion—the testing following upon the very uncertainty in construing success or failure inherent in a religious system whose gods communicated so indirectly. It thus merits notice that in Dionysius of Halicarnassus's telling, the statue of Juno at Veii not only replies in a loud voice, but does so twice: "For the soldiers, doubting whether it was the statue that had spoken, asked the same question again and received the same reply."[74] Second, and crucially, the relationship between god and landscape is not merely an affective one. It is, rather, rooted in the materiality of the gods themselves. The need for Poseidon to notice Odysseus on his raft is one expression of this; likewise the tradition that the people of Tyre tried to restrain Apollo from deserting them during Alexander's siege of their city by throwing chains over his statue.[75] But closer analogs at Rome might be the behavior of those men and women on the Capitol who offered documents to Jupiter for his inspection or dressed the hair of Juno and Minerva—"standing far away not only from their images but from their temples the women moved their

---

73. Livy 5.54.7; cf. Livy 1.55.4 and Festus s.v. *nequitum* (160L), quoted at p. 114 n. 72.

74. Dionysius of Halicarnassus 13.3.2.

75. Diodorus 17.41.7–8; Curtius 4.3.19–22; Plutarch *Alexander* 24.3–4. On this and kindred stories see Merkelbach 1970/71.

fingers like dressing maids, while others held up mirrors"[76]—or better still, the story that circulated about the Tarpeian head:[77]

> During the digging of foundations for a shrine on the Tarpeian Hill there was discovered a human head. For an interpretation envoys were sent to Olenus of Cales, the most distinguished seer of Etruria. Perceiving that the sign portended glory and success, Olenus tried by questioning to divert the blessing to his own people. He first traced with his staff the outline of a temple on the ground in front of him, and then asked: "Is this, then, Romans, what you say? 'Here will be the temple of Jupiter, All-good and Almighty; here we found the head?'" The *Annals* most firmly insist that the destiny of Rome would have passed to Etruria had not the Roman envoys, forewarned by the seer's son, replied: "Not exactly here, but it was in Rome that we say the head was found."

Camillus, too, cited some of the stories that circulated about the *pignora imperii,* the material guarantors of empire, of which the Palladium was only the most famous.[78] About those stories, I wish here to call attention only to their location at Rome, and in particular to the power that the story grants to the material words of the Romans, to bind the operations of Fortune in contravention of their veracity, a power both physically and metaphysically equivalent to that housed in the head itself.

This focus on materiality returns us to the statue of Juno, to its speech, its movement, and its nod. When I spoke above of the Romans' "confounding of gods and statues, in both language and ritual" I was alluding to an earlier age of scholarship, one reliant upon a Platonic theology and theory of representation alike. In its critique of idolatry, it reserved special

---

76. Seneca *De superstitione* fr. 36 Haase (quoted at Augustine *Civ.* 6.10).

77. Pliny *Nat.* 28.15–16: "Cum in Tarpeio foedientes delubro fundamenta caput humanum invenissent, missis ob id ad se legatis Etruriae celeberrimus vates Olenus Calenus praeclarum id fortunatumque cernens interrogatione in suam gentem transferre temptavit. scipione prius determinata templi imagine in solo ante se: Hoc ergo dicitis, Romani? hic templum Iovis optimi maximi futurum est, hic caput invenimus? constantissima annalium adfirmatione transiturum fuisse fatum in Etruriam, ni praemoniti a filio vatis legati Romani respondissent: Non plane hic sed Romae inventum caput dicimus. iterum id accidisse tradunt, cum in fastigium eiusdum delubri praeparatae quadrigae fictiles in fornace crevissent, et iterum simili modo retentum augurium."

78. On the *pignora imperii* see also below, chapter 7, pp. 182–83.

condescension for that tendency among the uneducated to confuse image and prototype, material and divine.[79] For that tradition we have been urged to substitute another view, which sees the behavior of the women on the Capitol as ludic, indeed, almost postmodern, self-consciously ironizing— or at least self-conscious—in its engagement with representation as an issue in the *cultus deorum*.[80] But was it representation that was at issue? To the importance of cult objects in *evocationes* we might oppose the form that the gods took at *lectisternia,* the ritual of expiation whose central rite consisted in feasting the gods, whose first performance is described—*mirabile dictu*— in Livy's book 5.[81] In that rite, though the gods had simply to move from their temples—not so far, in other words, as from Veii to Rome—their cult statues were not employed. Rather, stand-ins were used, replicas only of their heads, made from wicker.[82] But according to a scholiast on Horace, it was not wicker heads, but *numina,* the gods themselves, who rested on *pulvinaria* in this rite, that they might seem the more lofty.[83] Is it still a problem of representation if they conceived it as one of identity?

Now on the one hand, this opposition between statues and wicker heads urges just the sort of caution proposed above, against seeking a single logic in all testimonia for a rite, or for all testimonia, for all rites. That Juno of Veii was, somehow, her cult statue—that she nodded, and seemed light and easily moved—does not require that the gods at *lectisternia* somehow also be the wicker heads, or just their cult statues, or somehow both. We must avoid pressing our data as though, whatever their origins, Roman rituals developed and converged in their philosophical presuppositions, on the grounds, presumably, that their performances were centrally orchestrated by a body—dare I say "caste"?—of priests whose central role in the history of religion was precisely the denaturalization and mystification of disparate native rites.[84] This is not an original observation. At the same time, it urges reflection upon the margins of state cult, to look

79.   On this tradition of criticism see above, chapter 2, pp. 22–23.

80.   Feeney 1998, 95.

81.   On the first performance see Livy 5.13.4–8 and Dionysius of Halicarnassus 12.9. For later performances see Livy 7.2.2, 7.27.1, 8.25.1, and 40.59.7.

82.   Festus s.vv. *capita deorum* (56L), *stroppus* (410L), and *struppi* (472L); Livy 40.59.7.

83.   pseudo-Acro *ad* Horace *Carm.* 1.37.3: *PULVINAR DEORUM* pulvinaria dicebantur aut lecti deorum aut tabulata, in quibus stabant numina, ut eminentiora viderentur.

84.   Rüpke 1996a, Scheid 2006.

not only to the engagement of individuals with the gods of the civic pantheon, like the figures on the Capitol, nor solely to the light that private
religion might shed upon public cult, but also to the development of state
ritual under pressure from private practice and the presuppositions that
informed it. For as our evidence makes abundantly clear, the authority of
specialists and magistrates in matters of religion went only so far. As Macrobius recorded, when Julius Caesar changed the calendar, he altered the
date of the Saturnalia, from the fourteenth to the sixteenth day before
the kalends of January. Ironically, though Caesar came close to fixing its
date in absolute terms, some refused to play along and continued to employ the traditional date. The result was total confusion, and people became convinced that the holiday was actually supposed to last for three
days, from the sixteenth to the fourteenth—a practice presumably at vari-
ance with the desire of the traditionalist and the plans of Caesar alike, but
one ultimately confirmed as law by an edict of Augustus.[85]

This issue is no less urgent for the student of *evocatio:* for as it turns out,
it was not in the late classical period a ritual restricted to warfare, or even
to public cult as performed by magistrates holding *imperium.* According
to Ulpian, commenting on a praetorian interdict on sacred places (*ad Edictum* bk. 68 frr. 1482–83):

> Sacred places [*sacra loca*] are those that have been publicly dedicated,
> whether in the city or in the country. It must be understood that a
> public place can only become sacred if the emperor has dedicated it
> or has granted the power of dedicating it.
>   The interdict concerning sacred places does not apply to *sacraria.*
> It should also be observed that a sacred place is one thing, a *sacrarium*
> another. A sacred place is a place that has been consecrated, but a
> *sacrarium* is a place in which *sacra* have been deposited. This could even
> be in a private building, and it is customary for those who wish to free
> such a place from its religious scruple to call forth [*evocare*] the *sacra.*

Unpacking this text, what lay chronologically prior to such private evocations was the placement in a particular topographic and material context of a cult statue, a material object, by human hands; but that action

85. Macrobius *Sat.* 1.10.2 and 23–24.

must have been understood as concordant with the *voluntas* of the god that the cult object somehow was and represented. For if the god had not wanted to be there, it would, like the *dei Penates*, have displayed its will by moving elsewhere and, if tested, by moving again. And that expression of will, though spurred by private rather than magisterial action, impelled the exercise of analogy, within both ritual and law, and created the need to ask the god's permission to remove it from its chosen place.

With this understanding in mind, let us return to Livy's book 5. As it happens, neither Camillus's speech nor Livy's narrative remains consistent in situating Rome at the center of some sacred topography. For among the motions that Camillus put to his fellow citizens—and carried—was one extending *hospitium publicum* to the people of Caere: "For they had received the sacred objects of the Roman people and their priests, and by virtue of that benefaction the *honos deum immortalium* had not been interrupted."[86] Rather than ask why these *sacra* could be moved, indeed, without the ritual asking of their permission, where the other rites and objects mentioned by Camillus seemingly could not, and then seeking to exploit the dissonance thus excavated, I close by urging reflection upon the limitations of a religious system so ordered. For it is not clear how it would sustain the simultaneous performance of cult in multiple locations, how one would ask *dei decuriones,* whose worship was bounded by their city's walls, to express their will in eternal attenuation. That surely was a problem for an empire without end.

86. Livy 5.50.3.

7

THE PALLADIUM
AND THE PENTATEUCH

Historians of religion in late antiquity tend to adopt one of two perspectives. Either we seek to understand Christianization, a process ultimately reducible to acts of individual choice whose aggregate effects can be described in purely demographic terms, or we investigate the demise of paganism, a set of discrete rituals and practices, some of which survived in Christian Europe, robbed of their religious significance through cult acts and conciliar decrees.

Understood in these terms, the Christianization of the Roman empire passed a milestone in the early fifth century, the last age attesting a senator who publicly professed paganism. Similarly, paganism was either dying from the moment of its conception, as its constituent practices fell into abeyance, or it survives to this day.[1] The self-understandings of these religions, developed in fractious dialogue with each other, thus yield incompatible narratives and inconsistent periodizations. Assuming rather than interrogating the ontological integrity of their taxonomies, histori-

An earlier version of this chapter appeared in *Phoenix,* Journal of the Classical Association of Canada, 55 (2001), 369–410.

1. For recent literature on the historiography of Roman paganism see above, chapter 1, p. 13, and chapter 5, p. 98.

ography grounded in these perspectives can be erudite, but it cannot explain anything.[2]

If we are now to forge histories of religious change in late antiquity that do more than count Christian conversions or pagan survivals, we must avoid conceptual categories derived from the failed apologetics and willful misconstruals of pagan-Christian dialogue. We must also shun easy reliance on the distorted and misleading claims to novelty of Christian hagiography, a modern counterpart to the faith that late antique ecclesiastical historians placed in divine providence. We should have asked long ago whether the transfer of charisma from one individual to another did in fact constitute a change in the locus of the sacred. Insofar as that transfer did not require contemporaries to reconceptualize the holiness of individuals or the nature of divine immanence, the answer is no. Change in the religious mentality of late antique Europe should instead be charted first at an epistemological level, one prior, as it were, to religious or doctrinal commitment.

This chapter adumbrates such an approach by juxtaposing and conjoining two famous problems: the surge in antiquarianism in the West in the early fifth century and the contest for supremacy between Rome and Constantinople. Scholars have tended to assume that Christians and pagans thought about the sacralization of landscape in very different ways: insofar as paganism consisted of rites bereft of theological significance, pagans (it is assumed) sacralized space through ritual actions governed by pontifical and augural law. Christians, on the other hand, relied on sacred narratives and sacred relics, conducting pilgrimages to the lands where Jesus actually walked or to sites sacralized by the contingencies of martyrdoms and miracles.[3] These distinctions are misleading. Sacred topographies may have been maintained through ritual, pilgrimage, and liturgy; but spaces were made holy by actions of the gods, their particular identities notwithstanding.

Proponents of particular sacred topographies in late antiquity therefore faced two problems, one of theology and one of memory. How to un-

2. Cf. Smith 1990 *passim,* esp. 36–53.

3. See Salzman 1999 on Rome, and Fowden 1978 on the eastern provinces, which largely treat the Christian appropriation of pagan holy sites as a political problem. For rather different portraits of classical Roman thought on the sacralization of space see Cancik 1985/86, and chapter 5 above.

derstand the actions of the divine in this world? What traces did it leave, and how should one memorialize them? Understood in these terms, the differences between pagan and Christian arguments for Rome and Constantinople begin to dissolve, and the contemporaneous political significance of antiquarianism in their respective historical and religious traditions in the fifth and sixth centuries emerges with greater clarity.

This approach has ramifications for how we periodize religious change in late antiquity. Concentrating on the rise of holy men, the importance of relics and pilgrimage, or the prominence of Constantinople and the Holy Land does not, I would argue, allow one successfully to distinguish the classical and late antique. On the contrary: understood in philosophical terms, Christian and pagan sacred topographies for the late Roman empire can be shown to rest on similar theological presuppositions. Above all, they both assumed theories of materiality that bound human and divine to concrete landscapes and endowed word and action with like power and equivalent metaphysical status. We might once have described Macrobian antiquarianism as nostalgic or, at best, as a retreat from cult and its topographic concerns to the discursive world of texts; we might similarly have accused Hesychius of pedantry or superstition when he sought to locate the Palladium. We would have been in error.

Through its ability to narrate a particular sacred history, language enabled Macrobius to establish a sacred topography for the empire no less cogent than those grounded in a purely materialist devotion to sacred objects. In fact, these ready binarisms of word and object, speech and action, here break down. For even as discursive topographies describe the sacralization of space as a function of historical action and divine immanence, so sacred objects derive their meaning and continued legitimacy from their inscription in sacred histories and utility in reconstitutive ritual actions. Adherents of Athens and Jerusalem, or Rome and Constantinople, all required, even as they assumed, understandings of history and theology that stand apart from the Platonizing metaphysics that have dominated histories and historians of religion, and theories and theorists of matter, to this day.

.   .   .

In the first six decades of the twentieth century, scholars could be described with some confidence as having reached a general consensus on the conflict between pagans and Christians in the fourth century.[4] Most agreed that pagans and Christians actively disliked each other and that each side sought to do the other harm, at least to the extent permitted by the government. Of the work published in that era, the studies of Andreas Alföldi and Herbert Bloch remain notable for their rigor and influence. Each scholar attempted to identify pagans in the city of Rome and to prove their commitment to traditional religions and their corresponding opposition to Christianity. Alföldi launched his program in 1937 with his study of coins representing Isis and Serapis from the mint of Rome and followed it with volumes on the so-called contorniate medallions and his essay on the religious policies of Constantine. Throughout he attempted to document the "relentless struggle" of "the last representatives of the old Roman traditions against Christianity" "in defense of the religion of their fathers," as well as the increasing "religious intolerance" of the church and state from Constantine to Theodosius.[5]

Bloch first conducted a prosopographical study of holders of priesthoods in the later fourth century and subsequently argued that committed pagans had been responsible for reading, copying, and editing classical texts.[6] Together these scholars persuaded many of the existence of a circle of committed pagan aristocrats at Rome, whose leader was undoubtedly Vettius Agorius Praetextatus but which they called the circle of Symmachus largely because our knowledge of them comes predominantly from the preserved letters of Quintus Aurelius Symmachus.[7] Finally, the intellectual and religious interests of the circle's members were documented by a contemporary witness, Macrobius, who made Praetextatus, Symmachus, Servius, and their acquaintances interlocutors in his *Saturnalia*. What is more, Macrobius borrowed heavily from Iamblichus

---

4. In addition to the historiographic remarks below, I have reviewed the history of late antiquity as a discipline in "The End of Antiquity" (Ando forthcoming b) and as an object of study more generally in "Decline, Fall, and Transformation" (Ando 2007a).

5. A. Alföldi 1937, 1942–43, 1948, and 1952.

6. H. Bloch 1945 and 1963. English-speaking scholars tend to ignore Bloch's debts to earlier work, especially Marrou 1932. Marrou's essay well illustrates the greater nuance that Continental scholars brought to the study of religious conflict and cultural history in this period.

7. Cf. Robinson 1915, 92, labeling Symmachus "one of the most distinguished members of the aristocratic pagan party" while admitting that evidence for the party "is supplied chiefly by the works of Symmachus himself."

and Porphyry, and in so doing declared an allegiance to Hellenic philosophy and religion, even if he and his friends—the "last pagan generation"—"did not dare make a frontal attack on Christianity triumphant."[8]

Many of these trends received classic treatment in a famous collection of lectures delivered at the Warburg Institute and edited by Arnaldo Momigliano.[9] Although that volume was no doubt intended to provoke further work, in many ways it marked the end of an era. For while that book was in production, Peter Brown and Alan Cameron subjected the foundations of earlier scholarship to what seemed to be devastating scrutiny. First, in 1961 Brown advanced what we might call his pillow-talk theory of Christianization. Proceeding from the observation that the conversion of the Roman aristocracy had taken much longer than a single generation, Brown argued that the religious legislation passed by Theodosius in the last years of his reign could account for neither the scope nor the pace of senatorial conversions. His central thesis arose from his observation that "it is the wives, themselves, that are often an insoluble problem."[10] He concluded that aristocratic women converted first and then converted their husbands through their gentle powers of persuasion.

A few years later, Alan Cameron disbanded the circle of Symmachus and assigned Macrobius to the early 430s, confirming an hypothesis advanced by Santo Mazzarino three decades earlier.[11] He then subjected the editorial work of fourth-century and fifth-century intellectuals to similar scrutiny. Following Henri-Irénée Marrou, he argued that both Christians and pagans read, copied, and corrected classical texts: literary culture was literary, and nothing more.[12] The consequences for readers of Macrobius were stark: the *Saturnalia* had to be seen as the product of "sentimental

---

8.   Courcelle 1969, 13–47, provides a characteristically accurate representation of much earlier work on Macrobius, his aims, and his sources; the quotation is from p. 46.

9.   Momigliano 1963.

10.   Brown 1961, 7 (= 1972, 173).

11.   Alan Cameron 1964; Mazzarino 1937/38, 255–58; Alan Cameron 1966. Cameron persuaded all but a few—Syme 1968, 146, hesitates, while Flamant 1977, 96–141, and Döpp 1978 disagree—and his work has been confirmed by Panciera 1982.

12.   Alan Cameron 1977 (see, e.g., 28: "The fact that these authors were also Christian favorites only underlines how little specifically pagan content was left to this literary paganism"), 1984, and 1999. Matthews 1967, 507–9, anticipates some of these arguments: the *Saturnalia* is a "stage in the refinement of late Roman paganism into a literary paganism which is quite consistent with Christianity." Whose Christianity?

antiquarianism and nostalgic idealization of the past," while its paganism was "essentially nostalgic and literary" and its participants appeared "simply as great and learned men of an almost incidentally pagan past."[13]

Brown's and Cameron's arguments have shaped the study of religious conflict in the fourth and fifth centuries, particularly in the English-speaking world.[14] Indeed, some of their arguments have received valuable support. Two decades of counting Christians have suggested that the conversion of the aristocracy began sooner, and proceeded more regularly, than late antique narratives would have us believe.[15] And yet, if the government did genuinely favor Christians in the distribution of honors, we might expect public declarations of religious allegiance to respond accordingly, and patterns of apostasy and indictments for hypocritical conversions largely bear out this suspicion.[16] Others have subjected Christian historiography to scrutiny and concluded that it constructed its relationship with paganism as one of latent hostility, punctuated by persecutions and periods of conflict: in other words, generations of historians saw religious history in late antiquity as a sequence of crises because that is what they were intended to see.[17]

Revisiting the religious politics of the fourth and fifth centuries will require a return to the figures who were once central to this period and who have been largely ignored by those studying "the transformation of the classical heritage."[18] For what we have not learned in the last quarter-century is what Symmachus, Servius, Praetextatus, and Macrobius thought they were doing, if they were not engaged in the preservation of a cultural system then under assault by the government of their empire. After all, late antique Christians were not alone in viewing their age

13. Alan Cameron 1966, 36; and 1977, 23, and cf. 28. Matthews 1970, 466, was typical in its praise—Cameron's dating of the *Saturnalia* "deeply undermines most current assumptions of the intellectual nature and political coherence of paganism in Roman senatorial society in the late fourth century"—but typical, likewise, in its inability to develop some new interpretive framework to accommodate that text.

14. Notable participants in this tradition are O'Donnell 1978 and 1979, and Salzman 1990. Alan Cameron 1999 cites some recent voices of dissent in Europe.

15. Eck 1971, van Haehling 1978, T. Barnes 1987 and 1995.

16. Ando 1996, 198–205; and 1997, 88.

17. Thelamon 1981, and cf. Brown 1961, 3 (= 1972, 166); 1993, esp. 95–96; and 1995, 3–8.

18. For a recent, delightfully partisan review of the question, see Alan Cameron 2004b, following on idem 1999.

as one of struggle. Some pagans certainly understood the threat posed by Christianity's imperialist impulse. For Antoninus the son of Sosipatra, for example, the destruction of the Serapeum heralded the end of his way of life: after his death, he predicted, that temple would fall into a formless shadow, while an awesome darkness would seize power over the beautiful things of this world.[19] The *Asclepius* could be understood to depict religious change in similar terms: "A penalty of so-called laws will be laid down against religion, piety, and acts of worship. This most holy land, the home of shrines and temples, will overflow with graves and corpses. . . . I call upon you, most holy river, and I predict your future: you will burst your banks, filled by a torrent of blood."[20] Again, as Julian denounced Constantine as "an innovator and destroyer of hallowed laws and ancient tradition," so Julian's partisans described him as "the restorer of Roman religion."[21] What is more, but two decades before Macrobius indulged his "literary paganism" in an extended exercise in nostalgic antiquarianism, Augustine had been drafted by Marcellinus to respond to the legions of pagan critics who blamed Christianity and its emperors for the fall of Rome.[22] For Servius and Macrobius, Vergil preeminently deserved the title *pontifex maximus*.[23] Should they not be numbered among the *parvuli* whose tender souls were intoxicated by that great and most fa-

---

19. Eunapius *V. Soph.* 6.9.17. The significance of this event lingered long in Christian memories. See Rufinus *Hist. eccl.* 11.23–25 and 29–30: the Serapeum was the *caput idolatriae;* once it was overthrown, no temple of any other god could remain standing. See also Augustine *Div. daem.* 1.1, written ca. 407, Socrates 5.16, and Sozomen 7.15.

20. *Asclepius* 24, cited in its extant Latin version for the first time in Augustine *Civ.* 8.23–24. For useful cautions about the dating of *Asclepius* see Lane Fox 1990, 237–38. While I am tempted to agree with Hunink 1996 that Apuleius could have written this text, I am concerned here with its reception in the aftermath of 392. Alan Cameron 1965, 24 n. 48, argues brilliantly for dating the text to 391, but it is not clear to me that his argument requires dating the whole text to that period; cf. Frankfurter 1998, 247 and 252–53, discussing its initial reception.

21. Ammianus 21.10.8; *ILS* 752, from Numidia: *Iuliano pio felici* [*Aug.*] . . . *invicto principi, restitutori libertatis et Romanae religionis ac triumfatori orbis.*

22. Marcellinus at Augustine *Ep.* 136. On pagan and Christian literary recriminations in the years following 410, see Courcelle 1964, 56–77; on Augustine in particular see T. Barnes 1982 and, more briefly, O'Daly 1999, 27–33.

23. See, e.g., Macrobius *Sat.* 1.24.16. Cf. 1.24.17, where Flavianus finds in Vergil *tantam scientiam iuris auguralis* that it alone would make him famous, even if he lacked all other knowledge; 1.24.13, a passage of unmistakable religious significance (*sed nos, quos crassa Minerva dedecet, non patiamur abstrusa esse adyta sacri poematis, sed arcanorum sensuum investigato aditu doc-*

mous poet, who did not see, as Augustine did, the truths about Rome's conquered gods that Vergil had been forced by Veritas to confess?[24]

About the *Saturnalia* in particular we might ask, What does it mean that a text once presumed to be thoroughly pagan dates from a time when the Roman aristocracy publicly and almost unanimously professed Christianity? The intellectual and religious interests of its interlocutors were, of course, many and varied, whether measured by the words of Macrobius or by independent evidence of their activities. Others have investigated the ideological bases of fourth-century grammar and education: to adapt Gellius, Servius and Macrobius were fully aware that *humanitas* does not properly indicate indiscriminate goodwill toward all human beings, but rather "learning and training in the liberal arts."[25] It is eloquent testimony to the power of Cameron's work that sophisticated readings of Servius and Macrobius as religious figures have only recently begun to appear. Philippe Bruggisser, for example, has argued that Servius deliberately presented Romulus and Remus so as to deflect Christian criticisms of the fratricide, all the while participating in contemporary political debates over the concord of imperial brothers, while Sabine MacCormack and Charles Hedrick have revisited with renewed vigor and insight pagan and Christian modes of reading and interpreting Vergil and the politics of editing classical texts.[26]

The political and religious implications of antiquarian research in the fifth century cannot emerge from a reading of the *Saturnalia* so long as prejudice about the nature of religious history overdetermines those readings, nor, in fact, can they be elucidated by reading the *Saturnalia* alone.[27]

---

torum cultu celebranda praebeamus reclusa penetralia) and 5.1.18–20. Servius: see pp. 178–80 below. On Vergil's significance in late antique pagan life see Klingner 1965, 527–78, esp. 543–44; and MacCormack 1998. Turk 1963 is often described as having discussed Servius's description of Vergil as pontifex (see, e.g., Alan Cameron 1968, 101–2; and Hedrick 2000, 85), but he cites not a single passage from that author.

24. Augustine *Civ.* 1.3.

25. Gellius 13.17.1. On grammar as a marker of class, Kaster 1978 and 1980, Uhl 1998, and Alan Cameron 1999, 119–20.

26. Bruggisser 1987, esp. 125–60; MacCormack 1998; Hedrick 2000, esp. 171–213; and cf. Kahlos 1998. Syske 1993 does not fulfill its promise to discuss the "aims" of Macrobius (2–3).

27. Cf. Hedrick 2000, 210: "It is too simple to draw a sharp line between the 390's and 430's, to see Flavian the younger and his fellows ca. 431 as either straightforward Christians or crypto-pagans, either utterly assimilated or intransigent reactionaries."

Antiquarian research did not take place in ivory towers. In this chapter, I examine the actions of "the last pagan generation" and the role played by their researches into the Roman past in one arena of undeniable contemporary importance, the rivalry of Rome and Constantinople and the construction of a sacred topography for the later Roman empire. Macrobian antiquarianism emerges from this inquiry as a reaction to the suppression of those mechanisms whereby his heroes, those men who used to belong to the circle of Symmachus, had formerly debated the locus of the holy in the later Roman empire. That Macrobius made claims on behalf of Rome in language of immediate intelligibility and undeniable contemporary import is best seen by reading the very similar claims and language deployed on behalf of Constantinople in the same period. The ancient past emerges from their works as more than a guide to the constitution of the present. Rather, by concretizing presuppositions about relations between corporeal and divine reality, narratives of the past legitimated particular visions of the sacralization of space and took their place beside philosophy, politics, and law among the tools of late antique political life.

THE TOPOGRAPHY OF THE ROMAN EMPIRE IN THE FOURTH CENTURY

Until Constantine founded his new capital on the Bosporus, no one had questioned and certainly no one had threatened the centrality of Rome. Neither titulature nor iconography distinguishes the Tetrarchic foundations or residences in this way, nor is it possible to detect in literature of the early fourth century any sense that these detracted from the ideological and religious preeminence of Rome.[28] Constantinople was clearly different, and this was true already at its dedication. As early as 324, Porfyrius described that city as "another Rome," and a decade later Constantine allowed that he called his city an *urbs aeterna* at the behest of his God.[29]

---

28. Bréhier 1915, 241, 247, 249–50; Lathoud 1924, 294; A. Alföldi 1947, 12; *contra* Mango 1985, 24.

29. Porfyrius *Carm.* 4.5–6; for its date of composition see T. Barnes 1975, 179 and 184–85. Constantine: *CTh* 13.5.7 (*Pro commoditate urbis, quam aeterno nomine iubente deo donavimus*). Cf. *CJ* 1.17.1.10: *Romam autem intellegendum est non solum veterem, sed etiam regiam nostram, quae deo propitio cum melioribus condita est auguriis.* Themistius wrote his fourth oration thirty-three years later, but referring specifically to November 324 he called Constantinople πόλις ἡ τῆς βασιλείας ἡλικιῶτις (*Or.* 4.58b). On "the names of Constantinople" see Georgacas

The foundation of Constantinople altered the topography of the empire in several ways. The new capital on the Bosporus rapidly assumed an iconographic status roughly equivalent to that of Rome.[30] By the middle of the fourth century a hierarchy had developed that accorded preeminence to Rome and Constantinople and second rank to Antioch and Alexandria, Carthage and Trier, with partisans advancing the claims of their city and contesting those of their rivals within each rank.[31] Writers in both East and West took note of the competition between Rome and Constantinople, and very soon after Constantine's foundation it was commonly understood that he had intended the new capital to rival the old.[32] We can trace the institutional and ideological rivalry of the cities in a number of ways, but most easily—and perhaps most deceptively—through the privileges and ranks accorded to their respective Senates and senators.[33] In 379, for example, Themistius led an embassy from the Senate of Con-

---

1947 and cf. Dagron 1984b, 48–60. Too much as been made of the third canon of the Council of Constantinople in 381, the first "official" document to style Constantinople "New Rome."

30. J. Toynbee 1947 and 1953, and cf. Salzman 1990, 27–28.

31. Ausonius *Ordo urbium nobilium* (XXIV Green) 1–27 presents a somewhat idiosyncratic, Western view. More typical formulations are Libanius *Or.* 15.59 (ἀλλ' ἐν ταῖς μετὰ δύο τὰς πρώτας τετάγμεθα) and 33.24 (σὺ δ' ἐκείνους ἐπὶ πόλεως τοιαύτης οὐ μιμήσῃ ᾗ τοιαῦτα μὲν τἀρχαῖα, τοιαῦτα δὲ τὰ μετ' ἐκεῖνα, τοιαῦτα δὲ τα νῦν, ᾗ πλὴν δυοῖν πόλεων ἔνι τι πρὸς ἁπάσας εἰπεῖν περὶ αὐτῆς).

32. Libanius *Or.* 19.19 (τόν τε ἀντιθέντα τῇ Ῥωμαίων πόλει τὴν νέαν ὁμώνυμον) and cf. 20.24 (Λείπεται κἀκεῖνος τῶν σῶν δὴ τοῦτο ὁ τῇ Ῥώμῃ μὲν ὁμώνυμον ἐγείρας πόλιν, τὸ σχῆμα δὲ τὸ 'κείνης ἅπαν εἰς ταύτην εἰσαγαγών) and 30.37; *Origo Constantini* 6.30: "Constantinus autem ex <se> Byzantium Constantinopolim nuncupavit ob insignis victoriae <memoriam>. quam velut patriam cultu decoravit ingenti et Romae desideravit aequari, deinde quaesitis ei undique civibus divitias multas largitus est, ut prope in ea omnes thesauros <et> regias facultates exhauriret"; Eutropius 10.8.1: "Multas leges rogavit, quasdam ex bono et aequo, plerasque superfluas, nonnullas severas, primusque urbem nominis sui ad tantum festigium evehere molitus est, ut Romae aemulam faceret"; Festus 9.4: "Ita dicioni rei publicae sex Thraciarum provinciae sunt adquisitae: . . . Europa, in qua nunc secundae arces Romani orbis sunt constitutae: Constantinopolis." See also Claudian *Ruf.* 2.54 ("urbs etiam, magnae quae ducitur aemula Romae") and *Gild.* 61–63 ("cum subiit par Roma mihi divisaque sumpsit aequales Aurora togas, Aegyptia rura in partem cessere novae"), as well as Zosimus 2.30.1 (πόλιν ἀντίρροπον τῆς Ῥώμης ἐζήτει). Our picture might be clearer if we had the letters of Constantine in which he justified the privileges he granted to Constantinople's food supply and grain dole, but we know of his establishment only through references in later legislation (e.g., *CTh* 14.16.2 and 14.16.12).

33. Dagron 1984b, 119–210; Vanderspoel 1995, 53–66.

stantinople to Gratian. Although he styled Constantinople the equivalent of Rome—they were the two metropoleis of the world, the cities of Romulus and Constantine—he did so in order to justify the request with which he closed: Gratian should glorify the Senate of the East with honors, so that it would truly be his city, a second Rome.[34] And if the organization of Constantinople around seven hills and fourteen regions can indeed be traced to Constantine, his intentions become even clearer.[35]

The religious politics of the age lent the rivalry between the two capitals additional import and complexity. We cannot now know what Constantine did or did not do at the *limitatio, consecratio, inauguratio,* and *dedicatio* of his city.[36] What is clear is that Christians almost immediately understood and represented Constantine's foundation as a religious act and his city as the new, Christian capital of a Christian empire. Immediately after Constantine's death, Eusebius insisted that he had "celebrated his eponymous city by dedicating there magnificent *martyria* and spectacular buildings" and had "consecrated his city to the God of the martyrs," while purging it of all traces of idolatry and superstition.[37] To display the power of his triumphant God, Constantine likewise stripped the idols from temple precincts throughout the East and displayed them as *spolia* in his new city.[38] Some of these idols, we are told, he tore from their pedestals by heaping them with ropes and pulling them along the ground, as though they were captives. He also ordered soldiers to scrape the gold and silver leaf from any idols they did not confiscate and to pluck away their decorative gems.[39] An idiosyncratic eighth-century guidebook to the public monuments of Constantinople insists, quite plausibly, that Con-

---

34. Themistius *Or.* 14.182a and 183a–184a (τότε ἀληθινῶς ἔσται δευτέρα Ρώμη σὴ πόλις, εἴ γε ἄνδρες ἡ πόλις).

35. Janin 1964, 4–7, 24, and 43–58.

36. See Cracco Ruggini 1980b; and pp. 187–94 below.

37. Eusebius *Vita Constantini* 3.48.

38. Eusebius *Vita Constantini* 3.54.2–4; cf. Eunapius *V. Soph.* 6.1.5. Libanius *Or.* 30.6 and 37 complains of expenditures on Constantinople and hints that this involved stealing religious art; Zosimus 2.31–32 writes in similar terms; John Malalas 13.7 mentions in passing statues taken from Ilium and Rome but does not suggest that these were part of a systematic transfer.

39. Eusebius *Vita Constantini* 3.54.1–2, 5–7. Eusebius signally fails to understand attitudes to religious statuary. In Gaza, even the Christians refused to walk on pavements made from smashed idols (Mark *Vita Porph.* 76); cf. Mango 1963.

stantine also took statues from Rome, including one of Augustus.[40] It may be that it was precisely his paganism that led Julian to disparage Constantinople, the city of his birth, by insisting that it surpassed all other cities by as much as it fell short of Rome, while noting that being second to Rome was a greater honor than preeminence over all other cities.[41]

Later Christians found this picture of Constantine and this image of Constantinople useful. Augustine numbered the foundation of Constantinople one of the blessings granted by the Christian God to its pious champion: "to him God granted that he should found a city, an aid to the Roman empire and the daughter, as it were, of Rome itself, but without any temple or image of demons."[42] Socrates acknowledged his debt to Eusebius but added details not present in that author's *Life:* Constantine made his city equal to "ruling Rome," named it Constantinople, and ordered by law that it should be called "Second Rome."[43] According to Socrates, this law was inscribed on a pillar near Constantine's equestrian statue. He also followed Eusebius in seeing Constantinople as a Christian foundation, connecting Constantine's dedication of churches there with his prohibitions against paganism and his humiliation of idols. We will return to Sozomen's much fuller narrative; let it suffice now to observe that he, too, attributed to Constantine the desire that his city "should rule equally with Rome and should share with her in the empire." Seeking to found a city "equal in honor to Rome," Constantine was directed by God to Byzantium, which city he renamed "New Rome" and "Constantinople" and designated as the capital for the eastern half of the empire. What is more, God revealed his power in the fervor with which the inhabitants of the city took to the faith of its founder.[44] Philostorgius likewise reports that Constantine named his city Alma Roma, "which in the Roman tongue means 'honored,'" and so established its government and buildings that its fame began to rival that of "the earlier Rome."[45]

40. *Parastaseis syntomoi chronikai* 60.

41. Julian *Or.* 1.6 (8b–c).

42. Augustine *Civ.* 5.25.

43. Socrates 1.16.1.

44. Sozomen 2.3.1, 2, and 5.

45. Philostorgius 2.9; cf. Hesychius *Patria* 1, naming Rome τῇ πρεσβυτέρᾳ Ῥώμῃ and Constantinople τὴν νέαν Ῥώμην and arguing that Constantine made the latter equal to the former.

Christian intellectuals thus valorized Constantinople for its lack of idols and idolatrous cult. In this they reveal an understanding of the sacred and of its immanence in the material world seemingly fundamentally different from that loosely shared by their pagan opponents. Christians almost universally regarded idols and cult statues as the proper and exclusive recipients of pagan worship, and their understanding of the mechanics of conversion developed from this simple fact. So, writing of Constantine's appropriation of religious art, Eusebius concluded that "those suffering from superstition then at last learned to think properly, when the emperor held up their baubles to the laughter and mockery of all beholders."[46] Similarly, when, in early July 399 Arcadius and Honorius ordered the destruction of pagan temples in the countryside, they claimed that their action would destroy "the material basis of all superstition" (*his enim deiectis atque sublatis omnis superstitionis materia consumetur*).[47] Yet progress won by methods based on these premises was slow. This is true in spite of Eusebius, who tended to magnify both the scope and the effects of imperial legislation against paganism.[48] As emperors knew better than bishops, "sudden changes are hard on subjects." An idolatrous city that consistently paid its taxes had to be subjected to gradual pressure: let civic honors be available only to Christians and the temples shut, and the people will eventually acknowledge the truth.[49] A pragmatic toleration or, perhaps, a pragmatic restraint from religious coercion, glossed by intolerant rhetoric from pulpits and rostra and interrupted by occasional bursts of local violence, thus governed religious politics between the accession of Constantine and the last decade of the fourth century.[50]

Between the foundation of Constantinople, then, and the outpouring of coercive Christian legislation in the 390s, how did pagans articulate the unique status of Rome? Through cult.[51] Symmachus provides both a pos-

---

46. Eusebius *Vita Constantini* 3.54.3.

47. *CTh* 16.10.16.

48. Cf. Bradbury 1994 and Drake 2000, 360–67, 402, and 419.

49. Mark *Vita Porph.* 41.

50. T. Barnes 1982, 68

51. Verbal expressions of patriotism by Greek and Latin authors in late antiquity have received a great deal of careful attention, but few have concentrated on the religious aspects and nonverbal expressions of patriotic sentiment. Among a vast literature see Dölger 1937; Klingner 1965; 645–66; Paschoud 1967; Klein 1986; and Brodka 1998.

itive and a negative formulation of this position. On the one hand, the goodwill of the gods, if not retained through cult, is lost.[52] On the birthday of Rome in 401, the state was disturbed by several omens, most particularly the crash of the suffect consul's chariot. Decorated with the insignia of his office, the magistrate had broken his leg. "Even narrating it causes me concern—doing so is unlucky—and so in this telling I will be brief."[53] An omen at Spoleto worried Symmachus, as a citizen with a duty to the public good: it should have been expiated *publico nomine*. As it was, eight victims improperly sacrificed had failed to satisfy Jupiter.[54] Symmachus changed the itinerary of his travels to take action on behalf of his ailing homeland, "since my security seemed to me quite worthless in comparison to the ills of the commonwealth." He therefore yielded to the demands of pontifical office.[55] Famine, likewise, could be averted by the gods, as it could be caused by their displeasure: "Gods of my fatherland, pardon the neglect of your rites! Stave off this pitiless famine."[56] Nothing illustrates the seriousness of Symmachus's commitment to the customs and institutions of the *maiores* more clearly than his determination to punish errant Vestals: the duty of a pontiff and the loyalty of a senator demanded no less. As he wrote when one Primigenia was proven guilty of breaking her vows, "it remains only to enforce the severity of the laws against those who have polluted the rites of the state by an unspeakable crime."[57] His son listed on his epitaph no religious office save the pontificate: the ceremonies of the gods and the rites demanded by divinity were known to him.[58]

52. Symmachus *Ep.* 1.46.2: *Benignitas enim superiorum, nisi cultu tenatur, amittitur.*

53. Symmachus *Ep.* 6.40.1.

54. Symmachus *Ep.* 1.49; the phrase *ut civis ad bonum commune genitus* is actually applied by Symmachus to Praetextatus.

55. Symmachus *Ep.* 1.51; cf. 1.47.1 (*me impedit pontificalis officii cura*), 2.59 (Symmachus was staying at his suburban villa along the Via Appia, whence he returned to Rome for the festival of Vesta), and 2.34, writing to his son: *Adornare te reditum, quod sacra Deum Matris adpeterent, arbitrabar.* At 1.71 he praises Caecilianus to Celsinus Titianus, writing that he loves that man because he is *religiosae civitatis commodis obsequentem.*

56. Symmachus *Ep.* 2.7.3. See also *Rel.* 3.15–16: Depriving the Vestals of support granted them by *lex parentum* had brought about a famine. The land was not at fault, nor was the wind: *sacrilegio annus exaruit.*

57. Symmachus *Ep.* 9.108, 147–48.

58. *ILS* 2946; Symmachus *Ep.* 2.53, writing to his brother: *notae nobis sunt caerimoniae deorum et festa divinitatis imperata.*

Symmachus also argued that proper worship earned the favor of the gods. As proof he offered the evidence of history: "Do not forget the argument from advantage, which more than anything reveals the gods to mankind. As all reason lies in the dark, from what source might we better draw our knowledge of the divine than from memory and the evidence of past benefactions?" In a *prosopopoeia* moments later Rome confirmed the sentiment: "*Hic cultus* subjected the world to my laws."[59] In the same decade on the other side of the empire, Libanius advanced an almost identical set of arguments in defense of pagan temples and the rituals practiced in them. Like Symmachus, Libanius insisted that the history of the empire proved the efficacy and truthfulness of traditional forms of worship: "And it was with these gods to aid them that the Romans used to march against their foes, engage them in battle, conquer them, and, as conquerors, grant the vanquished a condition of life better than that which they had before their defeat, removing their fears and allowing them a share in their own civil life."[60] In fact, Libanius took this argument a step further, describing the evolution of religious practices as part and parcel of the increasing complexity of societies and development of technology.[61]

Libanius was not so foolish as to believe that the extension of the franchise and expansion of the empire had correspondingly diluted the gods' interest in Rome. On the contrary: "If the security of the empire rests on the sacrifices performed there, then we must believe sacrifice everywhere to be profitable. Indeed, just as the gods in Rome give greater things, so those in the fields and the other villages give lesser things."[62] The theological basis of this position deserves careful scrutiny. It was not that the gods could not or did not receive worship in multiple locations, nor even that the Capitoline triad was resident on the Capitol. By the fourth century, Capitolia existed in cities throughout the empire, from Spain to Africa to Egypt and throughout the Danubian provinces.[63] But if the gods of

59. Symmachus *Rel.* 3.8–9.

60. Libanius *Or.* 30.5 (translation Norman); cf. 30.31: Εἰπάτω γάρ μοί τις τῶν τὰς μὲν πυράγρας καὶ σφύρας καὶ ἄκμονας ἀφέντων... ποτέροις ἀκολουθοῦντες οἱ τὰ μέγιστα ἀπὸ μικρῶν καὶ φαύλων τῶν πρώτων ἀφορμῶν Ῥωμαῖοι δυνηθέντες ἐδυνήθησαν, τῷ τούτων ἢ οἷς ἱερὰ καὶ βωμοί, παρ' ὧν ὅ τι χρὴ ποιεῖν ἢ μὴ ποιεῖν διὰ τῶν μάντεων.

61. Libanius *Or.* 30.4.

62. Libanius *Or.* 30.33 (translation after Norman).

63. Barton 1982 and Ando 2000, 208.

Rome were not Platonic gods, whose interest in sacrifice and whose figural representation required elaborate and somewhat illogical defense, neither did they become the objects of a complex theological tradition.[64] When in *On the Laws* Cicero contrasted Persian cult and its theological basis with that of the Greeks and Romans, he provided as careful an articulation of the issue as now survives: "I propose that 'there should be shrines in cities.' On this issue I do not follow the magi of Persia, on whose authority Xerxes is said to have burned the temples of Greece, because the Greeks confined the gods within walls, although all places should be open and free to them as this entire world is their home and temple. The better position is that adopted by the Greeks and by us, who desire to increase piety toward the gods and so have wanted them to live in the same cities that we inhabit." Men will be more chaste, Cicero concludes, following Thales, when they believe that all things are full of gods.[65]

Symmachus thus subscribed to the theology of Cicero and spoke to the concerns of Libanius when he wrote of the altar of Victory: "Where shall we swear to obey your laws and decrees? By what scruple will the deceitful mind be terrified, lest it perjure itself under oath? To be sure, all things are full of god, nor is any place safe for perjurers. Nevertheless, the presence of a god is a powerful inducement to a fear of wrongdoing."[66] It is insufficient to say that Symmachus has elided the distinction between image and prototype, because more is at stake than a philosophy of representation. He presupposed a notion of divinity, and a theory of materiality, fundamentally at odds with those of Platonic or Christian metaphysics; and within the theology of a Symmachus or Libanius, the gods have interests in and attachments to particular landscapes, of which humans take account through the performance of ritual, and it was through ritual that humans might affect or alter the gods' attachments.[67]

If the theological underpinnings of these arguments on behalf of Rome did not then require articulation and therefore elude satisfactory expli-

---

64. See, e.g., Sallustius 15–16.

65. Cicero *Leg.* 2.26.

66. Symmachus *Rel.* 3.5.

67. The theological basis of Roman ritual, particularly in its understanding of topography and materiality, requires more attention than it has received. For a review of literature and some significant reprints, see Ando 2003b, 141–46, 164–89, and 252–72.

cation today, we can grasp their implications more clearly by studying the place of Rome in the religious landscape mapped and inhabited by Ammianus Marcellinus.[68] Writing in the early 390s of events some three decades earlier, Ammianus described the events at Rome in the prefecture of Tertullus. The Eternal City was gripped by fear of a coming shortage of grain: harsher storms than usual and unpredictable squalls disturbed the seas. But the fears of the populace were rapidly allayed: "Soon, by the will of that divine *numen* that nurtured Rome from its infancy and promised that it would last forever, while Tertullus the prefect was sacrificing at Ostia before the temple of the Dioscuri, tranquillity calmed the sea, the wind became a gentle southern breeze, and ships full of grain entered the port and refilled the stores of grain."[69] Ammianus highlights the place of Rome in the sacred topography of the later empire most pointedly when he juxtaposes events at Rome and elsewhere so as to reveal the centrality of the capital. So, for example, just prior to the successful assassination of Silvanus in Gaul in 355, "the people at Rome in the Circus Maximus [*Romae in Circo maximo populus*] shouted in a loud voice, 'Silvanus is conquered'—whether the populace was aroused by some report or by a presentiment is unknown."[70] Ammianus more clearly attributed to divine causes knowledge at Rome of events around the empire when he narrated the election of Valentinian in 364: the emperor-elect had to travel from his post at Ancyra to the army, and so for ten days no one held the helm of the empire. "This fact the *haruspex* Marcus reported to have happened at the time, when he inspected entrails at Rome [*extis Romae inspectis*]."[71]

Ammianus reported on religious matters at no time more densely than during Julian's Parthian campaign. At its start he provided a list of the omens that presaged ill for that undertaking. Closing the list, in a position of priority, is a report from the Sibylline books at Rome (*Romae super hoc bello libros Sibyllae consultos*): in clear language they forbade the em-

68. Camus 1967, 133–269, is far the best treatment of Ammianus's religious thought.
69. Ammianus 19.10.4.
70. Ammianus 15.5.34.
71. Ammianus 26.1.5. In her note on this passage, Marié 1984, 205 n. 12, cites 15.5.34 and compares Gellius 15.18. See also Camus 1967, 209, writing of divination without concern for where it takes place.

peror from leaving his own borders that year.[72] Soon after leaving Antioch, Julian was disturbed by dreams. Upon waking, he ordered that careful watch should be taken for omens throughout the day, 19 March 363: "As it was afterwards learned, on that same night, in the prefecture of Apronianus, the temple of Palatine Apollo in the Eternal City burned; had aid of every kind not been brought to bear, the magnitude of the fires would have consumed even the songs of the Cumaean Sibyl."[73] Other events on the campaign are merely dated by the ritual calendar of the Eternal City, and Julian himself attempted to establish a temporal and sacramental connection with Rome through cult: "Six days before the kalends of April, on the day when the annual processions for the Mother of the Gods are performed at Rome and the cart in which her image is carried is said to be washed in the waters of the Almo, the solemnity of the rites was performed in hallowed fashion, and Julian slept well, passing the night in happy confidence."[74]

Julian himself testified to his interest in Cybele in the hymn he addressed to her. Like Symmachus writing of Victory, Julian's narrative of her arrival in Rome elides the distinction between image and goddess. Although it was a most holy image ($\tau\hat{\eta}s$ $\theta\epsilon o\hat{v}$ $\tau\dot{o}$ $\dot{a}\gamma\iota\dot{\omega}\tau a\tau o\nu$ $\ddot{a}\gamma a\lambda\mu a$) of the goddess that sailed to Rome, the goddess herself revealed that the ship transported no lifeless idol ($\xi\dot{o}a\nu o\nu$ $\ddot{a}\psi v\chi o\nu$); rather, the object taken from the Phrygians held some greater and more divine power ($\delta\dot{v}\nu a\mu\dot{\iota}\nu$ $\tau\iota\nu a$ $\mu\epsilon\dot{\iota}\zeta\omega$ $\kappa a\dot{\iota}$ $\theta\epsilon\iota o\tau\dot{\epsilon}\rho a\nu$).[75] Of course, Julian did not doubt that one could honor the Great Mother at shrines outside Rome. He himself visited her ancient temple at Pessinus.[76] But it is equally clear that she was present at Rome, and Rome was thus privileged through and by the contingent presence of her most sacred image in that city. Anyone who doubted his narrative, Julian added, could read its details as preserved on bronze statues in the most powerful and god-beloved city of Rome.[77]

72. Ammianus 23.1.7.

73. Ammianus 23.3.3

74. Ammianus 23.3.7. Cf. Prudentius Peristephanon 10.151–60.

75. Julian Or. 8.2 (5.159c–160a): Η δὲ ὥσπερ ἐνδείξασθαι τῷ Ῥωμαίων ἐθέλουσα δήμῳ ὅτι μὴ ξόανον ἄγουσιν ἀπὸ τῆς Φρυγίας ἄψυχον, ἔχει δὲ ἄρα δύναμίν τινα μείζω καὶ θειοτέραν ὃ δὴ παρὰ τῶν Φρυγῶν λαβόντες ἔφερον.

76. Ammianus 22.9.5.

77. Julian Or. 8.2 (5.161b).

Ammianus nowhere asserted the centrality of Rome in the sacred topography of his world more vigorously than when he described the arrival in Rome of a giant obelisk taken from the temple of the Sun at Thebes. Augustus, he argued, had thought of moving this obelisk but had refrained, not because the obelisk was too big, but because it had been dedicated as a special gift to the Sun and had been placed within the shrine of its glorious temple. But Constantine, Ammianus continued, rightly thought that he was committing no sacrilege if, having torn the obelisk from one temple, he should rededicate the obelisk at Rome—that is, in the *templum totius mundi,* the temple of the entire world.[78] As much as this remark reveals about Ammianus and his feelings for Rome, it also reveals his ignorance. In point of fact, Constantine had intended the obelisk as another decoration for Constantinople, and it was Constantius who misunderstood the significance of that desire and sent the obelisk on to Rome, to celebrate his capture of the city and victory over the usurper Magnentius.[79]

At the enigmatic center of modern essays on Roman religious life stands Vettius Agorius Praetextatus, augur, pontifex of Vesta, pontifex of the Sun, *quindecemvir, curialis* of Hercules, a devotee of Liber and the Eleusinian Mysteries, hierophant, overseer of temples, and initiate of the *taurobolium.*[80] Praetextatus and his wife, Fabia Aconia Paulina, lived together for forty years, marked by piety and mutual devotion. While initiation in all the mysteries made Paulina the friend of the gods, Praetextatus "concealed in the recesses of his mind secrets discovered in sacred rites and, being learned, worshipped the manifold and divine *numen.*"[81] Scorning those offices and dignities sought by other men, Praetextatus wished to be known only as a priest of the gods.[82] For Praetextatus, then, as for Symmachus, religious devotion was properly expressed through ritual, and it

78. Ammianus 17.4.12–13: *nihilque committere in religionem recte existimans, si ablatum uno templo miraculum Romae sacraret, id est in templo totius mundi.*

79. *ILS* 736, esp. lines 1–6: "patris opus munusque suum tibi, Roma, dicavit Augustus toto Constantius orbe recepto, et quod nulla tulit tellus nec viderat aetas condidit, ut claris exaequet dona triumfis. Hoc decus ornatum genitor cognominis urbis esse volens, caesa Thebis de rupe revellit."

80. *ILS* 1259, front, lines 2–7; on the "centrality" of Praetextatus see Alan Cameron 1999, 111–15.

81. *ILS* 1259, right side, line 2; back, lines 13–15 and 25; on Paulina's initiations see also *ILS* 1260. On the *divum multiplex numen* see Nock 1972, 37–41, and cf. Camus 1967, 134–38.

82. *ILS* 1259, back, lines 18–21.

was through ritual that men interacted or united with the divine.[83] Like Symmachus, Praetextatus and Paulina honored Vesta and the Vestals: dedicating a statue of Caelia Concordia, they spoke of her outstanding modesty and noteworthy piety toward the cult of the gods.[84]

Nothing typifies the form of piety exhibited by Praetextatus better than his restoration of the images of the *di consentes*. In the first century B.C.E. their golden images had stood around the Forum, six male and an equal number female, and scattered inscriptions attest their worship in Dacia, Moesia, and in Italy at Picenum, Ocriculi, and Reate.[85] During his prefecture of the city in 367/8, Praetextatus repaired and replaced their sacred statues, decorated their site with all possible care and, most particularly, restored their cult to its ancient form.[86] This interest in performing rites according to their ancient form in a particular hallowed location mirrors the attention paid by Julian, Libanius, and Symmachus to the evidences of history; it formed the basis of Julian's criticism of Constantine; and it will be the clarion call of the last generation of pagans in the West: "Verily do I promise that I will maintain and preserve, so long as I am able, that which has been handed down and sanctioned by antiquity."[87]

WITHOUT CULT, WHITHER ROME?

The last two decades of the fourth century saw the government of the empire move with increasing severity against the institutions and prac-

---

83.   Cf. Sallustius 4 (πρέπουσι δὲ τῶν μύθων οἱ μὲν θεολογικοὶ φιλοσόφοις, οἱ δὲ φυσικοὶ καὶ ψυχικοὶ ποιηταῖς, οἱ δὲ μικτοὶ τελεταῖς, ἐπειδὴ καὶ πᾶσα τελετὴ πρὸς τὸν κόσμον ἡμᾶς καὶ πρὸς τοὺς θεοὺς συνάπτειν ἐθέλει), together with Nock 1926, xcviii–ci, as well as Libanius *Or.* 24.36.

84.   *ILS* 1261.

85.   Varro *De re rustica* 1.1.4 (Jupiter and Tellus, Sol and Luna, Ceres and Liber, Robigus and Flora, Minerva and Venus, and Lympha and Bonus Eventus); cf. Ennius *Ann.* 240–41 [Skutsch] (Juno, Vesta, Minerva, Ceres, Diana, Venus, Mars, Mercurius, Jove, Neptunus, Volcanus, and Apollo), almost definitely listing the twelve gods honored in the first *lectisternium,* whose inspiration and performance is described by Livy 22.10.9; but the sentence must be read with the whole paragraph in mind. On these gods see Wissowa 1912, 61 n. 6; and Latte 1967, 253 and 334. Dacia: *ILS* 4004–6. Moesia: *IGRR* 1.664; Picenum: *ILS* 4001. Ocriculi: *ILS* 4002. Reate: *ILS* 4007.

86.   *ILS* 4003: *deorum consentium sacrosancta simulacra cum omni loci totius adornatione, cultu in formam antiquam restituto, Vettius Praetextatus v.c. praefectus urbi reposuit.*

87.   Longinianus at Augustine *Ep.* 234.2; on their correspondence see Ando 1996, 192–93.

tices that ordered the religious lives of contemporary pagans. The stakes were clear. As Ambrose pointed out in his first letter to Valentinian on the altar of Victory, the presence of the altar in the Senate would force Christian senators to practice idolatry. Valentinian had to choose between two religions, and the choice for a Christian emperor was clear.[88] The general tenor of the conversation emerges from Christian reactions to the death of Praetextatus. A contemporary verse invective crowed that his divine knowledge, ascension of the Capitol, and three-month purification of the city had availed him naught: he had reached the limits of his life, suffering madness of soul and insanity of mind.[89] Writing a letter of consolation immediately after the event, Jerome compared the fate of a recently deceased Christian to that of Praetextatus, that sacrilegious devotee of idols, who had recently been dragged to Tartarus. In doing so, he alluded with savage irony to the epitaph Paulina wrote for her husband: "How great the change in affairs! That man, whom but days ago the heights of all honors preceded, who climbed the citadels of the Capitol as though triumphing over defeated enemies, whom the Roman people received with applause and ovations: at his death the whole city is disturbed. Now he is abandoned, naked, not in a milky palace in heaven, as his pathetic wife believes; rather, he is imprisoned in the squalid shadows."[90]

The events that led from the confrontation over the altar of Victory to the revolt and subsequent defeat of Eugenius at the hands of Theodosius lie buried in the pages of partisan historiography.[91] Whatever the motivation of Eugenius's supporters, the final battle at the Frigidus took place under the watchful eyes of opposing gods.[92] According to Ambrose, after his victory Theodosius "put away the images of the gentiles; his faith put away all worship of the idols; he laid waste all their ceremonies."[93] In

---

88. Ambrose *Ep.* 17.9, and cf. *Ep.* 18.31.

89. *Carmen contra paganos* 25–30; cf. Cracco Ruggini 1979, 84–89.

90. Jerome *Ep.* 23.2–3, interpreting *ILS* 1259 (back, lines 9 and 38–41) as alluding to an afterlife of the sort envisioned by Macrobius *Comm.* 1.4.4–5 and 1.15.1; cf. Jerome *Contra Ioann. Hieros.* 8.

91. On the history and historiography of these years see Hedrick 2000, 37–88, esp. 39–58; Cracco Ruggini 1979 is characteristically iconoclastic, insightful, and well documented.

92. Augustine *Civ.* 5.26; cf. Ambrose *De obitu Theodosii* 10, Rufinus *Hist. eccl.* 11.33, Socrates 5.25, Sozomen 7.24.3–7, and Theodoret *Hist. eccl.* 5.24.3–17.

93. Ambrose *De obitu Theodosii* 4.

point of fact, Theodosius had begun issuing increasingly severe legislation against paganism in 391, taking action first against public and then private forms of worship. He did not order pagans to convert, but simply outlawed all public and private behaviors intended to express devotion. No one could perform a sacrifice, visit a temple, or revere an altar; honors to the gods of hearth, home, and individual were forbidden, whether paid in incense, flame, light, or garlands.[94] Although earlier legislation had threatened pagans with dire punishments, those laws had rarely been enforced. Now Theodosius struck at the institutional and social supports of pagan practice: the property of anyone engaging in pagan rites would be confiscated, as would the land and buildings in which such activities took place. All privileges and exemptions for pagan priests of any description were now revoked. Five years later, Arcadius and Honorius granted two concessions, in the interest of public order: public holidays were to continue, so long as they were devoid of religious content, and pagan temples empty of illicit things were not to be destroyed.[95]

According to Augustine, Theodosius spared the sons of his slain enemies because he wanted them to take this opportunity to convert.[96] In the literary tradition, Theodosius entered Rome in triumph and addressed the Senate. The occasion, once invented, was too delicious to impugn. Prudentius depicted the arrival of Theodosius in Rome as a watershed. Theodosius addressed Rome itself and chastised it for its worship of the monstrous images of decaying gods. Rome silently and immediately converted: "Then for the first time, in its old age, did Rome blush and become docile; it was ashamed of its past, and hated the years spent in foul superstition."[97] Then, having named several great families that converted on that day, Prudentius confessed himself unable to list them all: "We could count hundreds of households sprung from the ancient blood of noble men that turned to the sign of Christ and raised themselves from the deep abyss of idolatry."[98] Prudentius offered the caveat that all did not convert, and indeed evidence of

---

94. *CTh* 16.10.10–12, on which see Matthews 1975, 231–37.

95. For "illicit things" see 16.10.18: *Aedes inlicitis rebus vacuas nostrarum beneficio sanctionum ne quis conetur evertere.*

96. Augustine *Civ.* 5.26.

97. Prudentius *Symm.* 1.511–13.

98. Prudentius *Symm.* 1.408–577 at 566–68.

publicly professing pagans survives for another forty years.[99] In sum, a rebuke from Theodosius produced immediate assent and silent contrition, and thus were the remnants of the pagan aristocracy converted.

What Prudentius does not provide—indeed, what he consigns to oblivion—is any report or summary of the arguments that might have been advanced for paganism on that occasion. For that, we must turn to Zosimus. In the pages of his history, Theodosius summoned the Senate and chided its members for clinging to their ancestral ways and not yet choosing to despise the gods. He exhorted them to renounce their "error, as he called it," and adhere to the faith of the Christians.[100] According to Zosimus, no one heeded his invitation, nor did anyone choose to depart from the customs handed down from the time when the city had been founded: by maintaining their ancestral customs they had already occupied Rome, unsacked, for twelve hundred years, and they did not know what would happen if they exchanged those customs for new ones. Theodosius then said that the treasury was burdened by expenditures for rites and ceremonies and that he wanted to end them all. "Those speaking for the Senate affirmed that the rites could not be performed duly and properly [μὴ κατὰ θεσμόν] without public support."[101] "Religious scruple being abandoned for this reason, and such cults as had been handed down by ancestral custom falling into abeyance, [they argued that] the Roman empire would weaken gradually and become a habitation for barbarians or that, in the end, deprived of inhabitants, the empire would be reduced to such a state that no one would recognize the sites where its cities once stood." As Zosimus reminded his audience, a simple narrative of subsequent events would clearly reveal that this did in fact eventuate, and he observed with some satisfaction that Theodosius handed over the lands of the West to his son Honorius and immediately succumbed to disease, even before he could return to Constantinople.[102]

Christians responded to the actions and arguments of late fourth-century pagans on two levels. First, they drew attention to what they regarded as the immorality or illogicality of pagan cult. The Palladium, the

99.   Chastagnol 1956.

100.   Zosimus 4.59.1.

101.   Mendelssohn identified a lacuna at this point; Paschoud agrees (1979, 329).

102.   Zosimus 4.59.3–4.

Lares of Priam, Vesta and her virgins, and hallowed forms of divination—all dear to Praetextatus, Symmachus, and their friends—these were attacked in sermons, books, and verse invective.[103] Praetextatus earned particular scorn for his faith in the purification offered by the *taurobolium*.[104] Just as Praetextatus had restored the statues of the *di consentes,* whom Varro had identified as gods of ancient Rome, so his "heir," Quintus Aurelius Symmachus himself, built a temple to Flora, whose worship at Rome, Varro claimed, had begun in the regal period; in doing so he, too, earned the disapprobation of his Christian contemporaries.[105] It is easy for readers of the *City of God* to argue, incorrectly, that Augustine attacked paganism's literary heritage and not its content or practice. If anything is clear from Christians' obsession with the rites for Cybele, it is that they had seen them performed.[106]

Christians also responded to pagans' privileging of Rome and its religious traditions on intellectual grounds. Among such critics, Augustine is by far the most famous, not least because his response to the sack of Rome in 410 led him to reflect more generally on whether Christian teachings were opposed to the *mores* of the *res publica*. Was it in fact true that great woes had befallen the state because Christian emperors esteemed the church before the commonwealth?[107] In the immediate aftermath of the disaster, Augustine had taken the radical position that Rome was a city like any other, and that cities fall. Earthly kingdoms end.[108] But Augustine also argued the subtler point that it had been only Rome's walls and

103. *Carmen contra paganos* 1–5; pseudo-Paulinus *Carm.* 32.52–67 and 128–50. For the date of pseudo-Paulinus see Cracco Ruggini 1979, 124–28, inclining to the 380s.

104. *Carmen contra paganos* 57–62; on the controversial history of this rite in Christian invective and modern scholarship, see McLynn 1996.

105. *Carmen contra paganos* 112–14; Varro *Ling.* 5.74. On the identity of the *heres* see Cracco Ruggini 1979, 110–12.

106. See esp. Augustine *Civ.* 7.26: *itemque de mollibus eidem Matri Magnae contra omnem virorum mulierumque verecundiam consecratis, qui usque in hesternum diem . . . per plateas vicosque Carthaginis*. Cf. Ambrose *Ep.* 18.30; pseudo-Cyprian *Carmen ad senatorem* 5–24; *Carmen contra paganos* 72–77; pseudo-Paulinus *Carm.* 32.6–24; Prudentius *Symm.* 2.51–52 and *Peristephanon* 10.151–60 and 1056–75. For fourth-century dedications to the Great Mother and Attis see H. Bloch 1945, 245–47; and Duthoy 1969.

107. Marcellinus to Augustine at Augustine *Ep.* 136.2. On Augustine's feeling for and writings about Rome see MacCormack 1998, 175–224. Zwierlein 1978 considers Augustine's arguments alongside those of his Christian contemporaries.

108. Augustine *Serm.* 81.8–9, delivered late in 410 or early in 411 (Verbraken 1976, 73).

buildings that had suffered in Alaric's attack. Alluding to Cicero, he asked what Rome was, if not the Romans.[109] And among the material detritus of a city were its idols, whether or not the pagans understood them thus:[110]

> Behold the sort of guardians to whom those learned men entrusted Rome: they have eyes and do not see. If they had the power to save Rome, why did they perish first? [The pagans] say, "Rome perished afterwards." Nevertheless, [their guardians] perished. "They themselves did not perish," they say; "only their images did." So? How were they going to protect your buildings, if they were not able to protect their own images? Alexandria once lost such gods. Constantinople has become a great city, because it was founded by a Christian emperor; it, too, lost its false gods once upon a time. Nevertheless, it grew, and grows, and abides. For as long as God wants, it abides. But he did not promise eternity to that city merely because we say so.

Augustine later returned to precisely the problem of the status of those pagan idols and pagan gods that had failed to save the city of Rome.[111] In books 2 and 3 of the *City of God,* he refuted those who insisted that divine favor followed on cult, piously and properly performed (*Civ.* 3.18):[112]

> If the idols were not able to repel fire from themselves, how were they going to help the city whose safety they were thought to guard, in the face of fire and flame? Events have shown that they were not able to help at all. We wouldn't put forward these attacks if those people would only say that their idols had been established not to protect purely temporal goods, but to signify eternal ones. Saying that, they could argue that when their idols happened to perish because they were corporeal and

---

109.   Augustine *Serm.* 81.9: *Roma enim quid est, nisi Romani?* Cf. *Serm. de excidio urbis* 6: *An putatis, fratres, civitatem in parietibus et non in civibus deputandum?* On Cicero's definition of *civitas* and its influence on Augustine and Macrobius see Ando 2000, 9–10; on Roman understandings of the significance of the destruction of cities see Laurence 1996.

110.   Augustine *Serm.* 105.9.12, delivered 410–11 (Verbraken 1976, 79).

111.   The mutual recriminations that followed the sack of Rome were complicated by the temporary revival of pagan cult immediately prior to the arrival of Alaric in Italy: Olympiodorus fr. 7.5 Blockley = Sozomen 9.6.1–5.

112.   *Civ.* 1.36 announces the topic of the next two books: *Sed adhuc mihi quaedam dicenda sunt adversus eos, qui Romanae rei publicae clades in religionem nostram referunt, qua diis suis sacrificare prohibentur.*

visible, nothing was detracted from those things because of which they were established. And then their idols could eventually be restored for the same purposes as before. As it is, with remarkable blindness they think that the terrestrial and temporal happiness of the city could be prevented from perishing by idols that could themselves perish. Hence, when they are shown that harm and unhappiness fell upon their city even when their idols still existed, they are ashamed to change a belief that they are unable to defend.

What Augustine here accepts and elsewhere advocated is a theory of materiality that recognizes further hypostases beyond the idol's irreducible materiality and the cult statue's "relation of iconic resemblance to some immaterial reality."[113] Indeed, according to Augustine, many misrecognized the metaphysical status of spiritual creatures, believing their imperceptibility to be a sign of their power and worth.[114] But Augustine recognized the existence of matter not susceptible to sense perception—he named it *spiritalis substantia* (spiritual matter)—and in his metaphysics creatures of spiritual substance, like the anthropomorphic idols that figuratively represented them, stood apart from the transcendent status of the divine.[115] Materiality was thus not defined by susceptibility to sense perception: no late antique metaphysician made that mistake. Not only was all matter, whether created ex nihilo or preexistent, not susceptible to sense perception prior to its formation, but spiritual matter remained both beyond the corporeal and insistently the product of analogous creative acts.[116] Augustine therefore understood the theological presuppositions of a Symmachus or Julian; he simply displaced Victory and Cybele from their positions of priority and situated them closer to those idols that they were powerless to protect. Similarly, when Augustine examined pagan allegorical interpretations of myth and ritual, he saw "nothing that could not be referred to temporal and earthly things and to a corporeal nature, or even to an invisible one—yet such a nature is still mutable, something that is in no way true of the true God."[117]

113. Pietz 1985, 7.
114. Augustine *Conf.* 10.42.67, on which see Ando 2001, 42.
115. Augustine *En. Ps.* 113.2.3 and 6.
116. See chapter 2 above.
117. Augustine *Civ.* 7.27.

Augustine disposed of the evidences of history in a similar fashion. In the years after the fall of Rome he came to adopt a position closer to that of his fellow Christians, viewing Rome as one in a succession of divinely ordained world empires, although he resisted assigning to it the eschatological significance that others did.[118] On the one hand, this chronological schema allowed him to situate Rome and its achievement in a much larger historical panorama, before which its significance faded considerably; it became one among several possible representatives of the terrestrial city, each of which might be contrasted with the heavenly one, both in their excellence and in their destiny.[119] It also contributed to his larger effort to challenge the significance of providentialist historiographies of human communities. It is perhaps not surprising that he dismissed the task of recounting all the disasters of Roman history—attempting to narrate them would make him no more than a writer of history; but his rejection of Christian histories that saw God as favoring Christian emperors merely because they were Christian sprang from a like impulse and a similar metaphysics.[120]

Other Christians also contested the usefulness of historical arguments. What Symmachus called the *mos maiorum*, Prudentius called the *superstitio veterum avorum*.[121] According to him, *mos* itself was blind, passing from one depraved generation to another.[122] To arguments that privileged a purely Roman tradition, Prudentius contrasted Christian history and Christian revelation. On the one hand, he asked Symmachus why one should privilege ancient customs over new revelations, over faith in the truth, and over the rules of the correct religion; on the other, he insisted that historical arguments again favored his side: "Even if we grant your love and concern for ancient custom and your reluctance to depart from traditional rites [*si tantus amor est et cura vetusti moris et a prisco placet haud discedere ritu*], there exists *in antiquis libris* a noble example, which shows that people worshipped a single god already at the time of the Flood, and

---

118. Cf. Ando 2000, 343–51.

119. See, e.g., *Civ.* 18.2 (Rome is one of *plurima regna terrarum, in quae terrenae utilitatis vel cupiditatis est divisa societas*) and 22 (Rome is *velut altera Babylon et velut prioris filia Babylonis*), and MacCormack 1998, 202 and 207–8.

120. Augustine *Civ.* 3.18 and 5.24–26.

121. Prudentius *Symm*.1.38–39; cf. 1.213 and 2.368–69.

122. Prudentius *Symm* 1.244; cf. 2.295.

even before it, indeed, all those did so who then cultivated the newborn fields and dwelled in that empty world."[123]

With cult forbidden, how were pagans at Rome to assert the preeminence of their city? What new understanding of their way of life did they forge? The actions of Symmachus and Libanius were no longer possible; their arguments were suspect. Although some had construed the sack of Rome as the result of neglected rites, no text of their arguments survives.[124] To the victor, to Augustine, belonged the spoils.

If the public profession of paganism was no longer possible, one could still love Rome. Some two decades after the city was sacked, Macrobius Ambrosius Theodosius wrote his *Saturnalia,* a loving and passionate investigation of Rome's pagan past.[125] In the lead role he cast Vettius Agorius Praetextatus, a man whom the gods themselves chose for preeminence in matters of religion.[126] He alone, his interlocutors declared, knew the secret nature of the gods; he alone had the spirit to apprehend the divine and the talent to express what he knew; one praised his memory, another his learning, and all his piety.[127] Another participant was Nichomachus Flavianus, the senator most closely associated with the revolt of Eugenius, whose devotion to paganism profoundly shaped the understanding and representation of his cause, then and later.[128]

As a foil for Praetextatus, Macrobius introduced a Christian, Evangelus, who displayed a passion for sarcasm and a talent for ignorance in equal measure.[129] Macrobius exploited the moment of his arrival to discuss explicitly the political and legal implications of religious affiliation in that era. Looking around at the assembled company, Evangelus recognized something that united them and excluded him, and he asked whether they wished to continue without witnesses present. "If that is the case, as I think it is, I will depart rather than mix myself up in your secrets."[130] "Se-

---

123. Prudentius *Symm.* 2.269–76 and 2.335–42.

124. For a review of such limited evidence as does exist see T. Barnes 1982, 71 and 73–74.

125. For the date and name see Alan Cameron 1966.

126. Macrobius *Sat.* 1.17.1

127. Macrobius *Sat.* 1.24.1.

128. On Flavianus, his career, and its reception, see Hedrick 2000.

129. Macrobius *Sat.* 1.7.1–2.

130. Macrobius *Sat.* 1.7.4.

crets" could mean many things, but it had long had as one of its meanings religious mystery; and in that meaning it had been employed by Symmachus and attracted the attention and ridicule of Ambrose and Prudentius.[131] Praetextatus rapidly revealed that he had understood Evangelus to be suggesting that their secret was a shared devotion to illicit religious practices. He immediately cited a maxim from Seneca, that one should talk among humans as though the gods were listening, and with the gods as though men were listening. Having said that, he added that their activities were in any event going to be legal: they had gathered in honor of the sacred holidays, the Saturnalia. "For if, during the performance of religious rites, no scruple forbids our cleansing a stream with sacred rites, while human and divine law permit us to dip our sheep in health-giving water, why can respect not be paid to religious scruple by passing these holy days in the study of sacred texts?"[132] Macrobius thus drew attention to precisely what one might or might not do in the charged atmosphere of his own age, for such constraints as Praetextatus imagines in the text had not existed in his lifetime.[133] In 430 the locus of the holy for pagans had moved from ritual spaces in an urban landscape to the world of texts, and it is from and through texts that Macrobius would seek to define anew the centrality of Rome.

The participants began their conversation by seeking to know the origins of the Saturnalia. For an answer they turned to Praetextatus: as a pontifex, he was uniquely knowledgeable about all rites and could reveal their origins and causes. But Praetextatus hesitated: "It is permissible for me to reveal the origin of the Saturnalia only insofar as it is discussed in literary myths or revealed to the vulgar by philosophers, but not as it relates to the hidden nature of divinity. For even during the rites themselves it is not permitted to reveal the hidden principles flowing from the fountain of truth, and anyone who pursues them is ordered to keep them within his conscience."[134] What could be openly discussed was the text

131. Ambrose *Ep.* 18.8; Prudentius *Symm.* 2.87–103; cf. Ando 1996, 188–90.

132. Macrobius *Sat.* 1.7.8.

133. Cf. Alan Cameron 1999, 116–17, arguing that Servius's mid-fourth-century source described cults using verbs in the present tense, which Servius, writing perhaps around 420, attempted systematically to correct to imperfects.

134. Macrobius *Sat.* 1.7.18.

of Vergil, the sacred text to which Praetextatus alluded in his rebuke of Evangelus. The sacred knowledge it contained lay beyond arts of grammar, with its focus on the elucidation of the poem's words. "But we, whom crude wisdom displeases, will not allow the innermost shrines of this sacred poem to remain hidden. Rather, by exploring the approach to its sacred and incommunicable meanings we will allow its hidden sanctuaries to be celebrated in cult by the learned."[135]

Yet one thing must have been clear to Macrobius in the early fifth century, as it is clear to us now. The sacred and incommunicable meanings inscribed in Vergil's poem in the Augustan age could not speak to his own in simple and unproblematic language. Jupiter's nod, like his promise of empire without end, now betokened information that lay beyond the exegetical powers of the grammarian: the passage of time, the rise of Christianity, and the deeds of Alaric had conspired at once to elevate and to obscure the meanings of that most holy text. If, as Servius knew, it had once been possible to read the *Aeneid* as a simple historical narrative, as an authoritative telling of the *gesta populi Romani,* in the political, religious, and discursive aftermath of 410 the *Aeneid* offered less narrative and more allegory, contained less history and more secrets, and provided not confirmation of one's ambitions but sanctuary for one's dreams.[136] How then did Vergil replace the armaments of cult in debating the sacred topography of the empire?

In two ways. First, Macrobius, like Symmachus and Praetextatus, looked to ancient history. According to Furius Albinus, who was learned in ancient lore, "if we would be wise, we must always revere *vetustas,* antiquity."[137] Like Prudentius, Macrobius looked beyond the deeds of the Roman people and inquired of history prior even to the foundation of Rome. In doing so he constructed historical explanations that connected the secular past that he shared with all his contemporaries with a particular sacred history. Where Augustine looked past Rome to Babylon, where Prudentius looked past Romulus to Noah and to Adam, Macrobius looked

---

135. Macrobius *Sat.* 1.24.13. Cf. *Sat* 1.17.2: *Tum Vettius: cave aestimes, mi Aviene, poetarum gregem, cum de dis fabulantur, non ab adytis plerumque philosophiae semina mutuari.*

136. Servius *ad Aen.* 6.752. On the import of *historia* and the role of this concept in Servian hermeneutics see Dietz 1995.

137. Macrobius *Sat.* 3.14.2.

to Saturn. When Janus ruled Italy from a city called Janiculum, he received Saturn and learned from him the arts of agriculture and in gratitude shared his kingdom with him. He also struck coins bearing Saturn's portrait, and their joint reign was commemorated by Vergil through an allusion, if not in narrative.[138] Thus the very fact that the Saturnalia originated with Saturn showed "how very much older the festival is than the city of Rome."[139] Mythic history thus concretized the actions of the divine and located them within a material and historical landscape that remained visible and numinous even in the fifth century.[140] The consecration of particular loci by Roman priests thus did no more, and no less, than circumscribe, respect, and order the presence of the holy in the Roman landscape. For Macrobius, the materiality of the landscape did not divorce it from the divine; rather, it was for humans through ritually correct speech and action to understand and respect the divine in the world.

Macrobius was not alone in this historical project. Christian definitions of historical time had shifted the parameters of debate. The history of Rome in and of itself no longer sufficed to reveal the workings of divine providence and the rewards of piety. Christians citing the books of Moses trumpeted their claims to chronological priority, and these had to be met or refuted.[141] Fourth-century pagans chose to respond in kind. The *Origo gentis Romanorum* contained in the Calendar of 354 began with Picus, "the son of Saturn, who ruled for thirty-eight years in the Laurentine plain even to that point where Rome now stands. At that time there were no cities or villages, but people lived a nomadic existence."[142] The similarly titled *Origo gentis Romanae* transmitted with Aurelius Victor's *Historia abbreviata* likewise aimed to reconstruct, through a reading of Vergil, the history of Italy from Janus and his alliance with Saturn down to Romulus and the foundation of Rome. That author showed a lack of scruple when he rehearsed the story of Hercules and Evander as told in the *libri*

138. Macrobius *Sat.* 1.7.19–24; cf. Servius *ad Aen.* 8.319 (and cf. on 7.180).

139. Macrobius *Sat.* 1.7.24.

140. Cf. MacCormack 1990, 10–11.

141. See, e.g., Augustine *Ep.* 102.8–15, where Augustine considers the sarcastic challenge posed by Porphyry Κατὰ Χριστιανῶν fr. 79 von Harnack: *Ut dimittam, inquit, tempora ante Latium regnatum, ab ipso Latio quasi principium humani nominis sumamus. In ipso Latio ante Albam dii culti sunt.*

142. *Origo gentis Romanorum* (NHLL § 531.5) in *Chron. min.* 1.143.

Pontificalium, even though he confessed that "our Vergil was afraid to follow this version."[143] In the face of this industry, which stretched back to
Ptolemy and Pliny, Hyginus and Cato, Servius occasionally threw up his
hands. It was not possible to learn by diligent inquiry the origin of the
city of Rome, for antiquity itself created uncertainty. And if clear reasoning was not possible about so great a city as Rome, there was little cause
for wonder that there should be disagreement about others: it was antiquity itself that created the error.[144]

The second way in which Macrobius defended the primacy of Rome
was by advocating the truth and efficacy of pontifical law. Earlier readers
of Vergil, Servius among them, had found his poem littered with allusions
to pontifical law and had argued that Vergil wished his readers to see Aeneas as a *pontifex maximus,* not least when, *ex persona Evandri,* he invited
Aeneas to enter a house artfully sacralized by pontifical law before there
were *pontifices.*[145] All Romans understood why Varro preceded his books
on divine antiquities with those on human affairs; only the introduction
of a Christian metaphysics, or post-Christian prejudice, could render his
premises opaque.[146] Even in the expanded imperial community of the second century, Varro's understanding of the human and the sacred still obtained. While in Nicomedia, Pliny learned that its citizens wished to move
an ancient temple of Magna Mater. He asked whether any particular *lex*
governed such actions and discovered that the form of dedication practiced in that city was different from that practiced at Rome. He sought
guidance from Trajan, who responded: "You can transfer the temple with-

143. *Origo gentis Romanae (NHLL* § 532.1) 7.

144. Servius *ad Aen.* 7.678; but cf. *ad Aen.* 1.273: Servius there provides one version of the
story of Amulius and Numitor, introducing it with the announcement that *historia hoc habet.*
In the longer version of Servius auctus, the note continues with the allowance that *sed de
origine et conditore urbis diversa a diversis traduntur.*

145. Servius *ad Aen.* 8.373, and cf. on 1.373, 2.2, 3.607, 8.470, 8.552, 9.298. Servius
identifies more than fifty passages in which Vergil demonstrates his awareness of, and strictly
adheres to, the niceties of *ius pontificum* (e.g., *ad Aen.* 1.179, 2.119, 2.141, 2.351, 3.64, 4.103,
6.176, 8.363, 8.552), or *disciplina pontificalis* (*ad Aen.* 2.693, 4.577, 7.190, 9.298, 9.641; and
ad Georg. 1.270), or *ritus pontificalis* (*ad Aen.* 4.262, 6.366, 8.275, 10.228; *ad Buc.* 5.20; and
ad Georg. 1.21, 1.31, 1.268, 1.270, 1.344, 2.162), or even uses properly some *verbum pontificale*
(*ad Aen.* 1.519, 2.148, 3.35, 12.170, 12.603; *ad Buc.* 5.66; and *ad Georg.* 1.21, 3.16 and 17).

146. Augustine *Civ.* 6.3–4, summarized by the *Breviculus: Quod ex disputatione Varronis apud
cultores deorum antiquiores res humanae quam divinae reperiantur.* Cf. Momigliano 1987, 62–65;
and above, chapter 1, pp. 15–18, and chapter 4, pp. 83–86.

out concern for religious scruple. . . . Nor let it trouble you that no law of dedication can be found, since the soil of an alien country is not susceptible to such dedication as is performed according to our law."[147]

When, therefore, Macrobius devoted his book 3 to showing that Vergil in every way observed proper scruple and diction in his religious terminology and descriptions of rites, he implicitly tied Vergil to a particular landscape, to be sure. But insofar as Vergil's text was sacred and could reveal sacred and incommunicable truths, Vergil's propriety in matters of *Roman* pontifical law necessarily privileged Vergil's landscape. The nature and consequences of these assumptions emerge with particular clarity when Macrobius discusses the history of *evocatio,* the rite by which Romans called forth gods from objects they wished to move or cities they wished to conquer.[148] The rite presumed that every city was under the protection of some deity, a sentiment Macrobius shared with Symmachus, as with virtually all pagans in antiquity: "Everyone has their own customs, their own religious practices; the divine mind has assigned to cities different religious practices to protect them. As souls are given to babies, so to nations are distributed *genii* to watch over their destinies."[149] It was for this reason, Macrobius argued, that the Romans were careful not to reveal their tutelary deity or the secret name of Rome; what is more, the formulas for the rite, like the name of Rome, remained the special preserve of the pontiffs.[150]

If Praetextatus knew the secret name of Rome, he did not reveal it. Legend had it that one Valerius Soranus did just that, and he consequently came to a nasty end.[151] The contemporary relevance of this bit of antiquarian lore was clear even before 410, and not just to readers of Vergil. Claudian lamented in his *Gothic War* that the enemy had been allowed to

---

147.   Pliny *Ep.* 10.49–50. The final sentence reads: *nec te moveat, quod lex dedicationis nulla reperitur, cum solum peregrinae civitatis capax non sit dedicationnis, quae fit nostro iure.*

148.   Macrobius *Sat.* 3.9.2; Basanoff 1947, esp. 25–44, a fascinating essay but unreliable on the history of pontifical law.

149.   Symmachus *Rel.* 3.8, and see MacCormack 1975ʼ.

150.   Pliny *Nat.* 28.18; cf. 3.65 and Macrobius *Sat.* 1.10.7–8, on Angerona, who is represented *ore obligato.* On Angerona's candidacy as that god or goddess *in cuius tutela urbs Roma est* see Wissowa 1912, 241 and 338.

151.   Plutarch *Quaest. Rom.* 62 (*Mor.* 278F); Servius *ad Aen.* 1.277. On Valerius Soranus see Cichorius 1906 and Alfonsi 1948 and 1949.

escape when he might have been trapped and destroyed in central Italy. "But the destruction of the name and race of the Getae would have been too dearly bought. Let Jupiter on high instead prevent barbarian eyes from profaning with their sight the shrines of Numa or temples of Quirinus or learning the secret of this great empire [*arcanum tanti regni*]."[152] In 417 the Gallic pagan Rutilius Namatianus felt sure that Claudian's fear had been realized through the treachery of Stilicho: "So much more bitter is the crime of dread Stilicho, because he betrayed the secret of the empire [*proditor arcani quod fuit imperii*]. . . . He did more than betray Rome to the depredations of Gothic arms: he first burnt the books containing the Sibyl's aid. . . . and wished to cast headlong the fateful guarantors of our eternal rule [*aeterni fatalia pignora regni*]."[153]

"There were seven *pignora* that maintained the Roman empire: the stone of the Mother of the Gods, the terracotta chariot of the Veientines, the ashes of Orestes, the scepter of Priam, the veil of Iliona, the Palladium, and the *ancilia*."[154] The term *pignus* defies translation; the only English equivalent of any accuracy is "palladium," whose adoption here would cause confusion and whose usage would in any event beg several questions. In the translation just above I adopt "guarantor" rather than "guarantee" or "surety" or "pledge," because the *pignora* did not all function merely as material reminders or tokens, although some did.[155] Rather, the material objects themselves possessed power and exercised agency. Pliny the Elder compared the terracotta chariot of the Veientines to a human head discovered on the Tarpeian Hill during the digging of a foundation for a new shrine. Not knowing what the head portended but recognizing it as an omen, the Romans sent envoys to Olenus of Cales, the most famous seer (*vates*) in Etruria. He tried to transfer the blessing to his own people by tracing the outline of a temple and saying, "Is this, then, Romans, what you say [*hoc ergo dicitis, Romani*]? 'Here will be the temple of

152. Claudian *De bello Gothico* 99–103; Cracco Ruggini 1968 places the polemic against Stilicho in a much wider rhetorical and political context.

153. Rutilius Namatianus *De reditu* 2.41–42, 51–52, and 55–56.

154. Servius *ad Aen.* 7.188.

155. According to Ovid, for example, Jupiter gave the *ancile* to Numa after promising *imperii pignora certa* (*Fasti* 3.345–46). "Mindful that the fate of the empire was bound up in it" (*memor imperii sortem consistere in illo*), Numa arranged for the shield to be copied; hence the plural *ancilia* (*Fasti* 3.379–82).

Jupiter, All-good and Almighty; here we found the head?'" Warned by the seer's son that Olenus would attempt some trick, the Romans responded, "Not exactly here, but it was in Rome that we say the head was found [*Non plane hic sed Romae inventum caput dicimus*]."[156] The *Annals* are in complete and total agreement, concluded Pliny, that the destiny of Rome would have been transferred to Etruria but for this astute reply.

Pliny told the story to illustrate the power of words and songs, and his telling lays significant stress on the power of speech acts: had the Romans adopted the wording of Olenus, the power of the head would have passed to Etruria, quite in spite of the truth or falsity of their utterance. But the tale of the head is not one of divine perversity, either: the Romans received no ambiguous oracle that tested their resolve or cleverness. Rather, the head was just a head, and yet it carried "some greater and more divine power," to use Julian's description of "the stone of the Mother of the Gods." Julian's misgivings about the status of the stone were typical. Cybele's *baitulos,* her black meteorite, had long tested the boundaries of traditional theories of representation. As we have seen, the earliest complete narratives of her transfer to Rome both waver uncomfortably between viewing the stone as an image of the goddess and as the goddess herself. Livy initially allowed that the Romans brought back from Pessinus "the sacred stone that the natives say is the Mother of the Gods," but his narrative of her arrival in Rome always speaks of her and not of the rock: Cornelius Scipio met *her* at Ostia; he carried *her* to shore and gave *her* to the first women of Rome; the women passed *her* from hand to hand; they installed the *goddess* in temple of Victory on the Palatine.[157] Ovid only once alludes to the stone's ambiguous metaphysical status by describing it as "the image of the goddess"; otherwise he refers dozens of times to it as the goddess. It was the goddess herself who spoke from her innermost shrine (*et sic est adytis diva locuta suis*): "I wanted to be sought out; let there be no delay; let me go, as I am willing. Rome is a worthy place, to which every god might go."[158]

If the gods might go to Rome, there they might stay. We are returned to the sacred topographies of Libanius and Symmachus, and to the theological problems posed by Symmachus's equation of the altar and statue

---

156. Pliny *Nat.* 28.15–16.

157. Livy 29.11.7 and 14.11–14.

158. Ovid *Fasti* 4.179–348. For the *imago* see 317–18; for her speech see 268–70.

of Victory with the *praesentia numinis,* the presence of the god. What we must not do, in attempting to unravel the philosophical underpinnings of their arguments, is evade a profound ontological and metaphysical crux by labeling it one of representation. Symmachus did not employ Victoria in metonymy for her statue, nor did he simply believe that the statue and altar functioned allegorically to represent a goddess whom he could not see. Again, the problem lies not with the materiality of the Tarpeian head, or Great Mother's stone, or Victory's altar, nor again with the representational capacity of their matter, but with the understanding of matter and representation that underlay ancient religiosity. Like those Romans who knew without being told that the Tarpeian head was not just a head, we must confess abiding ignorance before that shield on the Capitol that said, "To the *genius* of the city of Rome, whether it be male or female." Servius compared this inscription to the opening formula of a prayer of the pontiffs: "Jupiter Optimus Maximus, or by whatever other name you wish to be called."[159] It may be that the shield was just a gift and that its inscription signified nothing more than ignorance of a god's name, in thanksgiving for a benefaction of unknown agency.[160] It could also be that the shield fell from heaven, like an *ancile* or *baitulos,* and so stood for, and also had once been, the *genius* of the city. The power of words and objects existed in complex symbiosis: just as the pontiffs took care that no one should name the gods of Rome, lest they be spirited away through acts of augury, so the presence of sacred objects (*sacra*) made any site into a *sacrarium,* and the religious scruple attached to such a site could be removed only by "calling forth" (*evocare*) the *sacra.*[161]

Macrobius did allow Praetextatus to quote the formulas for an *evocatio* and a *devotio,* which he claims to have found in book 5 of the *Res reconditae* of Sammonicus Serenus, who was himself quoting one Furius.[162] As I have said, it is at least possible that this citation is genuine and the prayer authentic, and that the Furius of Sammonicus Serenus should be identified

159. Servius *ad Aen.* 2.351.

160. Compare, perhaps, *ILS* 4015: *sei deo sei deivae sac. C. Sextius C. f. Calvinus pr. de senati sententia restituit.* On gods whose names one does not know see below, p. 190; above, chapter 3, p. 56; Basanoff 1947, 25–30 and 89–90; and Scheid 1999b, 198–200.

161. Servius *ad Aen.* 2.351, on *exauguratio;* cf. Ulpian at *Dig.* 1.8.9.*pr.*-2. On these texts see above, chapter 5, pp. 112, 129–30.

162. Macrobius *Sat.* 3.9.6–11.

with Lucius Furius Philus, consul 136 B.C.E. and friend of Scipio Aemilianus, who performed these rituals at Carthage.[163] What we can say for certain is that Servius in the late fourth century firmly believed that Juno had been summoned forth from Carthage and her rites transferred to Rome during the third Punic war, and Servius knew the same formula for this rite as did Macrobius.[164] Macrobius closed this chapter by listing cities whose gods had been summoned forth to Rome, whose identity he had discovered *in antiquitatibus*. His list includes several towns in Italy, Carthage, and Corinth, and closes with a flourish: "And many other armies and cities of the Gauls, Spaniards, Africans, Moors, and the other races of whom the ancient annals speak."[165] Accurate or not, the argument constitutes a stunning validation, from the perspective of pontifical law, of Rome as center, as the *templum totius mundi*.

Macrobius was not the first to construct a theological argument for the centrality of Rome, nor the first to see in it a defense for Roman imperialism. In fact, we know this tradition best from its Christian opponents. Minucius Felix, for example, criticized Roman polytheism for its lack of discrimination, though he allowed Caecilius, the advocate of paganism, to defend Roman piety as best he could. Every city has its own rites and local gods, Caecilius began, but the Romans worship them all. As the Romans' power and authority embraced the circuit of the earth, they continued to practice their particular form of piety. Even when besieged on the soil of the Capitol they worshipped gods whom others might have spurned as angry: "They go forth armed with the performance of religious scruple; while in captured cities, their victory still raging, they worship the conquered gods of their enemies, invite them to Rome as their guests, and make them their own. As they have taken up the rites of all people, so they have earned their empire."[166]

163.   See Fraenkel 1957, 238, arguing that Appian *Pun.* 639 describes a *devotio,* tacitly assuming (no doubt correctly) that a *devotio* presumed a successful *evocatio.* Wissowa 1912, 374 and 384, views the *evocatio* of Carthaginian Juno as an invention of the second century C.E., both because Appian *Pun.* 639 makes no mention of an *evocatio* and because Cicero's vague language at *De lege agraria* 1.5 and 2.51 is difficult to understand if Juno of Carthage had in fact been transferred and was at that time worshipped at Rome. See also above, chapter 6, pp. 130–31.

164.   Servius *ad Aen.* 2.244 and 12.841, and cf. Fraenkel 1957, 237–38.

165.   Macrobius *Sat.* 3.9.13.

166.   Minucius Felix *Octavius* 6.1–2.

Prudentius gave voice to the Christian critique of this tradition in its developed form: Roman piety may have created "a single home for every earthborn divinity," but the tradition began with "such *numina* as fled the flames of Troy."[167]

On this question—namely what it meant that the gods of Troy had been defeated and fled to Rome—there could be no satisfactory dialogue. Fortunately, the differing ethical and theological presuppositions of the participants in these debates lie outside my concerns.[168] What is worth noting is that the gods of Troy did not die in 410. They survived the flames of Troy and the sack of Rome and retained their potency and their function in the new Christian capital of the eastern Roman empire. It is to their fate in that city that I now turn.

THE PASSING OF THE PALLADIUM

The residency of these gods in Constantinople might well surprise. The citizens of that city should not have needed them to assert its priority over Rome. Constantine and Eusebius had supplied them with a foundation on which to base their claims, one, moreover, that supplied internal justification for denying any legitimacy to the arguments of Macrobius. If it was possible for Westerners like Prudentius and Augustine to privilege recent revelations and thus to denigrate Rome and its *mos maiorum,* it should have been easy for Easterners to do the same.

But old habits die hard. The rivalry of cities had a distinguished history in Greek and Roman culture, and, like diplomatic negotiations, it had long been conducted by continual reference to each city's legendary past.[169] Themistius, for example, urged that Constantine's act of refoundation, his ἀνανέωσις, had severed the Constantinopolitan present from the site's Byzantine past. He therefore told his fellow citizens that their metropolis "was not ancient Megara, whence sprang the people who first settled on the Bosporus, but that city that rules over others and rules together with ours." In so doing he accepted too uncritically Constantine's prop-

167. Prudentius *Symm.* 1.189–96.

168. Cf. MacCormack 1998,156–74.

169. In addition to the bibliography cited at Ando 2000, 55, see Curty 1995; Ando 1999, 10–11; and Jones 1999.

aganda without considering its ideological repercussions.[170] In the ancient Mediterranean, a city without a past was no city at all.

What is more, by the middle of the fifth century, Rome was no longer a pagan city, to be dismissed as the dying relic of an earlier age. The heirs of Theodosius in the fifth century could not claim to have converted the Senate of Rome without weakening what had been fourth-century Constantinople's salient claim to primacy. Nor did Christianity itself provide any assistance. Christian understandings of God's immanence in this world did not allow for any obvious mechanism for sacralizing particular spaces or negotiating the topography of cities and empires.[171] By identifying within Christ a human nature, certain Christologies accepted through Christ a form of immanence that sacralized his world and so encouraged pilgrimage to Palestine, but Christ did not visit Rome or Byzantium. Rufinus might have believed that Constantine used the nails from the True Cross to render his helmet impermeable, but there is no evidence that Constantine did, in fact, transfer relics from Jerusalem to Constantinople. If anything, Constantine's endowments in Jerusalem made it the capital of Christianity.[172]

As we turn to Constantinople and its conceits in the middle of the fifth century, let me begin with a caution. Byzantine historians, travel writers, and theologians articulated their claims to preeminence primarily by retelling the foundation narrative of their city. It might be possible on the basis of their accounts to determine, with greater or lesser certainty, what Constantine actually did on 13 November 324 or 11 May 330 or sometime in 328 or 334 or whenever he did whatever it is he did.[173] But that

170.   Themistius *Or.* 23.298a–b. For the term "refoundation" or "renewal" see *Chron. Pasch.* (Bonn 528) and Malalas 13.7.

171.   MacCormack 1990, 12–14.

172.   The nails of the True Cross: Rufinus *Hist. ecl.* 10.8. Constantine's endowments in the Holy Land: Eusebius *Vita Constantini* 3.25–43, and cf. Dagron 1984b, 388–89.

173.   The most securely attested date remains 11 May 330: *Consularia Constantinopolitana sub anno* 330; Malalas 13.7–8; Hesychius *Patria* 1, 42. Malalas may have extrapolated from the date on which the city's anniversary was celebrated in his day, but the date of the festival surely originated somewhere. For 13 November 324 see Themistius *Or.* 4.58b. Starting work in 328, with dedication in 330: *Chron. Pasch.* (Bonn 528 and 529–30) and Theophanes s.a. 5821 (p. 28 lines 23–29 de Boor). Cf. *CTh* 2.8.19.2, declaring the *natales* of Rome and Constantinople to be holidays; and cf. Sozomen 5.17.8 and Cassiodorus *Hist. trip.* 6.30. The literature on the foundation narratives is large. Important contributions include Bréhier 1915; Lathoud 1924 and 1925; Frolow 1944; A. Alföldi 1947; Janin 1964, esp. 21–31; Dagron 1984b, esp. 13–47; Cracco Ruggini 1980b; and Mango 1985.

is not my concern here. My focus is on the role these narratives played at the moment of their telling, and the bases on which they sacralized Constantinople within the geography of the empire.[174]

First, by the end of the fifth century there was clearly a strong tradition that Constantine transferred to his new city the gods of Rome and the guarantors of its empire. One of these was the Palladium. The Palladium resembled the corpse of Iphigeneia: just about every city in Greece claimed to have it.[175] Indeed, insofar as Troy was supposed to have lost the Palladium, Rome had perhaps the least credible claim to possess it. Nevertheless, Romans had insisted at least since the age of Augustus that the Palladium was housed in the temple of Vesta, its existence becoming attached in the literary tradition to the actions of Lucius Caecilius Metellus, who saved the contents of that temple when it caught fire in 241 B.C.E.[176] Indeed, it is tempting to speculate that the Romans discovered their possession of it when the temple of Vesta burned in 14 B.C.E.[177] Its existence in Rome was known to Dionysius of Halicarnassus, who numbered the Palladium among the gods brought by Aeneas to Italy that could not by law be viewed by normal citizens.[178] Although Ovid did not know how the statue came to Rome, he understood its import, assigning to Apollo the admonition that Ilus and his descendants should "keep the heavenly goddess, and you will save your city: she transfers with herself the seat of empire."[179] Late in the fourth century, Servius, like Dionysius and Ovid before him, knew that the fate of the Palladium was contested, and yet he firmly believed that Vergil wrote as though Aeneas brought the Palladium with him. It was after its arrival in Rome, he observed, that

---

174. Dagron 1984a is essential to any understanding of the historiographic tradition surrounding the foundation of Constantinople.

175. See Dobschütz 1899, vol. 2; *RE* 19 s.v. "Iphigeneia" (Kjellberg), cols. 1589–98; *RE* 36.2 s.v. "Palladion" (Lippold), cols. 171–87; Burkert 1970, 360; Dubourdieu 1989, 460–67.

176. Ovid *Fasti* 6.419–36, Valerius Maximus 1.4.5.

177. Dio 54.24.2. To his account compare Tacitus on the great fire, who mentions the *delubrum Vestae* along with the *penates* (*Ann.* 15.41.1). Narrating the great fire under Commodus, Herodian is certain of his facts: his generation was the first to see the Palladium since it had reached Rome (1.14.4–5 and 5.6.3).

178. Dionysius of Halicarnassus 1.67–69, esp. 1.69.4, and 2.66.3–5.

179. Ovid *Fasti* 6.419–36 at 427–28 (trans. after Frazer).

Mamurius had made multiple copies of the original, to prevent its falling into enemy hands.[180]

In Byzantine tradition of the sixth century, Constantine brought the Palladium from Rome and buried it beneath his porphyry column.[181] Advocates of Rome and Constantinople continued to contest the issue. Procopius of Caesarea tells us that the Romans of his day continued to show visitors an image of the statue, chiseled on stone and set in the temple of Fortune, where it lay before a bronze statue of Athena. And, in his words, the image did not resemble any Greek statue of Athena, but looked like the work of ancient Egyptians. Without taking a stand on the issue, he observed that Constantinopolitans believed that Constantine removed the statue to his city and buried it in his forum.[182] In the same forum stood the Milion, Constantinople's analog for the Golden Milestone at Rome. The latter had been erected by Augustus to mark the point at which all the roads of Italy and the empire converged; it declared Rome the center of the *orbis terrarum*.[183] Constantinopolitan tradition naturally and probably correctly identified Constantine as the source of its Milion. It must have displayed a dedicatory text and was in any event grouped with portraits of Constantine, Helena, and the Tyche of the city. Like Constantine's other measures to reproduce in his city the ideological and material markers of a capital, this one required no explication.[184]

A similar tradition existed about the *genius* or Tyche of the city.[185] Constantinopolitans agreed that Constantine established a temple for the Tyche of his city and that he named her Anthousa, which was clearly intended to be a translation of *Flora* and was so understood by John Lydus.[186]

---

180. Servius *ad Aen.* 2.162–79, esp. on 166 and 178–79.

181. Malalas 13.7; *Chron. Pasch.* (Bonn 528), closing its almost identical narrative with the qualification ὥς τινες λέγουσι τῶν Βυζαντίων ἐκ διαδοχῆς ἀκούσαντες; *Patria* 2.45 (Preger 1901, 174); cf. Hesychius *Patria* 41, writing of δύο τῆς Παλλάδος ἱδρύματα.

182. Procopius *Bell. Goth.* 1.15.8–14, esp. 13; see also *Parastaseis syntomoi chronikai* 23.

183. Dio 54.8.4, Plutarch *Galba* 24.4. For further sources and a discussion of the monument's ideological significance see Ando 2000, 151–52.

184. *Parastaseis syntomoi chronikai* 34, 38; *Suda* s.v. Μίλιον (M 1065); *Patria* 2.42 (Preger 1901, 172–73); cf. Janin 1964, 51, 91–92, and esp. 103–4; and Dagron 1984b, 36.

185. See esp. Lathoud 1925, esp. 180–87; and Dagron 1984b, 43–45.

186. See, e.g., Malalas 13.7; *Chron. Pasch.* (Bonn 528). Lydus *Mens.* 4.75: Ῥώμη Φλῶρα καὶ ἡ Κωνσταντίνου πόλις ἤγουν Ἄνθουσα.

They disagreed on the origin of her cult statue: almost everyone, including Zosimus, John Lydus, and pseudo-Codinus, believed that Constantine had taken it from Rome, while Hesychius of Miletus insisted that Constantine had reused a cult statue of Rhea from an earlier Byzantine precinct.[187] The cult and temple of the city's Tyche was certainly well established in the fourth century, since we are told that Julian sacrificed to her in the basilica where she lived.[188] And by the end of the fourth century that temple required restoration, work financed by one Theodorus, prefect of the city. His generosity is celebrated by an epigram in the *Palatine Anthology* that insists his action honored Tyche and, by extension, "Rome of the Golden Shield."[189] It is very tempting to connect this name to the precious information provided by Servius on the *genius* of Rome: "Before the sack of a city, the *numina* are called forth from the enemy out of respect for religious scruple. That is why the Romans wish to keep secret the identity of that god in whose protection lies the city of Rome. Thus pontifical law forbids anyone from naming the *dii Romani,* lest anyone should augur them away. And there is on the Capitol a consecrated shield, on which the inscription runs, 'To the *genius* of the city of Rome, whether male or female.' And for the same reason, the *pontifices* pray, 'Jupiter Optimus Maximus, or by whatever other name you wish to be called.'"[190]

In spite of pontifical law and the secrecy it enjoined, John Lydus knew or thought he knew the laws and traditions about the names of Rome. Describing the foundation of Rome, he says that Romulus took up a holy war-trumpet—which the Romans, he observed, call a *lituus*—and called out the name of Rome, completing a sacred rite. "For that city has three names, its ritual name, its sacred name, and its political name. The ritual name in Greek is Eros, as if everything concerning the city lay in the power of the god Eros, wherefore the poet, writing allegorically in his *Bucolics,* calls the city Amaryllis." The poet, of course, is Vergil. About the same passage in the *Eclogues* Servius wrote: "Although he had left Galatea behind, he was detained by love of Amaryllis. Here the poet speaks alle-

---

187.   Zosimus 2.31.1–3; Lydus *Mag.* 2.10 (and cf. 2.12); pseudo-Codinus *Patria* 3.131 (Preger 1901, 257); Hesychius *Patria* 15.

188.   Socrates 3.11.4.

189.   *Anth. Pal.* 9.697.

190.   Servius *ad Aen.* 2.351.

gorically, saying, after I left Mantua behind I took myself to Rome: for he wants Galatea to be Mantua, and Rome to be Amaryllis."[191] Lydus continued: "The sacred name is Flora, in Greek *Anthousa,* whence comes the festival Anthesteria. The political name is Rome. The ritual name was known to all and used openly, but the sacred one was entrusted only to the *pontifices* for the completion of sacred rites."[192] As Servius might have told John, according to an ancient custom known to Vergil, the Romans built temples only after the proposed site had been freed from religious scruple and blessed by the augurs, then consecrated by the *pontifices;* then, at last, the *sacra* were dedicated on and to the site.[193]

We know from several sources that the Tyche of Constantinople was brought forth every year on the birthday of the city, paraded through the Hippodrome, and acclaimed with hymns, a celebration that, according to Byzantine tradition, had been started by Constantine as a ritual reenactment of the founding of the city.[194] John Malalas even explained how Constantine transferred these cult images away from Rome: he insisted that Constantine undertook a formal procession from Rome to Constantinople to dedicate his city in the spring of 330.[195] And according to Sozomen, Constantine established a council in his new city, which he called a Senate, and he arranged for his new city to celebrate "all those honors and festivals that were customary among the old Romans, since he wanted to show that the city that bore his name was, in every respect, equivalent to the Rome that is in Italy; nor did he fail in this desire."[196]

191. Servius *ad Buc.* 1.29.

192. Lydus *Mens.* 4.73, on which see Wittig 1910, 44–48.

193. Servius *ad Aen.* 1.446 and *ad Georg.* 3.16 and 17.

194. Malalas 13.8; cf. *Parastaseis syntomoi chronikai* 5, 38, and 56.

195. Malalas 13.7: καὶ ἐπὶ τῆς αὐτοῦ βασιλείας ἐνεκαινίσθη τό ποτε Βυζάντιον ἐπὶ τῆς ὑπατείας Γαλλιανοῦ καὶ Συμμάχου, τοῦ αὐτοῦ δὲ βασιλέως Κωνσταντίνου ποιήσαντος πρόκεσσον ἐπὶ πολὺν χρόνον, ἀπὸ Ῥώμης ἐλθόντος ἐν τῷ Βυζαντίῳ. Lydus may allude to this story at *Mag.* 2.10: Κωνσταντίνου γὰρ μετὰ τῆς Τύχης τὴν Ῥώμην ἀπολιπόντος. No dictionary adequately deals with the constitutional and ceremonial significance of the imperial *processus,* and LSJ omits its Greek derivative altogether; see instead A. Alföldi 1970, 95–97 and 146–48. Had Constantine made such a triumphal march, the significance of his direction would have been stunning: in the fourth century, imperial arrivals and imperial triumphs presupposed Rome (MacCormack 1981, 33–55).

196. Sozomen 2.3.6: βουλευτήριόν τε μέγα, ἣν σύγκλητον ὀνομάζουσιν, ἕτερον συνεστήσατο, τὰς αὐτὰς τάξας τιμὰς καὶ ἱερομηνίας, ἣ καὶ Ῥωμαίοις τοῖς πρεσβυτέροις ἔθος. ἐν πᾶσι δὲ δεῖξαι σπουδάσας ἐφάμιλλον τῇ παρὰ Ἰταλοῖς Ῥώμῃ τὴν ὁμώνυμον αὐτῷ πόλιν οὐ διήμαρτεν.

By the middle of the sixth century John Lydus could identify the moment and the ritual at which and through which Constantine endowed his city with its culture and identity: "As the monad is an archetypal form, and 'one' is an example of a monad, in just such a relationship was our blessed city in its first days considered in its relations with that Rome that used to surpass it in every way. For this reason Constantine never called it 'New Rome' prior to its consecration [κωνσεκράτιω], for that is what the Romans call its dedication [ἀποθέωσις]."[197] But Lydus is simply the most verbally precise in a long succession of historians who wrote in similar terms. As Sozomen's beliefs about the festival calendar of Constantinople make clear, by the middle of the fifth century many had begun to understand Constantine's foundational act in terms derived from pontifical law. It was, after all, Praetextatus the pontiff who in the *Saturnalia* explicated the organization and history of the calendar. According to his exposition, histories of the calendar ultimately relied on the "books of the pontiffs," and supervision of the calendar had originally been the responsibility of a *pontifex minor*.[198]

But the observance of pontifical law in the foundation of Constantinople grew more strict as the legends about that event developed. As early as 357, Themistius seems to have believed that Constantine traced the boundaries of his new city on the same day that he honored his son with the purple.[199] By the middle of the next century Philostorgius could claim that Constantine had performed a *limitatio,* tracing the boundaries of his new city with a spear.[200] How did Constantine know the proper formulas with which to perform these acts? According to John Lydus, he brought a young pontifex from Rome to supervise the ritual.[201] John digressed momentarily to explain to his readers that the *pontifices,* whom he calls οἱ Ῥωμαίων ἱεροφάνται, were a college of priests that supervised the cult of the Palladium. He also observed that the Greek word for *pontifex* was γεφυριστής, a translation based on etymology that can also be found

197. Lydus *Mag.* 2.30, and see Cracco Ruggini 1980b, 601–2.

198. Macrobius *Sat.* 1.12.21 and 1.15.9.

199. Themistius *Or.* 4.58b.

200. Philostorgius 2.9: καὶ τὸν περίβολον ὁριζόμενον βάδην τε περιιέναι, τὸ δόρυ τῇ χειρὶ φέροντα.

201. Lydus *Mens.* 4.2.

in Servius.[202] Whom did John cite as his authorities on pontifical law and religious affairs? The sources of Macrobius: Ateius Capito, Marcus Messalla, Gavius Bassus, Q. Lutatius Catulus, Serenus Sammonicus, M. Terentius Varro, Cornelius Labeo, Tarquitius Priscus, a certain Cincius who wrote on the calendar, and one Xenon, author of books on Italy.[203] And

202. Servius *ad Aen.* 2.166: "dicunt sane alii, unum simulacrum caelo lapsum, quod nubibus advectum et in ponte depositum, apud Athenas tantum fuisse, unde et γεφυριστής dicta est. ex qua etiam causa pontifices nuncupatos volunt: quamvis quidam pontifices a ponte sublicio, qui primus Tybri impositus est, appellatos tradunt, sicut Saliorum carmina loquuntur." Lydus *Mens.* 4.15: Ὅτι ποντίφικες οἱ ἀρχιερεῖς παρὰ Ῥωμαίοις ἐλέγοντο, καθάπερ ἐν Ἀθήναις τὸ πάλαι γεφυραῖοι πάντες οἱ περὶ τὰ πάτρια ἱερὰ ἐξηγηταὶ καὶ ἀρχιερεῖς—διοικηταὶ τῶν ὅλων—ὠνομάζοντο, διὰ τὸ ἐπὶ τῆς γεφύρας τοῦ Σπερχειοῦ ποταμοῦ ἱερατεύειν τῷ Παλλαδίῳ. πόντην γὰρ οἱ Ῥωμαῖοι τὴν γέφυραν καλοῦσι, καὶ ποντίλια τὰ γεφυραῖα ξύλα. ὅθεν καὶ πραξιεργίαι δῆθεν ἐκαλοῦντο ὡσανεὶ τελεσταί. τοῦτο γὰρ σημαίνει τὸ πόντιφεξ ἀπὸ τοῦ δυνατοῦ ἐν ἔργοις. See also Lydus *Mag.* 2.4, writing of Augustus: Ἐχρῆτο δὲ στολῇ ἐπ᾽ εἰρήνης, οἷα ποντίφεξ, ἀντὶ τοῦ ἀρχιερεὺς γεφυραῖος, πορφυρᾷ, ποδήρει, ἱερατικῇ, χρυσῷ λελογχωμένῃ. Cf. Varro *Ling.* 5.83 and Plutarch *Numa* 9.1–3. Plutarch cites different etymologies. Some derive *pontifex* from *potens;* others say that the name was assigned because the priests were charged to perform only such sacred duties as were possible (ἱερουργίας ... δυνατάς, which Plutarch has already translated πότηνς). But most writers, he adds, teach a laughable etymology: ὡς οὐδὲν ἀλλ᾽ ἢ γεφυροποιοὺς τοὺς ἄνδρας ἐπικληθέντας ἀπὸ τῶν ποιουμένων περὶ τὴν γέφυραν ἱερῶν, ἁγιωτάτων καὶ παλαιοτάτων ὄντων· πόντεμ γὰρ οἱ Λατῖνοι τὴν γέφυραν ὀνομάζουσιν. In official documents of the imperial era *pontifex* was either transliterated or, most commonly, rendered as ἀρχιερεύς (Magie 1905, 21, 39–40, 64, and 142; or, more briefly, Mason 1974, 77), although literary usage varied somewhat more widely (Magie 1905, 32, 142–43). Further etymologies common to Servius and Lydus include that of Quirinus (*ad Aen.* 1.292, *Mag.* 1.5); they cite the same passage of Asper on *sella* (*ad Aen.* 7.169, *Mag.* 1.7); they similarly distinguish between *clipei* and *scuta* (*ad Aen.* 9.368, *Mag.* 1.9); and they offer the same history and etymology for *ancile* (*ad Aen.* 8.664, *Mag.* 1.11); and many more such passages could be cited. On the sources of Lydus see Reifferscheid 1860, 466–67; Schultze 1862, 6–39, esp. 20–28; and Wittig 1910. Each of those scholars stands back from identifying any given author or authors as sources for Lydus. Reifferscheid is certainly correct that Suetonius received an enthusiastic reception in Byzantium; the number of correspondences between Servius, Macrobius, and Lydus is astonishing.

203. Lydus *Mens.* 4.1–2, citing Μεσσαλᾶς, Βάρρων, Γάβιος Βάσσος, and Λουτάτιος. M. Messalla: Macrobius *Sat.* 1.9.14. Macrobius and Lydus cite Varro continually. Gavius Bassus: Macrobius *Sat.* 1.9.13, 3.6.17, and 3.18.2–3. Macrobius does not quote Q. Lutatius Catulus but does list him as a pontiff: *Sat.* 3.13.11. Ateius Capito: Macrobius *Sat.* 1.14.5, 3.10.3 and 7, 7.13.11 (Capito is *pontificii iuris inter primos peritus*); Lydus *Mens.* 1.37, fr. 6 Wuensch. Serenus Sammonicus: Macrobius *Sat.* 3.9.3, 3.16.6, and 3.17.4; Lydus *Mag.* 3.32. Cornelius Labeo: Macrobius *Sat.* 1.16.29; Lydus *Mens.* 3.10, 4.1 and 25. Cincius: Macrobius *Sat.* 1.12.12–13, 18, and 20; Lydus *Mens.* 4.144. Xenon: Macrobius *Sat.* 1.9.3; Lydus *Mens.* 1.2.

who, according to John, was the pontifex who aided Constantine? Vettius Agorius Praetextatus.[204]

Easterners and Westerners continued for centuries to debate the merits of the old and new Rome, but the later tradition lies beyond the scope of this book. When the Christians did discover a Christian method for sacralizing Constantinople, they merely found their own palladia, among which the icon of Camuliana held pride of place, and insofar as their palladia were not made by human hands, they shared with the stone of the Great Mother a power and agency that transcended their materiality.[205] This much is clear: that the actions of Constantine and the preservation of specifically Roman customs remained central to this debate.[206] Hesychius of Miletus went so far as to rewrite early Byzantine history on analogy with Rome: Byzas had a half-brother named Strombus, with whom he quarreled at the foundation of his city; and Byzantium had been saved from the siege of Philip by the barking of dogs.[207] But in this endeavor he departed from common practice, which followed fourth-century authors in rejecting and ultimately erasing the city's Byzantine past.[208]

Here I suspect that the arrival of a new Tyche signaled a break with the past more severe than we can easily comprehend. Some knew that Byzantium must have had a Tyche before the arrival of Anthousa. Indeed, her name was Keroë.[209] But in the Byzantine imagination, Anthousa brought with her new customs, new holidays, a new identity, and a new history. The fifth-century appropriation of the Palladium and *genius* of Rome was masterful, on several levels, for even as Pallas and Flora endowed their new home with a sacred identity and mythological past, their departure deprived Rome of those same things.[210] And who in the middle of the fifth century could contest that Constantinople and not Rome had the true

204. Lydus *Mens.* 4.2: ὁ δὲ Πραιτέξτατος ὁ ἱεροφάντης, ὁ Σωπάτρῳ τε τῷ τελεστῇ καὶ Κωνσταντίνῳ τῷ αὐτοκράτωρι συλλαβὼν ἐπὶ τῷ πολισμῷ τῆς εὐδαίμονος ταύτης πόλεως.

205. See esp. Frolow 1944; cf. Kitzinger 1954, 111–15; Baynes 1955, 240–60; MacCormack 1975, 148–49, and 1990, 17–18 and 28; Averil Cameron 1978; and Geary 1986.

206. See, for example, Liudprand *Relatio de legatione* 50–51.

207. Hesychius *Patria* 19–20; on his work see Dagron 1984a, 23–29.

208. Cf. Themistius *Or.* 14.182a.

209. Malalas 13.7.

210. The *Constitutum Constantini* was, of course, equally brilliant in its appropriation of Constantine. Who better to undermine the legitimacy of his own foundation? See *Constitutum*

Palladium or that Constantine had brought it to the East in triumph? Whoever would admit its efficacy had to allow that it could not have been in Rome in 410.

THE POLITICS OF ANTIQUARIANISM

The pontifical lore and ancient artifacts through and with which Romans and Constantinopolitans contested the sacred topography of the Roman empire achieved a new importance in the fifth century, when neither city could claim preeminence for its episcopate or its relics. Their turn to antiquarianism was, under the circumstances, anything but nostalgic, interesting only to bookish pedants like John Lydus. Not only did Macrobius and Malalas write for their contemporaries about issues of contemporary importance, but their particular arguments appealed to their audiences—indeed, derived their power over them from their shared commitment to the traditions and beliefs that their narratives concretized. It meant something to passersby that the Palladium lay beneath Constantine's column, just as recycling building material from pagan temples did not desacralize them. The antiquarianism of Hesychius or the *Patria* acquired its power from a sense that the gods were, in fact, *in Rome*, as Libanius had said. It was that belief that made *evocatio* meaningful. This had been apparent even to Plutarch, the first Greek to discuss the ritual:[211]

> Why is it forbidden to mention or to inquire after or to call by name
> that deity, whether it be male or female, whose especial province it is
> to preserve and watch over Rome? . . . Is it because, as certain Roman
> writers have recorded, there are certain evocations and enchantments

---

12: *Atque decernentes sancimus, ut principatum teneat tam super quattuor praecipuas sedes Antiochenam, Alexandrinam, Constantinopolitanam et Hierosolymitanam, quamque etiam super omnes in universo orbe terrarum dei ecclesias.*

211. Plutarch *Quaest. Rom.* 61 (*Mor.* 278F): Διὰ τί τὸν θεὸν ἐκεῖνον, ᾧ μάλιστα τὴν Ῥώμην σῴζειν προσήκει καὶ φυλάττειν, εἴτ᾽ ἐστὶν ἄρρην εἴτε θήλεια, καὶ λέγειν ἀπείρηται καὶ ζητεῖν καὶ ὀνομάζειν... Πότερον, ὡς τῶν Ῥωμαϊκῶν τινες ἱστορήκασιν, ἐκκλήσεις εἰσὶ καὶ γοητεῖαι θεῶν, αἷς νομίζοντες καὶ αὐτοὶ θεούς τινας ἐκκεκλῆσθαι παρὰ τῶν πολεμίων καὶ μετῳκηκέναι πρὸς αὐτοὺς ἐφοβοῦντο τὸ αὐτὸ παθεῖν ὑφ᾽ ἑτέρων ὥσπερ οὖν Τύριοι δεσμοὺς ἀγάλμασι λέγονται περιβαλεῖν, ἕτεροι δ᾽ αἰτεῖν ἐγγυητὰς ἐπὶ λουτρὸν ἢ καθαρμόν τινα προπέμποντες οὕτως ᾤοντο Ῥμαῖοι τὸ ἄρρητον καὶ τὸ ἄγνωστον ἀσφαλεστάτην εἶναι θεοῦ καὶ βεβαιοτάτην φρουράν. On chained gods see Frazer 1913, 3:336–38; and Merkelbach 1970/71.

affecting the gods, by which the Romans believed that certain gods had been called forth from their enemies and had come to dwell among themselves, and they were afraid of having the same thing done to them by others? Accordingly, as the Tyrians are said to have put chains upon their images, and certain other people are said to demand sureties when they send forth their images for bathing or for some other rite of purification, so the Romans believed that not to mention and not to know the name of the god was the safest and surest way of shielding it.

If the power that Plutarch assigned to words ritually spoken and the link he posited between material idol and immaterial deity presumed beliefs that still defy satisfactory articulation, we should at least recognize in them the bases on which the sacred topography of the later Roman empire was negotiated.

Constantine's death on 22 May 337 was not the turning point it might seem to be. Rather, it opened the curtain on a new scene, in a drama that had begun whenever it was that Constantine ordered the construction of a mausoleum for himself and his family in "the imperial city," in Rome. It was there that he laid his mother to rest, perhaps in the same year that he consecrated Constantinople.[212] According to Eusebius, when Constantine died seven years later in Nicomedia, "those inhabiting the imperial city, namely the Senate and people of Rome . . . indulged in limitless grief. . . . They acclaimed his sons alone and no others Imperatores and Augusti, and with pitiful cries they asked that the corpse of their emperor be sent to them and that it be laid to rest in the imperial city."[213] Eusebius continued, effecting a dramatic shift in geographic perspective: "But those *here* looked after the one honored by God. The second of his children came to the city and sent forth his father's corpse, and he himself led the procession." Like the residents of Rome, Eusebius understood the power latent in Constantine's body, a power more potent and less contestable in death than it had been in life.

A little less than six decades later Theodosius lay dead at Milan. His corpse, too, was taken to Constantinople, although his son and successor

212. Her death and resting place: Eusebius *Vita Constantini* 3.47.1, but cf. Theophanes s.a. 5817 (p. 27, lines 10–14 de Boor). Further sources listed in *PLRE* I s.v. "Helena 3."
213. Eusebius *Vita Constantini* 4.69.

in the West, Honorius, did not accompany his body on that journey. A short while later, before an audience that included Honorius himself, Ambrose delivered a eulogy to the fallen emperor. Reflecting on the direction in which Theodosius then traveled, Ambrose offered no criticism and suffered no sense of loss. Speaking to Honorius in closing, Ambrose told him (*De obitu Theodosii* 56)

> not to fear lest his triumphant remains seem to lack honor wherever they go. Italy, who witnessed his triumphs, feels no such lack; Italy, twice freed from tyrants, celebrates the author of its liberty. Nor does Constantinople, who twice sent forth the emperor to victory, think him dishonored, although that city was not able to keep what it wanted. Constantinople awaited triumphal processions on his return and the titles of his victories; it awaited the emperor of the world, accompanied by the army of Gaul and supported by the strength of the whole world. But now Theodosius returns there stronger and more glorious; a throng of angels walks before him, and a crowd of saints follows. Clearly you are blessed, Constantinople, you who receive an inhabitant of Paradise, for through your august care over his buried corpse you will possess a citizen of the heavenly city.

Ambrose adhered at once to Christian doctrine and Christian politics. On the one hand, he dismissed any interest in the topography of this world and constructed instead a binarism contrasting this world and the next. On the other, he so privileged Constantinople as a Christian capital that he dispensed with the older Rome altogether. Of course, he had other reasons to cite Italy rather than Rome as the rival for Constantinople, not least a desire to include himself and his city among those who celebrated the author of their liberty. Nevertheless, in his mapping of the world, Rome has vanished from any contest for the affective heart of the empire, even of its western half. Ambrose died two years later; Prudentius perhaps a decade after that. Neither lived to rue their victories over Symmachus and the Roman past. Surrendering naively to the allure of a Christian capital, they sacrificed Rome, Italy, and the West to a Roman empire that numbered Pallas among the citizens of heaven.

BIBLIOGRAPHY

Adams, J. N. 2003. "'*Romanitas*' and the Latin language." *CQ* 53, 184–205.

Alföldi, A. 1937. *A festival of Isis in Rome under the Christian emperors of the IVth century*. Dissertationes Pannonicae, ser. 2, fasc. 7. Budapest: Institute of Numismatics and Archaeology of the Pázmány University; Leipzig: Harrassowitz.

———. 1942–43. *Die Kontorniaten: Ein verkanntes Propagandamittel der stadtrömischen heidnischen Aristokratie in ihrem Kampfe gegen das christliche Kaistertum.* 2 vols. Leipzig: Harrassowitz.

———. 1947. "On the foundation of Constantinople: A few notes." *JRS* 37, 10–16.

———. 1948. *The conversion of Constantine and pagan Rome.* Oxford: Clarendon Press.

———. 1952. *A conflict of ideas in the late Roman empire.* Oxford: Clarendon Press.

———. 1970. *Die monarchische Repräsentation im römischen Kaiserreiche.* Darmstadt: Wissenschaftliche Buchgesellschaft.

Alföldi, M. R. 1999. "Zur Frage der 'interpretatio Romana.'" In F.-R. Herrmann, I. Schmidt, and F. Verse, eds., *Festschrift für Günter Smolla,* 2:597–605. Wiesbaden: Selbstverlag des Landesamtes für Denkmalpflege Hessen.

Alföldy, G. 1985. "Epigraphica Hispanica, VI: Das Diana-Heiligtum von Segobriga." *ZPE* 58, 139–59.

Alfonsi, L. 1948. "L'importanza politico-religiosa della enunciazione di Valerio Sorano." *Epigraphica* 10, 81–89.

———. 1949. "L'importanza politico-religiosa della enunciazione di Valerio Sorano." *Epigraphica* 11, 47–48.

Ando, C. 1994. "Augustine on language." *RÉAug* 40, 45–78.

———. 1996. "Pagan apologetics and Christian intolerance in the ages of
Themistius and Augustine." *JECS* 4, 171–207.

———. 1997. Review of J. R. Martindale, ed., *The prosopography of the later Roman empire,* Part 3, A.D. 527–641 (Cambridge: Cambridge University Press,
1992). *Phoenix* 51, 86–88.

———. 1999. "Was Rome a *polis?*" *ClassAnt* 18, 5–34.

———. 2000. *Imperial ideology and provincial loyalty in the Roman empire.* Berkeley and Los Angeles: University of California Press.

———. 2001. "Signs, idols and the incarnation in Augustinian metaphysics."
Representations 73, 24–53.

———. 2002. "Vergil's Italy." In Levene and Nelis 2002 (q.v.), 123–42.

———. 2003a. Review of Goldhill 2001 (q.v.). *Phoenix* 57, 355–60.

———, ed. 2003b. *Roman Religion.* Edinburgh: Edinburgh University Press.

———. 2004. Review of Tim Whitmarsh, *Greek literature and the Roman empire:
The politics of imitation* (Oxford: Oxford University Press, 2001). *CPh* 99, 89–98.

———. 2006. "The administration of the provinces." In David S. Potter, ed.,
The Blackwell companion to the Roman empire, 177–92. Oxford: Blackwell.

———. 2007a. "Decline, fall and transformation." *Journal of Late Antiquity* 1
(forthcoming).

———. 2007b. "Exporting Roman religion." In J. Rüpke, ed., *A companion to
Roman religion,* 429–45. Oxford: Blackwell.

———. Forthcoming a. "Aliens, ambassadors and the integrity of the empire."
Law and History Review (forthcoming).

———. Forthcoming b. "The end of antiquity." In Alessandro Barchiesi and
Walter Scheidel, eds., *The Oxford handbook of Roman studies.* Oxford: Oxford
University Press.

Ando, C., and J. Rüpke, eds. 2006. *Religion and law in classical and Christian Rome.*
Stuttgart: Franz Steiner Verlag.

Andreau, J. 2000. "Commerce and finance." *CAH*[2] 11:769–86.

Asad, T. 1993. *Genealogies of religion: Discipline and reasons of power in Christianity
and Islam.* Baltimore: The Johns Hopkins University Press.

Auerbach, E. 1953. *Mimesis: The representation of reality in Western literature.* Trans.
W. R. Trask. Princeton: Princeton University Press.

Back, F. 1883. *De Graecorum caerimoniis in quibus homines deorum vice fungebantur.* Berlin: Schade.

Barasch, M. 1992. *Icon: Studies in the history of an idea.* New York: New York University Press.

Barnes, J. 1997. "Roman Aristotle." In J. Barnes and M. Griffin, eds., *Philosophia togata, II: Plato and Aristotle at Rome,* 1–69. Oxford: Clarendon Press.

Barnes, T. D. 1975. "Publilius Optatianus Porfyrius." *AJPh* 96, 173–86.

———. 1982. "Aspects of the background of the City of God." *Revue de l'Université d'Ottawa/University of Ottawa Quarterly* 52, 64–80.

———. 1987. "Christians and pagans in the reign of Constantius." *EntrHardt* 34, 301–43.

———. 1995. "Statistics and the conversion of the Roman aristocracy." *JRS* 85, 135–47

Barton, I. M. 1982 "Capitoline temples in Italy and the provinces (especially Africa)." *ANRW* 2.12.1, 259–342.

Basanoff, V. 1947. *Evocatio: Étude d'un rituel militaire romain.* Paris: Presses Universitaires de France.

Baynes, N. H. 1955. *Byzantine studies and other essays.* London: Athlone Press.

Beard, M. 1985. "Writing and ritual: A study of diversity and expansion in the Arval Acta." *PBSR* 53, 114–62.

———. 1986. "Cicero and divination: The formation of a Latin discourse." *JRS* 76, 33–46.

———. 1990. "Priesthood in the Roman Republic." In Beard and North 1990 (q.v.), 19–48.

———. 1991. "Writing and religion: Ancient literacy and the function of the written word in Roman religion." In *Literacy in the ancient world,* Journal of Roman Archaeology, Supplement 3: 35–58. Ann Arbor: Journal of Roman Archaeology.

———. 1998. "Documenting Roman religion." In Moatti 1998 (q.v.), 75–101.

Beard, M., and J. North, eds. 1990. *Pagan priests.* London: Duckworth.

Beard, M., J. North, and S. Price. 1998. *Religions of Rome.* 2 vols. Cambridge: Cambridge University Press.

Beaujeu, J. 1955. *La religion romaine à l'apogée de l'Empire.* Paris.

Bell, C. 1997. *Ritual: Perspectives and dimensions.* New York: Oxford University Press.

Bendlin, A. 1997. "Peripheral centres—Central peripheries: Religious communication in the Roman empire." In Cancik and Rüpke 1997 (q.v.), 35–68.

————. 2001. "Rituals or beliefs? 'Religion' and the religious life of Rome." *SCI* 20, 191–208.

Berger, A. 1953. *Encyclopedic dictionary of Roman law.* Transactions of the American Philosophical Society, 43.2. Philadelphia: American Philosophical Society.

Bergmann, B., and C. Kondoleon, eds. 1999. *The art of ancient spectacle.* Washington D.C.: National Gallery of Art.

Besançon, A. 2000. *The forbidden image: An intellectual history of iconoclasm.* Trans. J. M. Todd. Chicago: University of Chicago Press.

Bevan, E. 1940. *Holy images. An inquiry into idolatry and image-worship in ancient paganism and in Christianity.* London: Allen and Unwin.

Bispham, E., and C. Smith, eds. 2000. *Religion in Archaic and Republican Rome and Italy.* Edinburgh: Edinburgh University Press.

Bland, K. P. 2000. *The artless Jew: Medieval and modern affirmations and denials of the visual.* Princeton: Princeton University Press.

Bloch, H. 1945. "A new document of the last pagan revival in the West." *HThR* 38, 199–244.

————. 1963. "The pagan revival in the West at the end of the fourth century." In Momigliano 1963 (q.v.), 193–218.

Bloch, R. 1973. "Héra, Uni, Junon en Italie centrale." *RÉLatines* 51, 55–61.

Blomart, A. 1997. "Die *evocatio* und der Transfer fremder Götter von der Peripherie nach Rom." In Cancik and Rüpke 1997 (q.v.), 99–111.

de Borries, Bodo. 1918. *Quid veteres philosophi de idololatria senserint.* Göttingen: Officina Academica Dieterichiana.

Bostock, D. 1994. *Aristotle: Metaphysics, Books Z and H.* Oxford: Clarendon Press.

Bouma, J. W. 1993. "Architectural terracottas unearthed in a votive deposit in Borgo le Ferriere ('Satricum'), 6th–3rd centuries B.C." In E. Rystedt, C. Wikander, and O. Wikander, eds., *Deliciae fictiles: Proceedings of the first international conference on Central Italic architectural terracottas, Swedish Institute in Rome, 10–12 December 1990,* 291–97. Stockholm: Svenska Institutet.

Boyancé, P. 1972. *Études sur la religion romaine.* CÉFR 11. Rome: École Française de Rome.

Bradbury, S. 1994. "Constantine and the problem of anti-pagan legislation in the fourth century." *CPh* 89, 120–39.

Bradley, K. 1998. "Contending with conversion: Reflections on the reformation of Lucius the ass." *Phoenix* 52, 315–34.

Bréhier, L. 1915. "Constantin et la fondation de Constantinople." *Revue Historique* 119, 241–72.

Bremmer, J. 1991. "'Christianus sum': The early Christian martyrs and Christ." In G. J. M. Bartelink, A. Hilhorst, and C. H. Kneepkens, eds., *Eulogia: Mélanges offerts à Antoon A. R. Bastiaensen à l'occasion de son soixante-cinquième anniversaire*, 11–20. Steenbrugge: Abbatia S. Petri.

———. 1998. "'Religion,' 'ritual' and the opposition 'sacred vs. profane': Notes towards a terminological genealogy." In Graf 1998a (q.v.), 9–32.

Brodka, D. 1998. *Die Romideologie in der römischen Literatur der Spätantike*. Frankfurt: Peter Lang.

Brown, P. R. L. 1961. "Aspects of the Christianization of the Roman aristocracy." *JRS* 51, 1–11. [Reprinted with addenda in idem, *Religion and society in the age of Saint Augustine* (London: Faber and Faber, 1972), 161–82.]

———. 1963. "Religious coercion in the later Roman empire: The case of North Africa." *Historia* 48, 283–305

———. 1993. "The problem of Christianization." *PBA* 82: 89–106.

———. 1995. *Authority and the sacred: Aspects of the Christianisation of the Roman world*. Cambridge: Cambridge University Press.

Bruggisser, P. 1987. *Romulus Servianus: La légende de Romulus dans les commentaires à Virgile de Servius; Mythographie et idéologie à l'époque de la dynastie théodosienne*. Antiquitas, Reihe 1: Abhandlungen zur alten Geschichte, 36. Bonn: Habelt.

Bruun, C., ed. 2000. *The Roman middle Republic: Politics, religion and historiography c. 400–133 B.C.* Rome: Institutum Romanum Finlandiae.

Burkert, W. 1970. "Buzyge und Palladion: Gewalt und Gericht in altgriechischem Ritual." *Zeitschrift für Religions- und Geistesgeschichte* 22, 356–68.

———. 1987. *Ancient mystery cults*. Cambridge, Mass.: Harvard University Press.

Buxton, R., ed. 2000. *Oxford readings in Greek religion*. Oxford: Oxford University Press.

Cameron, Alan. 1964. "The Roman friends of Ammianus." *JRS* 54, 15–28.

———. 1965. "Palladas and Christian polemic." *JRS* 55, 17–30.

———. 1966. "The date and identity of Macrobius." *JRS* 56, 25–38.

———. 1968. "Gratian's repudiation of the pontifical robe." *JRS* 58, 96–102.

———. 1977. "Paganism and literature in late fourth-century Rome." *EntrHardt* 23, 1–40.

———. 1984. "The Latin revival of the fourth century." In W. Treadgold, ed., *Renaissances before the Renaissance*, 42–58. Stanford: Stanford University Press.

———. 1999. "The last pagans of Rome." In Harris 1999 (q.v.), 109–21.

———. 2004a. *Greek mythography in the Roman world*. American Classical Studies, 48. New York: Oxford University Press.

————. 2004b. "Vergil illustrated between pagans and Christians: Reconsidering the 'late-4th c. Classical Revival,' the dates of the manuscripts, and the places of production of the Latin classics." *JRA* 17, 502–25.

Cameron, Averil. 1978. "The Theotokos in sixth-century Constantinople: A city finds its symbol." *JThS* 29, 79–108.

Camodeca, G. 2006. "Comunità di *peregrini* a Puteoli nei primi due secoli dell'impero." In M. Gabriella Angeli Bertinelli and A. Donati, eds., *Le vie della storia: Migrazioni di popoli, viaggi di individui, circolazioni di idee nel Mediterraneo antico*, 269–87. Rome: Bretschneider.

Camus, P. M. 1967. *Ammien Marcellin.* Paris: Les Belles Lettres.

Cancik, H. 1985/86. "Rome as sacred landscape: Varro and the end of Republican religion in Rome." *Visible Religion* 4/5, 250–65.

————. 1999. "The reception of Greek cults in Rome." *ARG* 1, 161–73.

Cancik, H., H. Lichtenberger, and P. Schäfter, eds. 1996. *Geschichte—Tradition—Reflexion: Festschrift für Martin Hengel zum 70. Geburtstag.* Vol. 2, *Griechische und Römische Religion.* Tübingen: Mohr Siebeck.

Cancik, H., and J. Rüpke, eds. 1997. *Römische Reichsreligion and Provinzialreligion.* Tübingen: Mohr Siebeck.

Cancik-Lindemaier, H. 1996. "Der Diskurs Religion im Senatsbeschluß über die Bacchanalia von 186 v.Chr. und bei Livius (B. XXXIX)." In Cancik, Lichtenberger, and Schäfter 1996 (q.v.), 77–96.

Catalano, P. 1978. "Aspetti spaziali del sistema giuridico-religioso romano: Mundus, templum, urbs, ager, Latium, Italia." *ANRW* 2.16.1, 440–553.

de Cazanove, O. 2000a. "I destinatari dell'iscrizione di Tiriolo e la questione del campo d'applicazione del senatoconsulto de bacchanalibus." *Athenaeum* 88, 59–68.

————. 2000b. "Some thoughts on the 'religious Romanization' of Italy before the Social War." In Bispham and Smith 2000 (q.v.), 71–76.

Chastagnol, A. 1956. "Le sénateur Volusien et la conversion d'une famille de l'aristocratie romaine au bas-empire." *RÉAnciennes* 58, 241–53.

Chastagnol, A., S. Demougin, and C. Lepelley, eds. 1996. *Splendidissima civitas: Études d'histoire romaine en hommage à François Jacques.* Paris: Publications de la Sorbonne.

Cichorius, C. 1906. "Zur Lebensgeschichte des Valerius Soranus." *Hermes* 41, 59–68.

Clerc, C. 1915. *Les théories relatives au culte des images chez les auteurs grecs du IIème siècle après J.-C.* Paris: Fontemoing.

Cloud, D. 1994. "The constitution and criminal law." *CAH²* 9:491–530.

Cohen, S. J. D., and E. S. Frerichs, eds. 1993. *Diasporas in antiquity.* Atlanta: Scholars Press.

Cooley, A., ed. 2000a. *The epigraphic landscape of Roman Italy.* London: Institute of Classical Studies.

———. 2000b. "Politics and religion in the *ager Laurens.*" In Cooley 2000a, 173–91.

Cornell, T. J. 1989. "Rome and Latium to 390 B.C." *CAH²* 8.2:243–308.

———. 1995. *The beginnings of Rome: Italy and Rome from the Bronze Age to the Punic Wars (c. 1000–264 B.C.).* London: Routledge.

Courcelle, P. P. 1964. *Histoire littéraire des grandes invasions germaniques.* 3rd ed. Paris: Études Augustiniennes.

———. 1969. *Late Latin writers and their Greek sources.* Trans. H. E. Wedeck. Cambridge, Mass.: Harvard University Press.

Cracco Ruggini, L. 1968. "*De morte persecutorum* e polemica antibarbarica nella storiografica pagana e cristiana: A proposito della disgrazia di Stilicone." *Rivista di Storia e Letteratura Religiosa* 4, 433–47.

———. 1979. *Il paganesimo romana tra religione e politica (384–394 d.C.): Per una reinterpretazione del Carmen contra paganos.* Atti della Accademia Nazionale dei Lincei, Classe di Scienze Morali, Storiche e Filologiche, ser. 8, vol. 23, fasc. 1. Rome: Accademia Nazionale dei Lincei.

———. 1980a. "Nuclei immigrati e forze indigene in tre grandi centri commerciali dell'impero." In D'Arms and Kopf 1980 (q.v), 55–76.

———. 1980b. "Vettio Agorio Pretestato e la fondazione sacra di Constantinopoli." In *Miscellenea di studi classici in onore di Eugenio Manni,* 2: 593–610. Rome: Bretschneider.

Crawford, M. H., ed. 1996. *Roman statutes.* London: Institute of Classical Studies.

Curty, O. 1995. *Les parentés légendaires entre les cités grècques.* Hautes Études du Monde Greco-Romain, 20. Geneva: Droz.

Dagron, G. 1984a. *Constantinople imaginaire: Études sur le recueil des "Patria."* Bibliothèque Byzantine, Études, 8. Paris: Presses Universitaires de France.

———. 1984b. *Naissance d'une capitale: Constantinople et ses institutions de 330 à 451.* 2nd ed. Bibliothèque Byzantine, Études, 7. Paris: Presses Universitaires de France.

D'Arms, J., and E. C. Kopf, eds. 1980. *The seaborne commerce of ancient Rome.* Memoirs of the American Academy in Rome, vol. 36. Rome: American Academy in Rome.

Derks, T. 1991. "The perception of the Roman pantheon by a native elite: The example of votive inscriptions from Lower Germany." In N. Roymans and F. Theuws, eds., *Images of the past: Studies on ancient societies in northwestern Europe,* 235–65. Amsterdam: Instituut voor Pre- en Protohistorische Archeologie Albert Egges van Giffen.

Detienne, M., ed. 1990. *Traces de fondation.* Bibliothèque de l'École des Hautes Études, Section des Sciences Religieuses, vol. 93. Louvain: Peeters.

De Zulueta, F. 1946. *The Institutes of Gaius.* 2 vols. Oxford: Clarendon Press.

Dietz, D. B. 1995. "*Historia* in the commentary of Servius." *TAPhA* 125, 61–97.

von Dobschütz, E.. 1899. *Christusbilder: Untersuchungen zur christlichen Legende.* 3 vols. Leipzig: Hinrichs.

Dölger, F. J. 1937. "Rom in der Gedankenwelt der Byzantiner." *ZKG* 56, 1–42.

Dondin-Payre, M., and M.-T. Raepsaet-Charlier, eds. 1999. *Cités, municipes, colonies: Les processus de municipalisation en Gaule et en Germanie sous le Haut Empire romain.* Paris: Publications de la Sorbonne..

Döpp, S. 1978. "Zur Datierung von Macrobius' 'Saturnalia.'" *Hermes* 106, 619–32.

Drake, H. A. 2000. *Constantine and the bishops: The politics of intolerance.* Baltimore: The Johns Hopkins University Press.

Dubourdieu, A. 1989. *Les origines et le développement du culte des Pénates à Rome.* CÉFR 118. Rome: École Française de Rome.

Dubourdieu, A., and J. Scheid. 2000. "Lieux de culte, lieux sacrés: Les usages de la langue; L'Italie romaine." In Vauchez 2000 (q.v.), 59–80.

Dubuisson, M. 1982. "Y-a-t-il une politique linguistique romaine?" *Ktema* 7, 187–210.

Durand, J.-L., and J. Scheid. 1994. "'Rites' et 'religion': Remarques sur certains préjugés des historiens de la religion des grecs et des romains." *Archives de Sciences Sociales des Religions* 85, 23–43.

Duthoy, R. 1969. *The taurobolium: Its evolution and terminology.* Leiden: Brill.

Dyck, A. R. 2004. *A commentary on Cicero, "De legibus."* Ann Arbor: University of Michigan Press.

Eck, W. 1971. "Das Eindringen des Christentums in den Senatorenstand bis zu Konstantin der Große." *Chiron* 1, 381–406.

———. 2000. "Latein als Sprache politischer Kommunikation in Städten der östlichen Provinzen." *Chiron* 30, 641–60.

Edmondson, J. C. 1999. "The cultural politics of public spectacle in Rome and the Greek East, 167–166 BCE." In Bergmann and Kondoleon 1999 (q.v.), 77–95.

Elsner, J. 1996. "Image and ritual: Reflections on the religious appreciation of classical art." *CQ* 46, 513–31.

———. 2001. "Describing self in the language of other: Pseudo(?) Lucian at the temple of Hierapolis." In Goldhill 2001 (q.v.), 123–53.

Estienne, S. 1997. "Statues de dieux 'isolées' et lieux de culte: L'exemple de Rome." *Cahiers du Centre Gustave Glotz* 8, 81–96.

Fears, J. R. 1981. "The cult of Jupiter and Roman imperial ideology." *ANRW* 2.17.1, 3–141.

Feeney, D. 1998. *Literature and religion at Rome.* Cambridge: Cambridge University Press.

Flamant, J. 1977. *Macrobe et le Néo-Platonisme latin, à la fin du IVe siècle.* Leiden: Brill.

Foertmeyer, V. A. 1989. "Tourism in Graeco-Roman Egypt." Dissertation, Princeton University.

Fowden, G. 1978. "Bishops and temples in the eastern Roman empire, A.D. 320–435." *JThS* 29, 53–78.

Fraenkel, E. 1957. *Horace.* Oxford: Clarendon Press.

Frankfurter, D. 1998. *Religion in Roman Egypt: Assimilation and resistance.* Princeton: Princeton University Press.

Frateantonio, C. 1997. "Autonomie in der Kaiserzeit und Spätantike." In Cancik and Rüpke 1997 (q.v.), 85–97.

Frazer, J. G. 1913. *Pausanias's description of Greece.* 6 vols. New York: Macmillan.

Frier, B. 2000. "Demography." *CAH²* 11:787–816.

Frolow, A. 1944. "La dédicace de Constantinople dans la tradition byzantine." *Revue de l'Histoire des Religions* 127, 61–127.

Funke, H. 1981. "Götterbild." *RAC* 11, 659–828.

Galsterer, H. 1987. "La loi municipale des romains: Chimère ou réalité?" *Revue Historique de Droit Français et Étranger* 65, 181–203.

———. 1988. "Municipium Flavium Irnitanum: A Latin town in Spain." *JRS* 78, 78–90.

Geary, P. 1986. "Sacred commodities: The circulation of medieval relics." In A. Appadurai, ed. *The social life of things: Commodities in cultural perspective,* 169–91. Cambridge: Cambridge University Press.

Geffcken, J. 1916/19. "Der Bilderstreit des heidnischen Altertums." *ARW* 19, 286–315.

Georgacas, J. G. 1947. "The names of Constantinople." *TAPhA* 78, 347–67.

Gerson, L. P. 2005. *Aristotle and other Platonists.* Ithaca: Cornell University Press.

Giovannini, A. 1998. "Les livres auguraux." In Moatti 1998 (q.v.), 103–22.

———. 2000. "Le droit fécial et la déclaration de guerre de Rome à Carthage en 218 avant J.-C." *Athenaeum* 88, 69–116.

Girard, J.-L. 1980. "Interpretatio Romana: Questions historiques et problèmes de méthode." *Revue d'Histoire et de Philosophie Religieuses* 60, 21–27.

Gladigow, B. 1985/86. "Präsenz der Bilder—Präsenz der Götter: Kultbilder und Bilder der Götter in der griechischen Religion." *Visible Religion* 4/5, 114–33.

———. 1990. "Epiphanie, Statuette, Kultbild: Griechische Gottesvorstellungen im Wechsel von Kontext und Medium." *Visible Religion* 7, 98–121.

———. 1994. "Zur Ikonographie und Pragmatik römischer Kultbilder." In H. Keller and N. Staubach, eds., *Iconologia sacra: Mythos, Bildkunst und Dichtung in der religions- und sozialgeschichte Alteuropas—Festschrift für Karl Hauck*, 9–24. Berlin: de Gruyter.

Gleason, M. 1999. "Truth contests and talking corpses." In J. I. Porter, ed., *Constructions of the classical body*, 287–313. Ann Arbor: University of Michigan Press.

Glinister, F. 2000. "Sacred rubbish." In Bispham and Smith 2000 (q.v.), 54–70.

Goldhill, S., ed. 2001. *Being Greek under Rome: Cultural identity, the Second Sophistic and the development of empire.* Cambridge: Cambridge University Press.

González, J. 1986. "The *Lex Irnitana*: A new Flavian municipal law." *JRS* 76, 147–243.

Goodman, M. 1994. *Mission and conversion: Proselytizing in the religious history of the Roman empire.* Oxford: Clarendon Press.

Gordon, R. 1979. "Production and religion in the Graeco-Roman world." *Art History* 2, 5–34.

———. 1990a. "From Republic to Principate: Priesthood, religion, and ideology." In Beard and North 1990 (q.v.), 179–98.

———. 1990b. "Religion in the Roman empire: The civic compromise and its limits." In Beard and North 1990 (q.v.), 235–55.

———. 1990c. "The veil of power: Emperors, sacrificers and benefactors." In Beard and North 1990 (q.v.), 201–31.

Graf, F., ed. 1998a. *Ansichten griechischer Rituale.* Stuttgart: Teubner.

———. 1998b. "Interpretatio, II: Religion." *Neue Pauly* 5:1042–43.

Grosso, G. 1973. "Riflessioni su 'ius civile', 'ius gentium', 'ius honorarium' nella dialettica fra tecnicismo-tradizionalismo giuridico e adeguazione allo sviluppo economico e sociale in Roma." In *Studi in memoria di Guido Donatuti*, 1:439–53. Milan: La Goliardica.

Gruen, E. S. 1982. "Greek πίστις and Roman *fides*." *Athenaeum* 60, 50–68.

Gustafsson, G. 2000. *Evocatio deorum: Historical and mythical interpretations of ritualised conquests in the expansion of ancient Rome.* Acta Universitatis Upsaliensis, Historia Religionum 16. Uppsala : Uppsala University.

Harries, J. 1999. *Law and empire in late antiquity.* Cambridge: Cambridge University Press.

Harris, W. V. 1980. "Towards a study of the Roman slave trade." In D'Arms and Kopf 1980 (q.v.), 117–40.

—————, ed. 1999. *The transformations of Urbs Roma in late antiquity.* Portsmouth, R.I.: Journal of Roman Archaeology.

—————. 2000. "Trade." *CAH²* 11:710–40.

Harrison, T. 2000. *Divinity and history: The religion of Herodotus.* Oxford: Oxford University Press.

Hedrick, C. W., Jr. 2000. *History and silence: Purge and rehabilitation of memory in late antiquity.* Austin: University of Texas Press.

Henig, M. 1986. "*Ita intellexit numine inductus tuo:* Some personal interpretations of deity in Roman religion." In Henig and King 1986 (q.v.), 159–69.

Henig, M., and A. King, eds. 1986. *Pagan gods and shrines of the Roman empire.* Oxford: Oxford University Committee for Archaeology.

Hennephof, H. 1969. *Textus Byzantinos ad iconomachiam pertinentes.* Byzantina Neerlandica, ser. A, fasc. 1. Leiden: Brill.

Hölkeskamp, K.-J. 2000. "*Fides—deditio in fidem—dextra data et accepta:* Recht, Religion und Ritual im Rom." In Bruun 2000 (q.v.), 223–50.

Hunink, V. 1996. "Apuleius and the *Asclepius.*" *VigChr* 50, 288–308.

Janin, R. 1964. *Constantinople byzantine: Développement urbain et répertoire topographique.* 2nd ed. Paris: Institut Français d'Études Byzantines.

Joachim, H. H. 1922. *Aristotle on coming-to-be & passing-away (De generatione et corruptione).* Oxford: Clarendon Press.

Jocelyn, H. D. 1982. "Varro's *Antiquitates Rerum Divinarum* and religious affairs in the late Roman Republic." *Bulletin of the John Rylands University Library of Manchester* 65, 148–205.

Jones, C. P. 1999. *Kinship diplomacy in the ancient world.* Cambridge, Mass.: Harvard University Press.

Kahlos, M. 1998. "Saeculum Praetextati." Dissertation, Faculty of Arts, Helsinki. Helsinki: Helsinki University Printing House.

Kallet-Marx, R. M. 1995. *From hegemony to empire: The development of the Roman imperium in the East from 148 to 62 B.C.* Berkeley and Los Angeles: University of California Press.

Karamanolis, G. E. 2006. *Plato and Aristotle in agreement? Platonists on Aristotle from Antiochus to Porphyry.* Oxford: Clarendon Press.

Kaser, M. 1993. *Ius gentium.* Cologne: Böhlau.

Kaster, R. 1978. "Servius and *idonei auctores.*" *AJPh* 99, 181–209.

———. 1980. "Macrobius and Servius: *Verecundia* and the grammarian's function." *HSCPh* 84, 219–62.

Kiechle, F. K. 1970. "Götterdarstellung durch Menschen in den altmediterranen Religionen." *Historia* 19, 259–71.

Kirwan, C. 1989. *Augustine.* New York: Routledge.

Kitzinger, E. 1954. "The cult of images in the age before iconoclasm." *DOP* 8, 83–150.

Klein, R. 1986. "Die Romidee bei Symmachus, Claudian und Prudentius." In F. Paschoud, ed., *Colloque genevois sur Summaque,* 119–44. Paris: Les Belles Lettres.

Kleve, K. 1963. *Gnosis theon: Die Lehre von der natürlichen Gotteserkenntnis in der epikureischen Theologie.* Oslo: Universitetsforlaget.

Klingner, F. 1965. *Römische Geisteswelt.* Munich: Ellerman.

Krueger, P., ed. 1954. *Corpus iuris civilis.* Vol. 2, *Codex Justinianus.* 11th ed. Berlin: Weidmann.

Kuhnert, E. 1883. *De cura statuarum apud Graecos.* Berlin: Calvary.

Lane Fox, R. 1987. *Pagans and Christians.* New York.

———. 1990. Review of G. Fowden, *The Egyptian Hermes: A historical approach to the late pagan mind* (Cambridge: Cambridge University Press, 1986). *JRS* 80, 237–40.

Lathoud, D. 1924. "La consécration et la dédicace de Constantinople." *Echos d'Orient* 23, 289–314.

———. 1925. "La consécration et la dédicace de Constantinople." *Echos d'Orient* 24, 180–201.

Latte, K. 1967. *Römische Religionsgeschichte.* Munich: Beck.

Laurence, R. 1996. "Ritual, landscape and the destruction of place in the Roman imagination." In J. Wilkins, ed. *Approaches to the study of ritual: Italy and the ancient Mediterranean,* 111–21. London: Accordia Research Center.

Lenel, O., ed. 1889. *Palingenesia iuris civilis.* 2 vols. Leipzig: Tauchnitz.

Levene, D. S., and D. Nelis, eds. 2002. *Clio and the poets: Augustan poetry and the traditions of ancient historiography.* Leiden: Brill.

Lieberg, G. 1973. "Die Theologia tripertita in Forschung und Bezeugnung." *ANRW* I.4, 63–115.

———. 1982. "Die Theologia tripertita als Formprinzip antiken Denkens." *RhM* 126, 25–53.

Lieu, J., J. North, and T. Rajak, eds. 1992. *The Jews among pagans and Christians in the Roman empire*. London: Routledge.

Lightfoot, J. L. 2003. *Lucian: On the Syrian goddess*. Oxford: Oxford University Press.

Linder, A. 1987. *The Jews in Roman imperial legislation*. Detroit: Wayne State University Press.

Linder, M., and J. Scheid. 1993. "Quand croire c'est faire: Le problème de la croyance dans la Rome ancienne." *Archives de Sciences Sociales des Religions* 81, 47–62.

Linderski, J. 1986. "The augural law." *ANRW* 2.16.3, 2146–2312.

———. 2000. "Religio et cultus deorum." *JRA* 13, 453–63. [Review of Beard, North, and Price 1998.]

Link, W. 1910. *De vocis 'sanctus' usu pagano quaestiones selectae*. Königsberg: Hartung.

Lund, A. A. 1998. "Interpretatio romana: Tacitus über die germanischen Kulte." *Temenos* 34, 95–110.

MacCormack, S. 1975. "Roma, Constantinopolis, the emperor, and his genius." *CQ* 25, 131–50.

———. 1981. *Art and ceremony in late antiquity*. Berkeley and Los Angeles: University of California Press.

———. 1982. "Christ and empire, time and ceremonial in sixth-century Byzantium and beyond." *Byzantion* 52, 287–309.

———. 1990. "Loca sancta: The organization of sacred topography in late antiquity." In Ousterhout 1990 (q.v.), 7–40.

———. 1997. "Sin, citizenship and the salvation of souls: The impact of Christian priorities on late-Roman and post-Roman society." *CSSH* 39, 644–73.

———. 1998. *The shadows of poetry: Vergil in the mind of Augustine*. Berkeley and Los Angeles: University of California Press.

MacMullen, R. 1993. "The unromanized in Rome." In Cohen and Frerichs 1993 (q.v.), 47–64.

Madyda, L. 1939. *De pulchritudine imaginum deorum quid auctores Graeci saec. II. p. Chr. n. iudicaverint*. Polska Akademia Umierjetnosci, Arciwum Filologiczne nr. 16. Kraków: Polish Academy of Letters.

Magedelain, A. 1986. "Le *ius* archaïque." *MÉFRA* 98, 265–358.

Magie, D. 1905. *De Romanorum iuris publici sacrique vocabulis sollemnibus in Graecum sermonem conversis*. Leipzig: Teubner.

Malaise, M. 1972. *Les conditions de pénétration et de diffusion des cultes égyptiens en Italie*. Leiden: Brill.

————. 1984. "La diffusion des cultes égyptiens dans les provinces européennes de l'empire romain." *ANRW* 2.17.3, 1615–91.

Mandouze, A. 1958. "Saint Augustin et la religion romaine." *RechAug* 1, 187–223.

Mango, C. 1963. "Antique statuary and the Byzantine beholder." *DOP* 17, 55–75.

————. 1985. *Le développement urbain de Constantinople (IVe–VIIe siècles).* Travaux et Memoires, Monographies 2. Paris: de Boccard.

Marié, M.-A. 1984. *Ammien Marcellin, Histoire.* Vol. 5, *Livres XXVI–XXVIII.* Paris: Les Belles Lettres.

Marrou, H.-I. 1932. "La vie intellectuelle au forum de Trajan et au forum d'Auguste." *MÉFRA* 49, 93–110.

Mason, H. J. 1974. *Greek terms for Roman institutions: A lexicon and analysis.* American Studies in Papyrology, vol. 13. Toronto: Hakkert.

Matthews, J. F. 1967. "Continuity in a Roman family: The Rufii Festi of Volsinii." *Historia* 16, 484–509.

————. 1970. "The historical setting of the 'Carmen contra Paganos' (Cod. Par. Lat. 8084)." *Historia* 19, 464–79.

————. 1975. *Western aristocracies and imperial court, A.D. 364–425.* Oxford: Clarendon Press.

————. 2000. *Laying down the law: A study of the Theodosian Code.* New Haven: Yale University Press.

Mazzarino, S. 1937/38. "La politica religiosa di Stilicone." *Rendiconti del Reale Istituto Lombardo di Scienze e Lettere, Classe di Lettere e Scienze Morali e Storiche,* ser. 3, vol. 71, 235–62.

McGregor, H. C. P., trans. 1972. *Cicero: The nature of the gods.* Harmondsworth: Penguin.

McLynn, N. 1996. "The fourth-century *taurobolium*." *Phoenix* 50, 312–30.

Merkelbach, R. 1970/71. "Gefesselte Götter." *Antaios* 12, 549–65.

Michels, A. K. 1976. "The versatility of *religio*." In *The Mediterranean world: Papers presented in honour of Gilbert Bagnani, April 26, 1975,* 36–77. Peterborough: Trent University.

Mirsch, P. 1888. "De M. Terenti Varronis Antiquitatum rerum humanarum libris XXV." *Leipziger Studien zur Classischen Philologie* 15, 1–144.

Mitthof, F. 1993. "Vom ἱερώτατος Καῖσαρ zum ἐπιφανέστατος Καῖσαρ: Die Ehrenprädikate in der Titulatur der Thronfolger des 3. Jh. n.Chr. nach den Papyri." *ZPE* 99, 97–111.

Moatti, C. 1991. "La crise de la tradition à la fin de la république romaine à travers la littérature juridique et la science des antiquaires." In M. Pani, ed., *Con-*

tinuità e trasformazioni fra repubblica e principato: Istituzioni, politica, società, 31–45. Bari: Edipuglia.

———. 1997. *La raison de Rome*. Paris: Seuil.

———, ed. 1998. *La mémoire perdue: Recherches sur l'administration romaine*. CÉFR 243. Rome: École Française de Rome.

———. 2001. "*Respublica* et droit dans la Rome républicaine." *MÉFRM* 113, 811–37.

———, ed. 2004. *La mobilité des personnes en Méditerannée de l'antiquité à l'époque moderne: Procédures de contrôle et documents d'indentification*. CÉFR 341. Rome: École Française de Rome.

Momigliano, A., ed. 1963. *The conflict between paganism and Christianity in the fourth century*. Oxford: Clarendon Press.

———. 1987. *On pagans, Jews, and Christians*. Middletown: Wesleyan University Press.

———. 1989. "The origins of Rome." *CAH*² 8.2:52–112.

Mommsen, T., ed. 1905. *Codex Theodosianus*. Vol. 1, pars posterior, *Theodosiani libri XVI cum Constitutionibus Sirmondianis*. Berlin: Weidmann.

Muth, R. 1978. "Von Wesen römischer 'religio.'" *ANRW* 2.16.1, 290–354.

Nicolet, C. 1979. *Rome et la conquête du monde Méditerranéen*. Paris: Presses Universitaires de France.

———. 1991. *Space, geography and politics in the early Roman Empire*. Ann Arbor: University of Michigan Press.

———. 1996. *Financial documents and geographical knowledge in the Roman world*. Oxford: Leopard's Head Press.

Nock, A. D., ed. 1926. *Sallustius: Concerning the gods and the universe*. Cambridge: Cambridge University Press.

———. 1933. *Conversion: The old and the new in religion from Alexander the Great to Augustine of Hippo*. Oxford: Clarendon Press.

———. 1972. *Essays on religion and the ancient world*. Ed. Z. Stewart. 2 vols. Oxford: Clarendon Press.

North, J. 1992. "The development of religious pluralism." In Lieu, North, and Rajak 1992 (q.v.), 174–93.

———. 1998. "The books of the *pontifices*." In Moatti 1998 (q.v.), 45–63.

Noy, D. 2000. *Foreigners at Rome: Citizens and strangers*. London: Duckworth.

Oakley, S. 1998. *A commentary on Livy, books VI–X*. Vol. 2, *Books VII–VIII*. Oxford: Oxford University Press.

Obbink, D. 1996. *Philodemos: "On piety," part 1*. Oxford: Clarendon Press.

O'Daly, G. 1999. *Augustine's "City of God": A reader's guide*. Oxford: Clarendon Press.

O'Donnell, J. J. 1978. "The career of Virius Nicomachus Flavianus." *Phoenix* 32, 129–43.

———. 1979. "The demise of paganism." *Traditio* 35, 45–88.

Ogilvie, R. M. 1965. *A commentary on Livy, books 1–5*. Oxford: Clarendon Press.

———. 1969. *The Romans and their gods in the age of Augustus*. London: Chatto and Windus.

Osborne, C. 1987. "The repudiation of representation in Plato's *Republic* and its repercussions." *PCPhS* 33, 53–73.

Ousterhout, R., ed. 1990. *The blessings of pilgrimage*. Urbana: University of Illinois Press.

Panciera, S. 1982. "Iscrizioni senatorie de Roma e dintorni, n. 38." In *Atti del Colloquio internazionale AIEGL su epigrafia e ordine senatorio, Roma, 14–20 maggio 1981*, 658–60. Rome: Edizioni di Storia e Letteratura.

Paschoud, F. 1967. *Roma aeterna: Études sur le patriotisme romain dans l'occident latin à l'époque des grandes invasions*. Bibliotheca Helvetica Romana, 7. Rome: Institut Suisse de Rome.

———. 1979. *Zosime: Histoire nouvelle*. Vol. 2, part 2, *Livre IV*. Paris: Les Belles Lettres.

Pease, A. S. 1955. *Marcus Tullius Cicero, De natura deorum liber primus*. Cambridge, Mass.: Harvard University Press.

———. 1958. *M. Tulli Ciceronis De natura deorum libri secundus et tertius*. Cambridge, Mass.: Harvard University Press.

———. [1920, 1923] 1963. *M. Tulli Ciceronis De divinatione libri duo*. Darmstadt: Wissenschaftliche Buchgesellschaft.

Pelikan, J. 1990. *Imago Dei: The Byzantine apologia for icons*. Washington, D.C.: National Gallery of Art.

Pépin, J. 1956. "La théologie tripartite de Varron." *RÉAug* 2, 265–94.

Pietz, W. 1985. "The problem of the fetish, I." *Res* 9, 5–17.

———. 1987. "The problem of the fetish, II: The origin of the fetish." *Res* 13, 23–45.

———. 1988. "The problem of the fetish, IIIa. Bosman's Guinea and the enlightenment theory of fetishism." *Res* 16, 105–23.

Pocock, J. G. A. 1996. "Classical and civil history: The transformation of humanism." *Cromohs* 1, 1–34.

Potter, D. S. 1994. *Prophets and emperors: Human and divine authority from Augustus to Theodosius.* Cambridge, Mass.: Harvard University Press.

———. 1999. "Roman religion: Ideas and actions." In D. S. Potter and D. J. Mattingly, eds., *Life, death, and entertainment in the Roman empire,* 113–67. Ann Arbor: University of Michigan Press.

Preger, T., ed. 1901. *Scriptores originum Constantinopolitanarum.* Leipzig: Teubner.

Rackham, H., trans. 1933. *Cicero: De natura deorum, Academica.* Loeb Classical Library 268. Cambridge, Mass.: Harvard University Press.

Rawson, E. 1973. "Scipio, Laelius, Furius, and the ancestral religion." *JRS* 63, 161–74.

———. 1974. "Religion and politics in the late second century B.C. at Rome." *Phoenix* 28, 193–212.

———. 1991. *Roman culture and society.* Oxford: Clarendon Press.

Reifferscheid, A. 1860. *C. Suetoni Tranquilli praeter Caesarum libros reliquiae.* Leipzig: Teubner.

Remy, E. 1930. "Du groupement des peuples en états d'après le *De officiis* de Cicéron I, 53." In *Mélanges Paul Thomas,* 583–93. Bruges: Sainte Catherine.

Richter, F. 1906. *De deorum barbarorum interpretatione Romana quaestiones selectae.* Halle: Kaemmerer.

Rives, J. B. 1995. *Religion and authority in Roman Carthage.* Oxford: Clarendon Press.

Robinson, D. N. 1915. "An analysis of the pagan revival of the late fourth century, with especial reference to Symmachus." *TAPhA* 46, 87–101.

Ross, W. D. 1960. *Aristotle's Physics.* Oxford: Clarendon Press.

Rüpke, J. 1990. *Domi militiae: Die religiöse Konstruktion des Krieges in Rom.* Stuttgart: Steiner.

———. 1995. *Kalender und Öffentlichkeit: Die Geschichte der Repräsentation und religiösen Qualifikation von Zeit in Rom.* Berlin: de Gruyter.

———. 1996a. "Controllers and professionals: Analyzing religious specialists." *Numen* 43, 241–61.

———. 1996b. "Innovationsmechanismen kultischer Religionen: Sakralrecht im Rom der Republik." In Cancik, Lichtenberger, and Schäfter 1996 (q.v.), 265–85.

———. 2005. *Fasti sacerdotum: Die Mitglieder der Priesterschaften und das sakrale Funktionspersonal römischer, griechischer, orientalischer und jüdisch-christlicher Kulte in der Stadt Rom von 300 v.Chr. bis 499 n.Chr.* Stuttgart: Steiner.

———. 2006. "Religion in the Lex Ursonensis." In Ando and Rüpke 2006 (q.v.), 34–46.

Sachot, M. 1991. "'Religio/superstitio': Historique d'une subversion et d'un retournement." *RHR* 208, 355–94.

Saddington, D. B. 1999. "Roman soldiers, local gods and *interpretatio Romana* in Roman Germany." *Acta Classica* 42, 155–69.

Salzman, M. R. 1990. *On Roman time*. Berkeley and Los Angeles: University of California Press.

———. 1999. "The Christianization of sacred time and sacred space." In Harris 1999 (q.v.), 123–34.

Scheid, J. 1981. "Le délit religieux dans la Rome tardo-républicaine." In *Le délit religieux dans la cité antique*, CÉFR 48, 117–71. Rome: École Française de Rome.

———. 1985a. "Numa et Jupiter, ou les dieux citoyens de Rome." *Archives de Sciences Sociales des Religions* 59, 41–53.

———. 1985b. *Religion et piété à Rome*. Paris: Découverte.

———. 1986. "Le flamine de Jupiter, les Vestales, et général triomphant: Variations romaines sur le thème de la figuration des dieux." In C. Malamoud and J.-P. Vernant, eds., *Corps des dieux*, Le Temps de la Réflexion 7, 213–29. Paris: Gallimard.

———. 1987. "Polytheism impossible; or, The empty gods: Reasons behind a void in the history of Roman religion." *History and Anthropology* 3, 303–25.

———. 1987/89. "La parole des dieux: L'originalité du dialogue des romains avec leurs dieux." *Opus* 6–8, 125–36.

———. 1989/90. "'Hoc anno immolatum non est': Les aléas de la *voti sponsio*." *Scienze dell'Antichità, Storia Archeologia Antropologia* 3–4, 773–83.

———. 1990a. "Rituel et écriture à Rome." In A.-M. Blondeau and K. Schipper, eds., *Essais sur le rituel*, vol. 2, Bibliothèque de l'École des Hautes Études, Section des Sciences Religieuses 95, 1–15. Louvain: Peeters.

———. 1990b. *Romulus et ses frères: Le collège des frères arvales, modèle du culte public dans la Rome des empereurs*. BÉFAR 275. Rome: École Française de Rome.

———. 1993. "Cultes, mythes et politique au début de l'Empire." In F. Graf, ed., *Mythos in mythenloser Gesellschaft: Das Paradigma Roms*, 109–27. Stuttgart: Teubner.

———. 1994. "Les archives de la piété." In S. Demougin, ed., *La mémoire perdue: À la recherche des archives oubliées, publiques et privées, de la Rome antique*, CNRS—Série Histoire Ancienne et Médiévale 30, 173–85. Paris: Publications de la Sorbonne.

———. 1995. "Les espaces culturels et leur interprétation." *Klio* 77, 424–32.

———. 1996. "Pline le jeune et les sanctuaires d'Italie: Observations sur les lettres IV, 1, VII, 8 et IX, 39." In A. Chastagnol, S. Demougin, and C. Lepelley, eds., *Splendidissima civitas: Études d'histoire romaine en hommage à François Jacques*, 241–58. Paris: Publications de la Sorbonne.

———. 1998a. "Les livres sibyllins et les archives des quindécemvirs." In Moatti 1998 (q.v.), 11–26.

———. 1998b. "Nouveau rite et nouvelle piété: Réflexions sur le ritus Graecus." In Graf 1998a (q.v.), 168–82.

———. 1998c. *La religion des romains*. Paris: Colin.

———. 1999a. "Aspects religieux de la municipalisation: Quelques réflexions générales." In Dondin-Payre and Raepsaet-Charlier 1999 (q.v.), 381–423.

———. 1999b. "Hiérarchie et structure dans le polythéisme romain: Façons romaines de penser l'action." *ARG* 1, 184–203. [Trans. Philip Purchase as "Hierarchy and structure in Roman polytheism: Roman methods of conceiving action," in Ando 2003b (q.v.), 164–89.]

———. 1999c. "'Livres' sacerdotaux et érudition: L'exemple des chapelles des Argées." In C. Batsch, U. Egelhaaf-Gaiser, and R. Stepper, eds., *Zwischen Krise und Alltag: Antike Religionen im Mittelmeerraum*, 161–70. Stuttgart: Steiner.

———. 2001. *Religion et piété à Rome*. 2nd ed. Paris: Michel.

———. 2006. "Oral tradition and written tradition in the formation of sacred law in Rome." In Ando and Rüpke 2006 (q.v.), 14–33.

Schenk, W. 1989. "Interpretatio Graeca—Interpretatio Romana: Der hellenistische Synkretismus als semiotisches Problem." In P. Schmitter and H. W. Schmitz, eds., *Innovationen in Zeichentheorien: Kultur- und wissenschaftsgeschichtliche Studien zur Kreativität*, 83–121. Münster: Nodus.

Schiavone, A. 2005. *Ius: L'invenzione del diritto in Occidente*. Turin: Einaudi.

Schilling, R. 1979. *Rites, cultes, dieux de Rome*. Paris: Klincksieck.

Schnapp, A. 1994. "Are images animated? The psychology of statues in ancient Greece." In C. Renfrew and E. B. W. Zubrow, eds., *The ancient mind: Elements of cognitive archaeology*, 40–44. Cambridge: Cambridge University Press.

Schofer, R., and D. Rice. 1977. "Metaphor, metonymy, and synecdoche revis(it)ed." *Semiotica* 21, 121–49.

Schubart, A. 1866. "Die wörter ἄγαλμα, εἰκών, ξόανον, ἀνδριάς und verwandte, in ihren verschiedenen beziehungen. Nach Pausanias." *Philologus* 24, 561–87.

Schultze, J. F. 1862. *Quaestionum Lydianarum particula prior*. Berlin: Calvary.

Sedley, D. 1989. "Philosophical allegiance in the Greco-Roman world." In M. Griffin and J. Barnes, eds., *Philosophia togata: Essays on Philosophy and Roman Society*, 97–119. Oxford: Clarendon Press.

de Sélincourt, A. 1965. *The war with Hannibal: Books XXI–XXX of Livy's History of Rome from its foundation*. Baltimore: Penguin.

Shaw, B. 2000. "Rebels and outsiders." *CAH²* 11:361–403.

Sherk, R. K., ed. and trans. 1984. *Rome and the Greek East to the death of Augustus*. Cambridge: Cambridge University Press.

Smith, J. Z. 1990. *Drudgery divine: On the comparison of early Christianities and the religions of late antiquity*. Chicago: University of Chicago Press.

Smith, R. B. E. 1995. *Julian's gods: Religion and philosophy in the thought and action of Julian the Apostate*. London: Routledge.

Sourvinou-Inwood, C. 2000a. "What is *polis* religion?" In Buxton 2000 (q.v.), 13–37.

———. 2000b. "Further aspects of *polis* religion." In Buxton 2000 (q.v.), 38–55.

Spickermann, W. 2001. "Interpretatio romana? Zeugnisse der Religion von Römern, Kelten und Germanen im Rheingebiet bis zum Ende des Bataveraufstandes." In D. Hopp and C. Trümpler, eds., *Die frühe römische Kaiserzeit im Ruhrgebiet*, 94–106. Essen: Klartext.

Stark, R. 1996. *The rise of Christianity*. Princeton: Princeton University Press.

Syme, R. 1968. *Ammianus and the Historia Augusta*. Oxford: Clarendon Press.

Syske, E. 1993. *Studien zur Theologie im ersten Buch der Saturnalien des Ambrosius Theodosius Macrobius*. Stuttgart: Teubner.

Taylor, L. R. 1935. "The sellisternium and the theatrical pompa." *CPh* 30, 122–30.

———. 1942. "Caesar's colleagues in the pontifical college." *AJPh* 63, 385–412.

Thelamon, F. 1981. *Païens et Chrétiens au IVe siècle: L'apport de l' "Histoire ecclésiastique" de Rufin d'Aquilée*. Collection des Études Augustiniennes, Série Antiquité, no. 86. Paris: Études Augustiniennes.

Thomas, Y. 1984. *Mommsen et "l'isolierung" du droit (Rome, l'Allemagne et l'état)*. Paris: Boccard.

———. 1988. "Sanctio: Les défenses de la loi." *Écrit du Temps* 19, 61–84.

———. 1990. "L'institution de l'origine: Sacra principium populi Romani." In Detienne 1990 (q.v.), 143–70.

———. 1996. *"Origine" et "commune patrie": Étude de droit public romain (89 av. J.-C.–212 ap. J.-C.)*. CÉFR 221. Rome: École Française de Rome.

Toynbee, A. J. 1965. *Hannibal's legacy*. Oxford: Oxford University Press.

Toynbee, J. M. C. 1947. "*Roma* and *Constantinopolis* in late-antique art from 312 to 365." *JRS* 37, 135–44.

———. 1953. "*Roma* and *Constantinopolis* in late-antique art from 365 to Justin

II." In G. E. Mylonas, ed., *Studies presented to D. M. Robinson on his seventieth birthday*, 2:261–77. St. Louis: Washington University Press.

Turcan, R. 1996. *The cults of the Roman empire*. Trans. A. Nevill. Oxford: Blackwell.

Turk, E. 1963. "Les *Saturnales* de Macrobe, source de Servius Danielis." *RÉLatines* 41, 327–49.

Uhl, A. 1998. *Servius als Sprachlehrer: Zur Sprachrichtigkeit in der exegetischen Praxis des spätantiken Grammatikerunterrichts*. Göttingen: Vandenhoeck and Ruprecht.

Vaahtera, J. 2002. "Livy and the priestly records: À propos *ILS* 9338." *Hermes* 130, 100–108.

Vanderspoel, J. 1995. *Themistius and the imperial court: Oratory, civic duty, and paideia from Constantius to Theodosius*. Ann Arbor: University of Michigan Press.

van Haehling, R. 1978. *Die Religionszugehörigkeit der hohen Amsträger des römischen Reiches seit Constantins I: Alleinherrschaft bis zum Ende der theodosianischen Dynastie*. Antiquitas, Reihe 3, Band 23. Bonn: Habelt.

Vauchez, A., ed. 2000. *Lieux sacrés, lieux de culte, sanctuaires: Approches terminologiques, méthodologiques, historiques et monographiques*. CÉFR 273. Rome: École Française de Rome.

Verbraken, P.-P. 1976. *Études critiques sur les sermons authentiques de S. Augustin*. Instrumenta Patristica 12. Steenbrugge: Abbatia S. Petri.

Vernant, J.-P. 1979. *Religions, histoires, raison*. Paris: Maspero.

———. 1985. *Mythe et pensée chez les grecs*. Paris: Découverte.

Walsh, P. G., trans. 1997. *Cicero: The nature of the gods*. Oxford: Clarendon Press.

Warde Fowler, W. 1911. *The religious experience of the Roman people, from the earliest times to the age of Augustus*. London: Macmillan.

Waszink, J. H., and J. C. M. van Winden. 1987. *Tertullianus "De idololatria."* Leiden: Brill.

Webster, J. 1995. "*Interpretatio:* Roman word power and the Celtic gods." *Britannia* 26, 153–61.

Weinstock, S. 1926. "Die platonische Homerkritik und ihre Nachwirkung." *Philologus* 82, 121–53.

White, J. B. 1990. *Justice as translation: An essay in cultural and legal criticism*. Chicago: University of Chicago Press.

Whitehouse, R. D. 1996. "Ritual objects: Archaeological joke or neglected evidence?" In J. Wilkins, ed., *Approaches to the study of ritual: Italy and the ancient Mediterranean*, 9–30. London: Accordia Research Center.

Wiseman, T. P. 2004. *The myths of Rome*. Exeter: University of Exeter Press.

Wissowa, G. 1904. *Gesammelte Abhandlungen zur römischen Religions- und Stadt-geschichte.* Munich: Beck.

———. 1912. *Religion und Kultus der Römer.* 2nd ed. Munich: Beck.

———. 1915. "Die römische Staatspriestertümer altlateinischer Gemeindekulte." *Hermes* 50, 1–33.

———. 1916/19. "Interpretatio romana: Römische Götter im Barbarenlande." *ARW* 19, 1–49.

Wittig, C. 1910. *Quaestiones lydianae.* Königsberg: Ex officina Kargiana et Man-neckiana.

Woolf, G. 1997. "Polis-religion and its alternatives in the Roman provinces." In Cancik and Rüpke 1997 (q.v.), 71–84.

———. 2001. "Representation as cult: The case of the Jupiter columns." In W. Spickermann, ed., *Religion in der germanischen Provinzen Roms,* 117–34. Tübingen: Mohr Siebeck.

Zack, A. 2001. *Studien zum 'römischen Völkerrecht': Kriegserklärung, Kriegsbeschluß, Beeidung und Ratifikation zwischenstaatlicher Verträge, internationale Freundschaft und Feindschaft während der römischen Republik bis zum Beginn des Prinzipats.* Göttingen: Duehrkohp and Radicke.

Zwierlein, O. 1978. "Der Fall Roms im Spiegel der Kirchenväter." *ZPE* 32, 45–80.

GENERAL INDEX

aetiology, xiii, 60–61
Alcinous, 37–39
allegory, 32
Ambrose, 26, 169
Ammianus Marcellinus, 137, 165–67
Amphiaraus, 7–9, 12–13
anonymous gods, 56, 184, 190
anthropomorphism, 32
antiquarianism. *See* history and
    historical argument
Apuleius, xvi, 38–39, 140–41
Arcadius, 161, 170
Aristotle, 34–36
Arnobius, 134–35, 139
Auerbach, Erich, xv, 26–27
Augustine, 4–5, 27, 31–32, 39–
    41, 52–53, 70, 89–90, 170, 172–
    74; as reader of Cicero, x, 89–
    90; as reader of Varro, 15–18,
    83–86
Aventine Hill, 114–15, 134

Bacchanalia, 10–13
Brown, Peter, 153

calendar, 147, 191, 194
Cameron, Alan, 153–54
Camillus, 110–11, 142–43, 145, 148
Carthage. *See* Juno Caelestis
Christianity, 3–4, 13–17, 28, 34, 59–
    65, 68–71, 88–91, 102, 105, 135–37,
    149–56, 159–61, 169, 172–73, 175,
    186–87, 194, 197
Christianization, 149–51, 168–71
Cicero, 2–3, 5, 6, 7, 9, 37, 56–57, 72,
    74, 75–79, 89–90, 105–106, 110,
    125, 164
civil law. See *ius civile*
Claudian, 181
Claudius, 118
Codex Justinianus. *See* Justinian *and*
    Index Locorum s.v.
Codex Theodosianus. *See* Theodosius II
    and Index Locorum s.v.
coercion, 70–71
colonies, 95–96, 118–19
communication of Romans with gods,
    17, 45, 85–86, 125–26, 143–44
Constantine, 63, 157, 159–60, 189, 196

INDEX LOCORUM

Text:	10.75/14 Bembo
Display:	Bembo
Compositor:	Integrated Composition Systems
Printer and binder:	Thomson-Shore, Inc.